HISTORY OF THE STAFFORDSHIRE POTTERIES

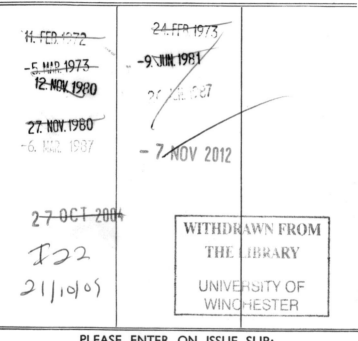
PLEASE ENTER ON ISSUE SLIP:

AUTHOR SHAW

TITLE History of the Staffordshire potteries

ACCESSION No. 52721

SIMEON SHAW

HISTORY OF THE STAFFORDSHIRE POTTERIES

Originally published in 1829

DAVID & CHARLES REPRINTS

S. R. PUBLISHERS LIMITED

0 7153 4889 2 *(David & Charles)*
0 85409 589 6 *(S.R. Publishers)*

Simeon Shaw is reputed to have been born in
Salford, Lancashire, c 1784-86. In addition to
the volume reprinted here, he wrote various
other works including *The Chemistry of the
Several Natural and Artificial Heterogeneous
Compounds Used in Manufacturing Porcelain,
Glass and Pottery* (London, W.Lewis, 1837)
and *Tables of the Characteristics of Chemical
Substances: Adapted to Facilitate Chemical
Analysis* (London, Sherwood, 1843).
In 1837-8 he started to write a comprehensive
history of the area covered by the Parliament-
ary Borough of Stoke-on-Trent. Parts I-VIII
of this, covering the first ten chapters, were
issued, but due to financial and other diffi-
culties Shaw was unable to proceed, and
the work was completed by John Ward as
*The Borough of Stoke-upon-Trent... Comp-
rising its History, Statistics, Civil Policy &
Traffic* (1843).
Shaw died in the County Mental Asylum,
Stafford, on 8 April 1859, and is buried in
the church yard at Bethesda Chapel, Hanley.

*This work was originally published by
the author, at Hanley, in 1829*

Reprinted in 1970 by
DAVID & CHARLES (PUBLISHERS) LIMITED
South Devon House Newton Abbot Devon
and
S.R. PUBLISHERS LIMITED
East Ardsley Wakefield Yorkshire

Printed in Great Britain by
Latimer Trend & Company Limited Whitstable

HISTORY

OF THE

STAFFORDSHIRE POTTERIES;

AND THE

Rise and Progress

OF THE

MANUFACTURE

OF

POTTERY AND PORCELAIN;

WITH REFERENCES TO GENUINE SPECIMENS,

AND NOTICES OF

Eminent Potters.

How pleasing, to the Patriotic Philanthropist,
The Landsape, with its devious hills and vales
Whose slopes exhibit many thousand roofs,
The comfortable homes of Laborants,
Whose Industry and Art transmute to Gold
The copious stores of useful Minerals,—
Coals, Clays, and Ores, derived from the mines,
Enriching much their Country and themselves.

Hanley;

PRINTED FOR THE AUTHOR,

By G. Jackson, Printer and Bookseller, Market-Place, Hanley.

—

1829.

TO

JOSIAH SPODE, ESQ.

IN RESPECTFUL ACKNOWLEDGMENT OF
UNSOLICITED KINDNESS, AFFORDED
WHEN MOST CALCULATED TO BENE-
FIT THE AUTHOR,

THIS VOLUME

IS GRATEFULLY DEDICATED,

BY HIS OBLIGED SERVANT,

SIMEON SHAW.

PREFACE.

THE Scroll of History presented a Blank, that might be filled up by others also with myself. How far my Attempt is worthy of the subject, the Public will not be long in giving me correct Information.

This Volume originated in the Reminiscences of many aged Persons, who had witnessed the time and manner in which the Art of Pottery had attained much of its importance. Facts and circumstances, which when they first occurred, merely excited momentary attention, have proved momentous in elucidating the Incidents which have been developed, while gratifying a rational and amusing curiosity concerning the Manufacture of the District, and the Persons whose genius and perseverance have raised it to its present celebrity. The prevention of illiberal prejudices and contracted views, and the entertainment afforded, by contemplating the first essays in an Art, and the important results, are adequate apology for my inquisitiveness, not to mention the greater service of rescuing from Oblivion much of these Materials, which probably would have been irretrieveably lost, thro' the demise of several since the Memoranda were first obtained, and the indifference or listlessness of others rapidly approaching the bourne which bounds the confines of the Eternal World.

In the Mercantile World generally, the meed of admiration and excellence has been assigned to some Potters, overlooking others whose ingenuity has been extremely beneficial. By divesting all, of those guises which during life perplexed the observer's judgment, they become subservient to general benefit as if they were our contemporaries; and thus some are presented as deserving the gratitude of posterity, of whom, but for this work, it might be said,

> " And what, no Monument, Inscription, Stone ?
> Their place, their dates, their Names, almost unknown :
> Go, search it there, where, to be born and die,
> Of rich and poor make all the history. "

I need not be told that the person who, disregarding poverty, difficulty, and privations, dares attempt to deserve well of his country by supplying Information alike improving and entertaining, must reckon on envy at his talents, and contempt of his indigence; and submit to be traduced, ridiculed, and despised, for this useful and most irksome labour,

On Indigency's barren track
Where man does every comfort lack,
Thrown on this sterile waste and tine
The strongest powers may sink and pine ;
Or shivering in misfortune's storm,
While half nutrition wastes his form,
The' unbending Author, proud tho' poor,
May hide in shades or dells obscure.

Some Readers there certainly will be, from whose candid Criticism I shall not re coil, but avail myself of all their suggestions for emendation, in an Appendix, for which while stating that all further Information from genuine Sources, shall be duly acknowledged, I gratefully mention my obligations for valuable Materials, already introduced, to E. Wood, Sen., T. Minton, Sen. W. Turner, T. Fenton, J. and R. Riley, H. Daniel, and G. Forrister, Esqrs., and Mr. Leigh, Attorney.—Is it possible to adduce higher Authority?

The Delay in Publication, tho' productive of much inconvenience to myself, has been embraced to introduce much additional information, entertaining to present readers, and pregnant with interest to posterity, which has been supplied while the work has been in progress.

S. S

SHELTON, OCT. 1st, 1829.

CONTENTS.

HISTORY

OF THE

Staffordshire Potteries.

CHAPTER I.

PRELIMINARY REMARKS.

ABOUT five miles north west, and five miles south east of Newcastle-under-Lyme, are the two extremities of that interesting and opulent district, named — THE POTTERIES,— because almost exclusively appropriated to Manufactories of Porcelain and Pottery, not yielding in the elegance, beauty, and utility of the productions, to those of China; and in extent of operations exceeding all others in Europe.

About a mile from the boundary of the county of Stafford, on the Moorlands, is the northern part, at Golden Hill; and at varying breadths from three to five miles, the district extends to its south-eastern part, at Mear Lane Furnace, in length *ten* miles; covering above *twenty thousand* acres with Towns, Villages, and Hamlets, and forming one of the most populous and industrious districts of equal extent in the nation.

A

There being about *fifty thousand* persons in the parishes of Stoke, Burslem, and Wolstanton, supported by the Manufacture, as operatives, colliers, and persons employed on the canal to bring the raw materials, and carry away the manufactured productions.

We may subdivide the District thus, (from the southern extremity;)—Lane End, with Mear, Furnace, Longton, and the Foley;—Lane Delph with Fenton;—Stoke, with Penkhull and Boothen;—Hanley and Shelton, with Etruria, Vale Pleasant, Cobridge, and Sneyd Green;—Burslem, with Hot Lane, Hamill, Dale Hall, Newport and Longport;—and Brown Hills, with Tunstall, Clay Hills, Greenfield, (formerly Smithfield,) Newfield, Sandyford, Golden Hill, and Green Lane. When Erdeswick wrote his Antiquities of the County (1590,) these places appear to have been mere fiefs of larger Estates; but at this day (1829,) they are distinct townships and liberties, important to the state on account of their wealth and manufactures.

The Enquiry has been frequently made—"Why did the Early Potters first establish themselves in this district; and why has the manufacture in this neighbourhood flourished more than in any other part of England, or perhaps of the World?"—The largest Potteries known, being Wedgwood's, Etruria; Spode's, Stoke; Wood's, Burslem; Davenport's, Longport; Minton's, Stoke; Bourne's, Fenton; Ridgways', Shelton; Dimmock's, Hanley; Hicks and Meigh's, Shelton; Meigh's, Hanley; with many others, considerable in themselves, but not equal to these in extent and importance.

We can offer only a conjectural Answer to the enquiry.

When the district was first selected as the Seat of the Manufacture of Pottery, we cannot accurately ascertain; but the considerable depth beneath the present surface, at which remains of Manufactories, and Pottery, have been discovered during the last and the present century, leads to the opinion that the Art was practised here during the time the country was tributary to the Roman power; if not even prior to that era: and authenticated specimens prove that it was in full operation in different places, near three centuries ago.

Certainly during a long period, the manufacture was rude and uninteresting; neither did the productions of the early periods present any earnest of the successive and important improvements for which the last sixty or seventy years are so distinguished. But it is probable, that if we could ascertain when our other staple manufactures first began to be improved and extended, we should find this Art beginning to obtain celebrity, and that it has prospered in proportion to the facility of disposing of it profitably. Perhaps also, the Sales of Porcelain from China, may have stimulated the British Potters to imitate that commodity.

We find various causes powerfully combining to give permanence to the Manufacture here; and are persuaded that the same peculiarities of situation and advantages cannot be found in an equal extent of ground in the United Kingdom.

The situation, on the ridge of the low part of the Moorlands, is so much diversified with hills and dales,

that however little might be its value for agricultural
purposes, or bleak and barren its aspect, no inconvenience is ever experienced by the inhabitants from the
volumes of smoke arising from the coal consumed in
making Bricks, Tiles, and Earthenware.   This part
of the ridge has less cause than any other to be called
the Moorlands; for, owing to the industry of its population, it has all the appearances of cultivated tracts
of country; tho' its surface is uneven, and generally
rochy, or gravelly clay.   Here also the potters enjoy
four of the chief natural benefits which can be connected
with human existence—air extremely salubrious, water of tolerable purity, the sun seldom obscured by
fogs, and an entire freedom from damp.

Other advantages for the Manufacture, which have
contributed to make this district a permanent seat, and
enabled it to triumph over every attempt at its removal,
are the *Coals* and *Clay* for the several purposes, being
readily obtained on moderate terms.   Different Strata
of Coals of various kinds, and Marls or Clays of different sorts and colours, some tenacious, some friable,
all over the district, at a depth easily accessible, present an almost inexhaustible store of two sorts of materials, indispensable in the manufacture of Pottery.
The Coals have a curvilineal range, much in the form of a
horse shoe; regarded from the mines at Lane End to
Ubberley and Bucknall; or from Shelton to Norton
and Biddulph; or from Burslem to the Stonetrough
mines; whence they suddenly return by Whitehill,
Kidsgrove, Harecastle, to the Neighbourhood of Red
Street.   In the former range, the dip is about *one* foot
perpendicular to every four feet in extent, westward;
but a few strata *stare*, i. e. are almost perpendicular
to the surface.   The other range dips south-east for
near four miles; and the mines of Silverdale dip eastward, and crop out westward.

The Strata vary in quality and quantity; there having been discovered in this Coal Field, *thirty four* different mines, from *one* to *ten* feet in thickness; and several thin veins not at present extracted. The names are varied in some places; and the quality and quantity vary also; but generally they are known by these Names:

1 Red Shag Mine,	18 Undermost of Two Little Mines,
2 Brief Furlong ditto,	19 Whitfield Mine,
3 Little Mine,	20 Church ditto,
4 Bass ditto,	21 Eight Foot ditto,
5 Little Row ditto,	22 Ten ditto ditto,
6 Peacock ditto,	23 Bowling Alley ditto,
7 Spend Croft ditto,	24 Sparrow Buts ditto,
8 Great Row ditto,	25 Holly Lane ditto,
9 Cannel Row ditto,	26 Iron Stone Coal ditto,
10 Thirty Inch Cannel ditto,	27 Flats ditto,
11 Chalky Row ditto,	28 Frog Row ditto,
12 Row Hurst ditto	29 Cockshead ditto,
13 Burn Wood ditto,	30 Lime Kiln ditto,
14 Little ditto,	31 Ridgway Cannel ditto,
15 Four Foot ditto,	32 Bullhurst ditto,
16 Easling ditto,	33 Badiley Edge ditto,
17 Topmost of two little mines,	34 Deep Badiley Edge ditto

There are also several thin veins of coal lying between the above mines, which are without names, and have never been worked.

Some of these are better adapted than others for making Pottery; and others are better for domestic purposes The great Row and Ten Foot coals are much used, because of their small portion of bitumen. There is a Cannel, or Pill, of a bituminous quality, a few inches thick, over the coals, like the cream on milk; and by some persons the cannel is considered the bitumen of these coals. E. Wood, Esq. recently discovered a rich mine of Cannel, *three* feet thick. The coals which have much bitumen, are here called *soldering*, because they are a long time in consuming, and tho' they do not give great heat, they rarely leave much ashes; as those of Apedale and neighbourhood.

A 3.

Connected with the Coal Strata, are very rich and productive veins of marl, particularly adapted for the saggers, and fire bricks of the potters' kilns, because scarcely impregnated with iron; and hence very much in requisition thro' the district. There are also many *Faults* in this Coal field; which in some places might be a great disadvantage; but in the Potteries, a most contrary result is obvious, in the great dispersion of the Coals to every part of the district. Had the Coals been all in one spot, the seat of the Potteries would have been there only; and had the surface of the ground been a plain, or a valley, the smoke could not have readily dissipated; and this pleasant and healthful district would have been the 'murkiest den' possible to be imagined.

In the early times the Coals were cropping out at different places; and nigh these the early potters fixed their sun pans and ovens, for convenience of coals and clay. Little labour being required to procure them, they were very cheap. In Dr. Plott's time (1686,) they were about 1s. 4d. the ton; in 1795, 4s. 6d.; and in 1829, 8s. 4d. The soil and clay only had to be removed, at first; and thus large and open pits were formed; like those now open in Lane Delph, and Woodiston in Shelton. These being liable to delays from wtaer, the miners resorted to the advantage of a gutter from the lowest Lands near, extended under all the coals above its level; which being drained by it, a supply of coals was obtained until the upper part of the mine was exhausted. In 1719, Lord Macclesfield thus drained about 150 acres of coals, by the gutter near Burslem Church, and plentifully supplied the neighbourhood more than sixty years. The gutters also are useful to convey the water from those mines whose depth exceeds its level. At first horse gins were employed to draw up large casks filled with water, and emptied in the gutter; but now powerful steam engines are used, to work *two* or *three* large pumps, with lifts of *forty* or *fifty* yards each.

In 1708, in a field near the Hamill, thro' which was a foot path, 'the rains had so affected the path', as to expose the hollow of a potters kiln, at a considerable distance from any other then known, and wholly beyond any traces of tradition. A few years subsequently, on removing a very old building that a new manufactory might be erected, under the foundations were discovered the remains of a potter's oven, with some very coarse saggers, containing the kind of Pottery formerly made. Other specimens have been discovered in levelling the hilly parts of the highways in the district; all exhibiting considerable ingenuity, and great antiquity, and carrying the judgment and imagination far back into a period of time, not even conjectured by persons acquainted with only the partial statements heretofore submitted to the public.

Were a person to place himself, in succession, on the hills, at Green Lane, Wolstanton, Basford, Harts Hill, and Fenton Park, and take a Bird's-eye view of the different parts, he would be much gratified with the many indications of the utility of well-directed industry, and its results, a vast increase of population; numerous and extensive manufactories, with beautiful mansions; maintenance for the employed, and opulence for the employers. While a close investigation of the places, will prove, that of the comfortable habitations of the thousands of industrious individual journeymen, a greater number reside in their own houses, the savings of their labours, than can be found in any other place of equal population in Great Britain.

Very recently great improvements have been made in all the highways from Tunstall to Lane End; and now good dwelling houses are being erected in different parts of them; so that only a few years may be expected to elapse before the whole district will appear, to a passenger, or traveller, a large manufacturing *town*, with distinct names for its subdivisions.

The Philanthropist at all times with peculiar pleasure contemplates the progressive developement of the human mind, where talent and diligence raise a community from ignorance to knowledge, from barbarity to refinement in civilization and the Arts;—the gradations and means, by which, under the influence of natural and moral causes, obstacles presented by a locality unpromising and unfavourable, have been disregarded or surmounted; and with success have been pursued, the improvement of manners and conduct, the acquirement of mental and physical science, and the attainment of that distinguished excellence, which contribute to the advancement and benefit of society. All the fraternity, actuated by the same spirit and resolution to promote the general interest by personal eminence in some particular branch of the manufacture, associate and form an indivisible connection for the important purpose of extending the knowledge and operations of peculiar manipulations and useful inventions; which alike dignify and more closely unite the individuals, cherish personal merit, enhance the comforts of society, promote general welfare, cement the links of the chain of mankind, and raise the people in the scale of nations.

This interesting and flourishing district most forcibly illustrates the results which may be expected from a cordial union of man's intellectual and physical powers; the researches of the mineralogist with the ingenuity of the artizan.   Little more than a century ago, its existence was scarcely noticed; it wore then a barren aspect, and was a mere range of straggling and detached hamlets, with few inhabitants, and little trade, (as we find in Dr. Plott's History of the County;) its rich and almost inexhaustible mineral treasures were unknown, and its agricultural advantages were considered very paucile.   But since then, by uniting talents and perseverance, the recesses of the earth have been explored to enrich its owners, and extremely rapid has been the advancement in population, manufactures, and commercial prosperity.   We have populous towns and villages, the abode of social comfort to multitudes; with regular markets, public edifices, extensive and commodious manufactories, elegant mansions, and comfortable habitations, for a busy and enterprizing community of *fifty thousand* persons.   The value of the productions of the district is greatly enhanced by the demand for them in making Porcelain and Pottery; and these latter are so much in request thro' the globe, as ultimately to cause their useful and ornamented productions, in all their varieties, to be exhibited in most markets of the Eastern and Western Continents.

As it is impossible for any person to determine which Earths not yet introduced, may form part of the materials of excellent pottery hitherto unproduced; or what brilliant Colours at present not thought of, may hereafter be obtained from the mineral kingdom, by the researches of mineralogists and the operations of chemists; it becomes every person, to cultivate the ability providence has conferred, and sedulously employ his genius to promote his advancement in his profession. For, even at this period, the manufacture is rising in celebrity constantly; and we are most agreeably surprised at the exhibition of new specimens of cultivated taste and well-directed ingenuity.

The Inhabitants of the Potteries, regarded as a body, possess the spirit of true patriotism. Parties there are, and sometimes they can scarcely 'agree to differ'; but, whatever differences may have occurred as to the *manner* of promoting the public good, all have united in the *desire* and *means* whereby it might be accomplished.

The fortunes which have been realized from small capitals, by individual talent and industry, are very numerous, considerable, and in some instances, almost princely; and with honour and comfort are they enjoyed. Most of the lands near the houses of the manufacturers, belong to the several estates; and the other in the vicinity of the towns now are cultivated either for variety or convenience, to support horses employed for numerous purposes, and milch cows to supply the wants of the population. The tenure is mostly freehold; altho' there are some copyholds; and other customary freeholds paying fines and rents certain.

Since 1780, the demand for Grain and Flour has been increasing to a vast amount; and new sources of supply from distant parts, have been opened by the Canal; so that the inhabitants need not fear either monopoly or scarcity; tho' the price of these and all other articles of food, will ever be higher in a district which produces so little, and consumes such large quantities.

The great demand for milk and butter, has diminished the number of acres appropriated to tillage. That part which is so employed, is usually let to the journeyman potter, at a small sum per rood, to plant with potatoes in his leisure hours. A crop of Wheat usually follows; then one of Oats succeeds. The Straw of both is an article in great demand for packing pottery; and always obtains a good remuneration to the agriculturist.

The Manure is often the refuse of the farm yard, and likewise lime, and, at times, both these, mixed with the soil of the sides of the roads, gutter clods, ditchings, and the drawings off the butts of pastures. On some lands, refuse salt is occasionally employed. The lime stone for these and other purposes, is brought from Cauldon Low. Great plenty of potatoes and other vegetables, are supplied from the neighbourhood of Bowers, Betley, and Lawton; and smaller supplies come from the neighbouring villages.

In the woods within many miles circuit, great quantities of hazel rods and coppice wood are cut at the successive growth of about seven or eight years, to supply the Crate Makers of the district with materials for Crates, in which Pottery is packed. A good price is paid for the heads and rods, so as to render their careful cultivation an object of interest to the Landowners.

The western extremity of the district, being hills, which arrest the progress of the clouds from the Atlantic ocean, and combined with the high rarefaction of the air by the immense combustion of coals in the Potteries, we always find the clouds brought by the westerly winds precipitating their waters. Yet not only is the district now productive of much pasturage for the horses and cattle; but the atmosphere is pure and healthful, and seldom are the people affected by epidemic diseases. However, we notice many instances

of Bronchocele, or thick neck, a very unseemly enlargement of the glands of the throat.

We may observe that it has happened with this
district, as with most other places where the increase
of trade from the industry of the manufacturers has
been rapid, that there remain many improvements to
be effected to promote the convenience of the inhabitants.   However, the whole district is now alert, as
we shall proceed to shew.

Until some time after the commencement of the
present century, workmen were rather scarce, because
of continual drains for the army and navy; and public attention was wholly absorbed by the principal and
primary source of wealth — the improvement of the
various branches of the manufacture, and in supplying
the foreign demands.   But, after the peace, when labour was become cheap, the attention of all classes
was directed to the improvement of the public roads of
this district, to render them good and direct; a truly
important object, and one indispensable to the interests
of commerce in a populous manufacturing district.
These facilitate the intercourse with commercial, intelligent persons, and animate and refine manners,
that in all ranks of society precede that improvement
in morals, which it is desirable this district should enjoy.   This object, at one period (1784,) caused a
complete insurrection; the lower classes being fearful
that by good roads their *trade* would be carried out of
the country; and only by great efforts on the part of
the Masters, were the results prevented from being
most prejudicial.   But much labour, and great sums
of money, have been expended on the highways; and
care has been exercised to secure regularity of building
in streets; and to supply them with Lamps and Water.

The Trustees of the several Markets avail themselves of every method to supply the Dealers with
most convenient stalls, and accommodate those persons
who attend as purchasers. And all the Markets are
well supplied with provisions and merchandise.

Many of the new Streets are distinguished by the
Name on the corners; but few of them have the Doors
of the Houses numbered. This might be done on a
very useful, simple, and convenient plan — all the *even*
Numbers might be on one side, and all the *odd* ones
on the other; a person would then be certain on
whether side was situated the house he was seeking.
The introduction of Gas Lamps with powerful burners,
in the streets, and most of the highways, is a very
convenient accommodation to all parties, strangers and
inhabitants.

Good Water is supplied from Reservoirs at Lane
End, and Hanley; but is more of a rarity in all the
Towns, than is desirable for the health and cleanliness
of the population. A stranger is surprized to see
water carts in the streets, selling at a *halfpenny* a
pailful, this essential article of human enjoyment.

In 1815, the Nobility and Gentry of the neighbourhood most promptly aided the exertions of the
Manufacturers in the Establishment of one of the
grandest methods of alleviating the Sufferings of the
afflicted classes of operatives. By their munificent
donations, with one of £500, from his Majesty, (then
Prince Regent,) and a Legacy of £1000, from the late
John Rogers, Esq. of the Watlands, this extensive
and populous district enjoys the advantages dispensed
by the NORTH STAFFORDSHIRE INFIRMARY.

B

It has a situation almost central, and one of the most eligible in the vicinity, being on a rising plot of Land, in the Liberty of Shelton, but so wholly free from surrounding buildings, that it is readily seen from many parts. The Edifice is now enlarged much from its original construction. It is of Brick, very spacious and commodious with numerous wards for the accommodation of numerous In-patients; besides all appropriate Apartments for the various purposes and Officers of the Establishment.

During more than ten years the Benefits had been dispensed to the neighbourhood; and with the increased population, an increased demand for the helps conferred, was experienced, and the Trustees at length resolved upon an enlargement, the better to meet the wants of the applicants. The Intention was published, and numerous donations were immediately received; but the chief Aid was wholly unexpected and unprecedented:—

A Gentleman, whose philanthropy is exceeded only by his urbanity and modesty, suggested the trial of a *Bazaar*, to augment the Funds. Some obstacles were presented, but were surmounted. The trial was made; and to the honour of the Ladies be it mentioned, the store of Articles of utility, elegance, and taste was so abundant, that the sales realized more than *Nine Hundred Pounds* additional to the funds for enlarging the Edifice. Thus a lasting benefit results to posterity, thro' the benevolent hints and exertions of Arthur Minton, Esq.

A Medical Library, and Museum of Subjects of Anatomy and Physiology, have been recently projected; and great expectations are raised in reference to the advantages they will afford.   The whole expence of the Establishment, is defrayed by Annual Subscriptions of the opulent, in addition to small weekly deductions from the Earnings of the operative classes.

The Most Noble the Marquis of Stafford, is the Patron; and the President, Vice-Presidents, and committee, are elected from the most worthy and estimable Persons of the neighbourhood.

The same high Personage is the Patron also of the POTTERY MECHANICS' INSTITUTION.   A truly noble Donation from him, was followed by extremely liberal Contributions, from Josiah Wedgwood, Esq. Richard Edensor Heathcote, Esq., M. P., Thomas Hawe Parker, Esq., E. J. Littleton, Esq., M. P., Sir John Wrottesley, Bart., M. P., and some other gentlemen; and which were applied to purchase a Library and apparatus, exclusively adapted to Philosophical Researches.   The Members contribute small sums annually, and have the Books regularly circulated amongst them.   Classes for particular Studies also are formed ; and those for Chemistry, Modelling, and Drawing promise to be very useful.   During the three Winters since its establishment, Courses of Lectures have been regularly delivered to the Members, free of expence ; and to visitors on payment of a small sum. Many of the intelligent manufacturers are honorary Members, and by their example excite their workmen to excellence in their particular branches.   In our times, it is readily admitted by all persons of true discernment, that to combine the gratifying and advantageous pursuits of science and literature with the energies required by commercial engagements, are highly beneficial ; because all corroding cares are alleviated or dissipated by them.

Without the partiality of friendship ascribing adscititious excellence; or the rancour of envy depreciating their real importance; the full meed of praise will be assigned by posterity unto all those Worthies, already demised, whose indefatigable exercise of ingenuity and industry, in introducing *fresh materials*, implements, or ornaments, have benefitted all with whom they were connected, by commencing and establishing the goodly fabric of a staple manufacture on a solid and durable foundation; and, likewise, to their successors and survivors, who, by having improved and advanced the Art to its present perfection, have completed a celebrious superstructure, every way worthy the talents of their eminent progenitors.

When it is considered, that nearly the whole of the Materials used are native productions, and that five parts in six of the manufactured articles are exported, few Branches of manufacture have greater claim to the gratitude and admiration of their countrymen, than these valuable establishments, and the persons who have founded, fostered, and advanced them. The late Mr. Wedgwood, in his day was a principal promoter of this advancement; and since his time additional and great improvements have been made by the united genius of the present Potters, Spode, Wood, Ridgways, Minton, Turner, &c. and it is a fair presumption that specimens of their productions will be found, not only in the cabinets of princes and opulent persons of taste, but in the markets of every state where British commerce extends.

We shall now proceed to describe the several Towns, according to their present appearance; and from a careful survey of their improved condition.

CHAPTER II.

THE POTTERIES.

TUNSTALL, AND ITS VICINITY.

TUNSTALL has risen, during the present century, from being a mere small street, of about *twenty* houses in the highroad, and about *forty* more in the lanes leading to Chatterley and Red-Street, into a town of moderate size, for the accommodation of whose inhabitants, a Church is to be erected by Government, at the expence of several thousand pounds.

The town is pleasantly situated on the declivity of a considerable eminence, allowing most of it to be seen (at the distance of two miles) from the new turnpike road from Newcastle to Lawton; being from the former place distant about *four* miles. It is on the highroad from Bosley to Newcastle, and from Lawton to Burslem. It is the chief liberty of the Parish of Wolstanton; has many respectable tradespeople in it; and its manufacturers rank high for talent and opulence. From it there are some very pleasing prospects, over much of the District, and its vicinity.

Mr. John Mear, Mr. T. Goodfellow, and Mr. Ralph Hall, have elegant Mansions connected with extensive manufactories. Of Mr. Hall, it may be justly stated, that his modesty and unaffected piety, are exceeded only by his philanthropy and assiduity in every good work for public or private benefit. There are other manufactories, of considerable extent, belonging to S. & J. Rathbone, J. Boden, Bourne, Nixon, & Co. Breeze, & Co, and Burrows, & Co.

B 3.

At the manufactory now owned by Mr. Good-fellow, Mr. Enoch Booth first introduced that most important improvement in the manufacture of pottery, —the fluid Glaze. Here also his son-in-law and successor Anthony Keeling, employed Enamellers, of the Porcelain, then commenced making under Mr. Champion's Patent, in copartnership with Samuel Hollins, J. & P. Warburton, and William Clowes. But very soon afterwards this was transferred to Shelton, under the firm of Hollins, Warburton, & Co.

Smith Child, Esq. has recently established a very commodious manufactory for Chemicals, at Clay Hills; near which are very extensive beds of excellent marl, employed in making Blue Tiles for Houses, Floor Quarries, and different kinds of Bricks, of superior quality for appearance and durability.

Each of the three denominations of Methodists has here a spacious Chapel, with which is connected a Sunday School; whose Libraries promote the moral improvement of the people. Here is also a very repectable Literary Society, unassuming in character, but assiduous in research.

In 1815, by a public subscription was formed a spacious Market Place, which is now well attended by dealers of every kind; also was erected an elegant Court House; with Lock-ups for Offenders. There are a large Windmill, and also a Steam Mill, for grinding grain. And at a short distance is Hostin Mill, for grinding Potters' Materials; concerning which, in 1826, several thousand pounds were expended in a Lawsuit, to determine in whether parish it is situated, Burslem or Wolstanton; and the decision fixed it in the former.

Tunstall belonged to John Frost, Esq. in the reign of Henry VIII.

The House at Hardingwood, a short distance from Golden Hill, has a peculiar situation. Whenever its inhabitants go to Church (that of Lawton,) they pass, out of the province of Canterbury into that of York; out of the county of Stafford into that of Chester; out of the diocese of Lichfield and Coventry, into that of Chester; out of the hundred of Pirehill, into that of Nantwich; being successively in three constableries, Tunstall, Chell, and Lawton; and in three parishes, Wolstanton, Audley, and Lawton.

Tradition mentions a Church having been at Tunstall in former Ages; but no traces of such a structure have been discovered at any time. Certainly human bones have been dug up in a field near the Wesleyan Chapel; but the bodies may have been buried here, because of the great distance from the Church; or, at one of the battles between the Normans and Saxons.

Closely connected with Tunstall, and much like one of its extremities, tho' in Burslem parish, we find on the Burslem road, HIGHGATE, and the FLASH; containing about *fifty* dwelling houses, chiefly for the operative classes. Also,

BROWNHILLS.—Here is one manufactory, belonging to Samuel Marsh & Co.; and another, moderately extensive, the property of John Wood, Esq., a gentleman of great worth for every manly feeling, who resides in an adjacent elegant Mansion; of a moderate yet convenient size, placed in a well-arranged paddock and gardens. from which there are beautiful prospects, and a delightful command of the Turnpike roads

to Longport and Wolstanton, also to Burslem and
Tunstall. At this place occurred that most remarkable and fatal catastrophe, in 1797, of Dr. Oliver
shooting the owner, father to the present proprietor,
a truly pious and good man, and an affectionate head
of his family.

On the road to Bosley, is GREEN FIELD (or
SMITH-FIELD) containing several strata of excellent
Coals and Marls, and some beautiful prospects. The
very elegant and commodious Mansion, seen from the
high road, has a truly picturesque appearance, in a
pleasant hanging wood, fronted by a fine lawn.

The present name has been substituted for that
which kept in remembrance the unhappy founder,
Theophilus Smith; who, in a fit of jealousy attempted
the life of his kind friend, Mr. Wainwright, (who still
survives, in the United States,) and subsequently in
goal perished by his own hand. This was late the
property of Jesse Breeze, Esq. whose daughters have
it in possession; but neither the Colliery nor the Manufactory is at this time (1829) in operation.

NEW FIELD is stated (by Pitt, p. 393, but no
reference is given to his authority,) as having been a
part of the extensive Town Fields of Tunstall, about
1613. Certain it is, that a descendant of the William
Badyley, who, in 10 Edw. IV. became seized of a
messuage and land here, now has it in possession.
This Gentleman is Smith Child, Esq. grandson of Admiral Smith Child; who, during the peace of 1763,
erected here a large manufactory, and a very spacious
and elegant Mansion, having extensive prospects over
much of the potteries. The very valuable mines of
coal with which this estate is enriched, were increased

in value during the minority of its present possessor,
by a sewer from the low level of the Canal being run
up under them to drain them most effectively.   In fact
the whole of this property was greatly improved by
the very judicious management of J. H. Clive, Esq.
one of the earliest and most successful introducers of
ornamental engraving into the Blue printing department of Pottery.

SMITH CHILD, Admiral of the Blue, who of late years
lived on this estate, settled on him by his maternal uncle,
Thomas Baddeley, was of Salopian descent, though his immediate ancestry were of Audley, in this county, — his great-
grandfather, Smith Child, having succeeded to Boyle's Hall
and other property in the latter township, (of which the Admiral was himself a native) on the demise of Margaret Smithe,
widow, about 1657.   In the peace of 1763, he married his kins-
woman, Margaret Roylance, and resumed, near the commencement of the American war, his naval duties, which were
continued to its termination.   While on shore, he ardently
participated in agricultural and other useful pursuits, and received the honorary freedom of Newcastle-under-Lyme, and
of Liverpool.

" He died of gout in the Stomach, at New-field, on the
21st January, 1813, aged 83.   He entered the service under
Earl Gower's auspices in 1747, as the nautical disciple of Lord
Anson, and served at the sieges of Pondicherry and Louis-
bourg.   He commanded the *Europe* in the two actions off the
Chesapeake, in 1781, with such credit as enabled him to obtain
preferment for most of her officers ; but, the following year,
his eldest son, (a youth who had evinced great intrepidity on
board the *Fame* upon the memorable *Twelfth of April*, and was
about to have joined the *Foudroyant*, commanded by Sir John
Jervis, then at home,) perished in the unfortunate *Ville de
Paris*.   In 1795 he took the command of the *Commerce de Mar-
seilles* of 120 guns, and attained his flag on Valentine's day,
1799.   The Admiral was, during great part of his life, in the
Commission of the Peace for Staffordshire, — a Deputy-Lieu-
tenant, &c. of the county, — and was most eminently and extensively beloved and revered."   His remains are deposited
at Wolstanton, under a plain tomb.

The following are copies of two ancient and curious deeds connected with this place.

" TUNSTALL.— At the Court there holden on Tuesday in the week of Penticost in the 10th Year of the Reign of King Edd. the 4th came William Badyley Son and Heir of Margery Handeson and took Seisin of the Lord of Audley of one Messuage and 20 Acres of customary Land in Tunstall of which the said Margery died seized To hold to the said William and his Heirs according to the custom of the Manor: and he gives to the said Lord at his entry 20d. In testimony whereof John Harryson Deputy Steward to this Copy hath affixed his Seal. Given as above."

" Be yt knowne to all true me In chryste In the wey of truthe yt I Phythyon of Tunstall dyd purchys a garden place yt lythhe in Tunstal at Hary of Tunstal my broders ye wch garden place I do set at my dysseasse to Margerye my wyffe and to Margyt my doughttd ye wyffe of John Banchcrofte & aftd ye dysseace of my wyffe hytt to remeyne to Margytt my doughttd & to hyr eyres the recorder of this Rychard of rydgways & to thys I set to my seale Gyvvyn ye last daye of Julye in ye yere & reyne of Kynge Harry ye Syxt yfter ye conquest of England x x x. & vij."

The Manufactory is now occupied by Joseph Heath & Co. --- The other manufactory, nigher Golden Hill, is occupied by James Beech and Abraham Lownds. The latter gentleman will long be remembered in this neighbourhood as a friend of mankind, and one of the Founders and chief supporters of the Large Tunstall Sunday School.

GOLDEN HILL. This extremity of the district can have claim to its high appellation, only in consequence of its valuable mines of Coals, Cannel, Ironstone, and Marl. In the sixteenth century, coarse Pottery, and more recently the brown, chequered, and Porto Bello wares have been made here. A few years ago, there was also a small establishment for the manufacture of Cream Colour, and Porcelain; but it is now discontinued; and very recently the buildings have been converted into dwelling houses. Only the Coarse Pottery is now manufactured, in new buildings. There are *three* taverns in this small place. A few years since, a number of new houses, also a Small Chapel and Sunday School, for the Wesleyan Methodists, were added to this liberty.

On the West of this place is LATEBROOK, where is a large Furnace for reducing the iron ore found in the neighbourhood in considerable quantity. On the North, are Kidsgrove and Whitehill Collieries, very extensive and productive; the property of Thomas Kinnersley, Esq. of Clough Hall.

At a short distance westward, are the two subterraneous Tunnels, the principal on the line of the Trent and Mersey Canal, under the Harecastle (Query—Air-castle) Hill. The Old Tunnel, which commences near Kidsgrove, and terminates near Clay Hills, was a work of immense labour and expense, in consequence of unforeseen difficulties. Its length is *two thousand eight hundred and eighty* yards; its height *twelve* feet, and its width *nine* feet, at the depth of *seventy* to *eighty* yards beneath the surface of the hill thro' which it is excavated, and lined and arched with bricks. The fall of Water, from this highest pond, to the northern extremity is *three hundred and twenty six* feet, by *thirty five* locks, and to the southern *three hundred and sixteen* feet by *forty* locks. The new Tunnel is of larger dimensions than the other; and a towing path, with a strong guard rail is formed along one of its sides. This stupendous undertaking was calculated to occupy the labour of five years, during which several hundred men would be employed in the excavation of the earth, and the construction of the Tunnel, independent of the numbers employed in conveying materials, &c. Contracts were made for bricks in every direction. The expence was calculated at *a guinea per inch*—the distance being about one mile and three quarters, or *two thousand eight hundred and eighty* yards, which *alone* make *one hundred and three thousand six hundred and eighty* guineas; and including all the materials, at a *quarter of a million sterling.* Shafts were sunk and steam engines erected for the raising of the earth, &c. at different points of the elevation — the tunnel averaging about *seventy* yards in depth from the surface of the hill. The Grand Trunk Canal was only begun in July 17th, 1766, and finished in 1777; yet such is the richness of the Company, and the business of the canal, that the money is no object compared to the advantage to be gained. On the plan of one tunnel, if a boat arrived but a few minutes after another, which had entered the Tunnel, it had to tarry *six* hours, for its turn, in either direction. By the additional one the different directions has each its separate tunnel of progress, by which the business of the canal is incalculably promoted in expedition.—Such is the ingenuity and adventurous disposition of man. Not only will he effect his purposes on the surface of the ground; but will even dare to penetrate into its internal recesses, to carry forward his designs where they can possibly be completed.—

Urged by curiosity, the author presumed to visit this monument of industrious perseverance. The strata cannot easily be ascertained from the interior, because of the brick work; but fossils of various kinds have been found in the substances excavated. After being wholly excluded from the light of day, and introduced into these dreary regions, suddenly is presented to view, glimmering in the distance, the lights of an extensive coal mine, where are busily employed the murky-visaged colliers; and small boats are seen approaching the tunnel by means of a small subterraneous canal. Passing forward, at a considerable distance, the first appearance of light adds a pleasing object to the vision, cheering the adventurer, like as the pole-star cheers the returning mariner who has unfortunately lost his compass;—the beams of light increase to the view, the land in the distance is faintly presented; and at length the bark emerges from the cavity, the visitor looks with eagerness for objects known or recognizable, and almost conjectures he has passed thro' the chambers of Hades, and entered upon the scenery of another world.

The northern extremity of Golden Hill, is GREEN LANE, formerly only the direct road into the Potteries; and having its name from its fertile and pleasing appearance, to the persons who employed gangs of horses. At this farthest extremity of the district in this direction, is a small and very old manufactory of coarse black ware. The situation has considerable elevation, and consequently a peculiarly pleasing, and particularly extensive and diversified Landscape. Looking southward and eastward, almost the whole of this interesting and populous district is presented to the eye of the beholder;—the towns, villages, mansions, churches, hills, dales and Canal, appear in every possible angle, and gratify while they interest the spectator. The contrary way presents much of the richly cultivated water bason of the County of Chester; having in the distance the towering hills of Lancashire in front; those of Wales on one side, and those of Derbyshire on the other; while the inte-

C

rior of this microcosm is richly interspersed with sheets of water, fine enclosures, woods, and elegant mansions of persons of rank and opulence.

BURSLEM, AND ITS VICINITY.

BURSLEM, the MOTHER OF THE POTTERIES, is now a populous Market-town, and a distinct Parish; having been separated from Stoke by Act of Parliament. More than three miles N. N. E. of Newcastle, it stands on a very prominent hill. In Erdeswick's "Antiquities," it is named *Bulwardslene;* and in Shaw's "General History," *Barcardeslim;* both names doubtless having reference to *Bullbaiting.* However, whether we admit the former name, as originating from some *Bull-keeper,* (bull-ward,) and the latter as from some dog-keeper, we shall easily find, on trial, that the rapid utterance of the words as *two* syllables, according to the known principle in Language of shortening all difficult words, will make the name be Burdslem, or Burslem the same as nigh as possible. Other local authorities of our day, give *Boar's Lane,* from a wild Boar which pestered the neighbourhood.

Whoever attentively surveys the structure and number of the old Buildings of Burslem, will be convinced that its antiquity is greater than any other place in the district. In fact, this cannot be doubted on any tenable ground. But it must be admitted not to have increased so rapidly, and to as great extent, as have some of the other towns. It is, however, a flourishing place. Many wide and spacious new streets of excellent dwelling houses, erected of bricks chiefly made on the spot, have nearly doubled the size of the town within the present quarter of a century.

In consequence of its situation on an elevated portion of the Moorland Ridge, it probably never experienced disadvantage, however much its inhabitants were formerly, for a few hours at a time, incommoded by the vast volumes of dense clouds of vapour proceeding from the ovens at the time of employing Salt for the purpose of causing the glazed inside and outside of the Pottery. They were always dispersed in a few hours; and never could become stagnant, because of the constant current of air from the hills of Derbyshire, or from the sea, over the Cheshire water bason.

This place is the most early and chief seat of the Manufacture in this district; from here can be traced the migrations of potters to the neighbouring hamlets and towns; and existing specimens warrant the belief that the coarse brown, cloudy, and mottled pottery have been made during many centuries, and, according to some opinions, since the Romans inherited the territory. The population was for a long period very scanty, and a straggling oven, and requisite buildings covered with thatch, and employing few persons, might be found at the junction of each of the roads, rendered common by frequent journeys of gangs of horses. The fabrication of common vessels, porrengers, jugs, cups, &c. had continued in the very rude state in which it was found by Dr. Plott, when he surveyed the county in 1686. His description regards such a state; yet is very respectful concerning Burslem, as having the largest Potteries then known to exist.

Nearly the whole of the Land on which the town now stands, as well as that which surrounds it, has at various times, in distant years, been deeply excavated for clay and ironstone; which at varying depths below almost the whole of the district, lie in valuable beds of

varied extent, differing in qualities and colours;
from which coarse materials, alone, or variously inter-
mixed, were made the clumsy articles transmitted to
our day; these were ornamented with clays, destitute
of elegance in the design, and the colours were not
only badly ground, but were applied with little taste
and design; the glaze also was lead ore, or pulverized
ironstone rock, or calcined lead, each deleterious to
the constitution, applied to vessels designed for culinary purposes.

Burslem was constituted a separate Rectory from
the Rectory of Stoke, by Act of Parliament, in 1805.
The Patron is William Adams, Esq. of Cobridge; the
Rector, Rev. Edward Whieldon. The Old Church
is dedicated to St. John; but merely the square tower
(1) remains of the first edifice; the present brick
structure having been erected early in the last century,
prior to any idea of the town becoming so populous
as it now is; else there would have been greater attention to provide accommodation. The very low si
tuation, and wholly unconnected with any houses, shew
that the other parts of the place were unsuitable for
such an edifice; the ground being liable to excavation,
or else mere heaps of shords. Very recently a fine
Peal of new Bells has been fixed in the tower.

Near the Old Church is the NATIONAL SCHOOL;
a spacious edifice, three stories high; supported wholly
by voluntary subscriptions, appropriated to educate
children of the labouring classes, both on Sundays and
during the week days.

---

1 Towards additional erections on the old Tower to raise
the whole, the late John Rogers, Esq. of the Watlands, left
£100. provided the same be effected within a specified period;
but this not yet being done, it is to be feared that the Legacy
has lapsed to the residuary Legatee.

At the top of the town stands the FREE SCHOOL; for educating a certain number of Boys and Girls. — The rent of a Farm and Land at Ipstones, should supply the Funds; but at present only a small sum is received for the proper purposes. The premises had suffered so much injury from time and neglect, that a large sum was required to repair them thoroughly; and the Farm House and Buildings were also in a delapidated condition; so that, for at least seven years, the rental of the Property will be required to pay off the Debts incurred by necessary repairs. When the whole estate again is available, we may fairly hope that this School will produce persons truly eminent for intelligence and industry.

In 1826, an Act of Parliament was obtained, constituting Burslem a Town, governed by a Chief Bailiff, with proper Officers, and a regular Police Establishment. The activity of those gentlemen who have hitherto filled the principal situation, has greatly promoted the general interests, by securing order and decorum, during the sabbath especially. The Public Offices are in the Town Hall.

The Town Hall was first erected in 1760, upon a plot of waste land called the May-pole bank; and the whole expence was defrayed by public subscription; about thirty of the masters contributing equal sums to those given by the then Lords of the manor, Sir Nigel Gresley, Bart. and Ralph Sneyd, Esq. £10. each. It is a brick edifice on an ashler basement; and is alike creditable to the public taste and spirit of the parties who founded it, and the purposes for which it is designed. It became the rallying point of the market people, and soon was surrounded by stalls, (for the various purposes of retail dealers, and butchers,) which remained fixed on the spot several years, until they were so injured by the weather, and the pilferage of boards, that they became almost a nuisance, and consequently were removed.

In the year 1824, the Town Hall underwent a complete repair both internally and externally, from the amount of money collected as Tolls in the market. The lower portion was divided into Watchhouse, Lockups. and a place for stalls, &c.; and the upper part into Offices for the Business of the Parish, and the Town; and also a spacious, well-furnished and beautiful Room, for Public Meetings, the holding of Petty Sessions every fortnight, and Public News Room for the respectable Inhabitants. In no town can there exist more unanimity on public affairs, than is evinced in Burslem.

The very extensive Manufactory of Enoch Wood and Sons, (which covers the sites of *five* old factories) has such a judicious arrangement, that it presents all the appearance of a most extensive Laboratory, and the Machinery of an Experimentalist. Here also is a MUSEUM, altogether *unique*, containing Specimens of the Progress of this Art, from very early times, previous to any authentic historical records, up to the present day; some of which were found under the foundations of these Manufactories, and of other manufactories dilapidated more than *eighty* years ago. Two other manufactories in the town, also are occupied and owned by these gentlemen. At the west front of the large manufactory, this venerable Father of the Potteries and truly eminent Antiquarian, has a spacious and elegant mansion, surrounded by convenient pleasure grounds, having an extensive prospect over the summit Pond of the Trent and Mersey Canal. Besides these, in the town there are about twenty six other manufactories of some extent, and several small ones. The largest of these are occupied and owned by Josh. Machin & Co., T. & B. Goodwin, T. Heath, J. Cormie, John Hall & Sons, and John Riley Marsh;— and from these we find every kind of Porcelain and Pottery regularly forwarded to all the marts of both continents.

The Bichers Colliery, a little above the town, affords the opportunity of contemplating the advantages to be derived from a judicious combination of the Principles which distinguish the Steam Engines erected by Savory, Boulton and Watt, and Trevethick. In 1806, E. Wood, Esq. having to erect a powerful Steam Engine at this place, attempted to connect the Air pump and condenser, as well as the patent high pressure principle; and was so successful, that this Engine by him constructed here, has more than thrice the power of any previously made. Adjoining, he erected a most commodious circular BATH, supplied with water, to any height of temperature, from 85° to 90°. The interior is beautifully painted in Landscapes, and marine views; and the public are admitted for a very small acknowledgment.

Near the northern extremity of the Market Place, is the Big House, so called, because when erected, it was indisputably the largest and best in the town of Burslem, if not in the whole District; but we incline to the latter conjecture. It is occupied by the younger Enoch Wood, Esq. well known and esteemed as a most intelligent manufacturer, and of the strictest integrity as a tradesman; and equally respected for his mental ability and the benevolence of his disposition. Another worthy brother resides in a beautiful mansion at Longport; and a third, eminent for his public and private virtues, is High or Chief Bailiff of Burslem.

The Wesleyan Chapel is very large, capable of accommodating *three thousand* persons, and adjoining it is a Sunday School, where *one thousand six hundred* children regularly receive literary and religious instruction. There are Six other Chapels for different religious parties; but to their credit be it spoken, most of them are beginning to forget their peculiar dogmas, and to regard only the ' New Commandment,' in their conduct towards each other.

A short distance below, at the end of the Waterloo Road, is a Residence, as unassuming in its appearance, as is its deservedly respected proprietor, Joseph Machin, Esq. one of the most early enamellers, and for some time a manufacturer of Porcelain and Pottery. During a long period he has been a member, and for many years Steward, and principal supporter, of the Wesleyan Methodist Society in Burslem. We do not recollect having heard a whisper of any kind to his discredit; but the general voice is in his praise. The influence of his piety, as well as the sincerity of his religious profession, have been constantly manifested in the blameless tenor of his transactions as a tradesman, his candour and benevolence as a friend, and his liberality towards every institution designed to ameliorate the condition of mankind. One of his Sons, who resides near, appears to emulate all the virtues of his worthy parent. The other is of much promise as a first rate artist.

At the lower part of the Furlong, or Newcastle road, is Portland House, late the residence of John Riley, Esq. deceased, and now of his disconsolate family. This gentleman and his Brother, Richard R. Esq. by perseverance amassed a very considerable property; but both died in the vigour of manhood. The latter had just completed, but not entered upon, a very beautiful Mansion above the Hamill, called Bank House. Both were highly esteemed for their integrity as tradesmen, and their kindness as masters; and the town of Burslem will long enjoy the benefit of their exertions with others for its aggrandizement.

On the south side, near Mrs. Riley's, Mr. John Ward, Attorney, has erected a beautiful Villa. And the large House on the opposite bank is the residence of Thomas Heath, Esq. of whom it needs merely be stated, that he ranks among the highest class of the district for every characteristic estimable by mankind.

In the vale below Burslem, July 26, 1766, the first clod was cut of the Trent and Mersey Canal, by the late Josiah Wedgwood, Esq. then recently appointed Potter to the Queen Consort of George III. In 1816, on the 50th anniversary, all the respectable manufacturers of Burslem assembled to celebrate the event, and to pay a respectful compliment to that gentleman, a native of this town. On this occasion, the chair was filled by E. Wood, Esq. who had a personal acquaintance with the deceased; to whose merits he paid very ample acknowledgments, and greatly added to the interest excited, by an exhibition of the several gradations of the manufacture during at least *one hundred and fifty* years. Indeed only those persons, who have seen the specimens, can form adequate ideas of the regular manner in which the numerous improvements have succeeded each other, from the coarse porrenger, and the Butter-pot, unto the fine Porcelain, and Jasper.

LONGPORT, & DALE HOLE, have in the present century rapidly increased in population; having one Square, and several streets of New Houses already erected, and others laid out. To accommodate these the New Church is being erected near these places. There is a neat Wesleyan Chapel, and Sunday School, in Longport. This name originated in its being the *last* wharf from Etruria south of the tunnel, and the *first* reached by the boats from the northern side. Formerly a long range of stepping-stones were placed across the swampy meadows, forming the LONG BRIDGE, but when the Canal had drawn more passengers on the road, a raised or high way was formed, still existing.

In the Dale Hole the New Church is in progress, adapted for the increasing demands for public accommodation at religious worship. The style is gothic; and the whole when completed will be a beautiful specimen of architecture. It is dedicated to St. Paul, and the following inscription is engraved on a Brass Plate deposited in the Foundation Stone.

Hujus Ecclesiæ Subparochiali, Sancto Paulo Dicatæ (partim publicis privatis, partim impensis extructæ,) vir honorabilis ac admodum Reverendus Henrycus Ryder, D. D. Episcopus Lichfieldiensis et Coventriensis, Lapidem angularem deposuit Regnante feliciter Georgio Quarto, Mensis Junii die XXIV. Anno salutis humanæ MDCCCXXVIII. Deo Gloria: Patriæ decus.

E. Wood, Pacis Curatore.

E. Whieldon, Rectore.
W. Adams, Patrono.

L. H. Rhead,
J. Clewes,
T. Weatherby,
T. Hancock.
} Ædituis.

L. Vulliamy, Architecto.

FREE TRANSLATION.

The Foundation Stone of this Parochial Chapel, erected partly by a National Grant, and partly by Private Contributions, was laid by the Honourable and Right Reverend Henry Ryder, D. D. Lord Bishop of Lichfield and Coventry, in the auspicious reign of George the Fourth, on the XXIV day of June, in the year of Redemption MDCCCXXVIII. The Glory be ascribed to God; the honour to our Country.

The situation is certainly low; and the population of Dale Hole, and Longport, will chiefly receive the advantages of the ministry in this place. Much anxiety was evinced to have a Church erected on the Jenkins, the most elevated spot in the town, and close adjoining to the Market Place; but whether the intention will be executed, cannot at present be with truth asserted.

At Longport is a very extensive and convenient manufactory of Pottery, Porcelain, and Glass, belonging to John Davenport, Esq. & Sons; also another near Newport, his Business Residence. J. Davenport, Esq. is well known as one of the most enterprizing and successful Manufacturers. Of his worth as a private person, the numerous instances of his benevolence are the best testimonials.

Messrs. Williamson, and Messrs. Phillips have extensive manufactories of Pottery; and the article produced at Dale Hole manufactory, belonging to Spencer Rogers, Esq. of the Watlands, is not excelled by any other production of the district.

The residence of Josh. Stubbs, Esq. has a very extended prospect southward along the Vale on whose northern banks the Potteries are established. The gentleman has long been esteemed for his excellencies of character.

Overlooking Longport, and a considerable portion of the District, is Porthill, the beautiful and almost sequestered residence of Mr. R. Daniel, (of the firm H. & R. D. of Stoke,) a gentleman equally esteemed for the virtues of his heart, and the stores of his mind.

Beyond, at a short distance, is Watlands, a superb mansion, and gardens, where Spencer Rogers, Esq. enjoys the sweets of domiciliary quiet, after the fatigues of commercial activity. This gentleman is well known as a manufacturer of superior talent, and his worth, as a member of the Community, is very highly prized.

In HOT LANE, besides other manufactories, is that of Warburton, & Co. at which the first Cream Colour Pottery was manufactured on the improvement of Mr. E. Booth's fluid glaze. From a descendant of the person, — Jacob Warburton, Esq. have been obtained some valuable remarks introduced in the proper places in this History.

COBRIDGE contains a number of houses, and is in both Burslem and Stoke Parishes. The elegant mansion of W. Adams, Esq. is in the former; while the neat and modest edifice belonging to J. Hales, Esq. is in the latter.

There is a Free School, erected about *seventy* years ago, and now occasionally beneficial to the poorer classes. A neat Chapel here belongs to the Methodist New Connection, with a Sunday School attached. Here is a very large Roman Catholic Chapel, and also a convenient School Room, for educating Youth by a method which embraces the *useful* of the systems of Bell and Lancaster, yet differs from both. At the Grange, near this place, formerly a very secluded spot, are the remains of an old Catholic Chapel, a mere thatched shed; probably the place of resort to that body of Christians, at the time when bigotry was rancorously pursuing its victims with merciless retaliation for real or supposed injuries.

At Cobridge are the Manufactories of R. Stevenson, J. & R. Clews. N. Dillon, Mansfield & Hackney, S. Godwin, S. Alcock, and some others not at present in operation. The various kinds of Pottery and Porcelain, are here manufactured in great perfection.

HANLEY & SHELTON; WITH THEIR VICINITY.

HANLEY & SHELTON are situated on the north-east of Newcastle, at the distance of about two miles and a half. They formerly were of little account in the topography of Staffordshire; for the only notice Erdeswick takes of Shelton is this; "Scelfitone was in the Conqueror's hands, 20th of his reign." — And the only *conjectural* notice of Hanley, is formed on the nearness of the *name* to that given, and the facts of being nigh to Bucknall, and property in the place having long been in the possession of the families mentioned :— "Bucknall and *Annesley* are allotted to Ralph De Hooton, by deed, Jan. 28,11th Richard II. — *Ansedeley* vulgariter *Annesley* and a part of Buckenhall — *Annesley*, a mile from the Dove (but more probably *Trent.*) Sir John Verdon, Knt. Lord of *Ansley*, Biddulph, and Bucknall. *Annesley* belonged to the family of Tole, (Talk) or Tock; after them to the Bougheys and Mainwarings, of Whit-

D

more.—Edward Mainwaring, Lord of Whitmore, has Nether Biddulph, *Annesley,* and a part of Buckenhall."

The *Testa de Nevill*, which is an ancient record preserved in the Exechequer, and compiled by John Nevill, a justice in Eyre, between the years 1234 and 1238, contains the following particulars of tenures within this manor by knight's service and socage:

KNIGHT'S FEES.—" John de Cnocton holds the vill of Cnocton *(now Knutton)* to fee-farm, paying yearly to the New Castle £4. 11s. 6d., also performing the guard of the same castle for forty days, at the cost of our Lord the King.

" Also, William de Erdinton holds the vill of Fenton to fee-farm, paying yearly to the said castle 7s. 4d., performing also the aforesaid guard for the aforesaid term.

" Also, William de Hanleg' holds the vill of Hanleg' *(now Hanley)* to fee-farm, paying yearly to the said Castle 6s. and performing, &c.

" Also, Ralph de Bevill holds the vill of Langeton *(now Longton)* to fee-farm, paying yearly 5s. to the said Castle, &c.

"Also, William Murell holds one yard-land within the said manor of New Castle, in the vill of Selton, *(now Shelton)* by the serjeanty of keeping *Haim* (the inclosure or park) of our Lord the King there, which is called the *Haia* of Clive *(now Cliff.)*

" Also, Henry de Audicheley holds within the said manor the vills of Tunstall, Chadderleg,' *(now Chatterley)* Bradewell, Turnedesfeld, *(now Thursfield)* and Normanecot, *(now Normacot)* by the serjeanty of serving on foot, with a bow and arrows, within the said Castle for eight days in time of war at his own cost."

SOCAGE TENANTS.—" The Knights Templars hold Kel, *(now Keel)* a member of New Castle, of the gift of our Lord King Henry, and pay nothing."

Hanley and Shelton were, by Act of Parliament, united into one Market Town, in 1812, and they now form the largest in the Potteries, and probably in the county of Stafford. They are situate on the gentle declivity of a large hill, with a south western aspect; and viewed from Woolstanton Church yard, present a beautiful object for contemplation; the Buildings and Streets rising gradually above the valley. In 1825, and 1828, Acts of Parliament were obtained to establish a regular Commission of respectable Inhabitants, for the purposes of Lighting and Watching the Towns, and directing an internal Police; and great public benefit has resulted from these Regulations.

Most of the Streets are *new*, having been formed, and the houses erected in the present century; and many others being now in course of erection. They are both wide, and regular in height, *(only two stories.)* and on each side is a good causeway for foot passengers, paved with hard bricks. And for public accommodation, the spirit of improvement has been extended to the removal of obstructions, and the rendering the public roads open and direct. There are some spacious and elegant houses, the residences of the more opulent Inhabitants, some of which are subsequently particularized.

The situation of the Market-place is such, that only by a circuitous route do the coaches from Burslem to Stoke pass through it. An inconvenience only to be remedied by opening the projected new line of Road between Burslem and Lane End. The Market is doubtless the largest in the district, and well supplied with every kind of produce, (except grain, the sale of which is discouraged, because of the Corn Market at Newcastle on Mondays,) and the Tolls, which now produce more than £700 annually, are appropriated for the improvement of the town. Saturday is the principal, and Wednesday the second market day. The Market-Place is extensive, and around it are many capacious Shops for every descrip-

tion of merchandize.   The establishments of Messrs.
Boulton and Robinson, and of Mr. T. Cox, for Dra-
pery, &c. are most capacious and elegant; the
former, second to none in the county; the other
equalled by very few.   The Shop of Mr. Wilson, for
Chemicals, is truly respectable; and its proprietor
deservedly ranks high in his profession.   The Swan
Inn is a first rate Commercial Traveller's Hotel; and
with other similar establishments, receives ample patronage.   At the upper part is a fine *Doric Column*,
of cast-iron, on a bold pedestal; beneath which is the
main valve of the Water Works; and from which an
ample supply of water for the use of the market, or
other public purposes, is readily obtained.   At the
top of the column is a large Gas Lamp, of great utility in that situation.   The *Market Hall* is a neat
structure, but is merely a species of *Shed* for Venders
of Poultry, Eggs, and Butter, on the Market Days,
and to cover the stalls during the time they are unem-
ployed.   In one corner is the watch-house, and another
two very secure dungeons, or lock-ups.   A room over
this edifice, would be not only very extensive, but of
great utility to the Inhabitants, who have not any
public Room of adequate dimensions for general
Meetings.

From the Market-Place, the Company of Proprietors of the Navigation from the Trent to the
Mersey, have a *Rail Road*, on which, by waggons,
they bring up all packages into the town, and return
with Crates, and Casks of Porcelain and Pottery, to
be forwarded to the places of consignment.   This
Rail Way terminates in the Vale Pleasant, near
Etruria, where are several offices, a large Wharf,
and Storehouses belonging to the Company, for the
several purposes of materials for the manufacturers.

We have been informed that Hanley and Lane End are indebted for their Churches to the liberality of a Gentleman, whom it would be criminal to overlook, tho' he was scarcely connected with the manufactures of the district. At the time when the method of ornamenting the Salt glazed white stone ware by Blue Painting, was beginning to attract attention; there resided, at Newcastle, a Gentleman, whose aquisitions of property appear to have only stimulated him to increased exertions how he might best promote the interests of the inhabitants of this then rising district. This was JOHN BOURNE, Esq. to whose munificence, Burslem owes chiefly its Grammar School, Hanley its Church, and Lane End its Church and Free School. At the time of Christmas, 1760 or 61, being on a visit at the house of Mr. Hollins, of the Upper Green, Hanley, father of the late Samuel Hollins, Esq. and Mrs. Chatterley, of Shelton; the conversation turned on the very severe weather, so unsettled as to render hazardous the attendance at Stoke Church for the Holy Communion of the Lord's Supper, at that high Festival of the Church. Mr. Bourne was intent on going, not apprehending any injury to his health thereby; but the reflection, that many others might be greatly inconvenienced by going, and grieved at being prevented by the weather, caused him to declare, that if a suitable plot of Land could be obtained, he would give £500. towards the erection of a Church. (The same amount he also gave towards Lane End Church.) Another Gentleman present, Mr. Adams, immediately supported this liberal offer, by a present of Land for the site and cemetry; and we believe a descendant of this gentleman, has given land at Burslem, for similar purposes of the New Church there. The Rev. Mr. Middleton preached the first sermon in Hanley Church, which proving much too small for the increasing popu-

lation, was taken down, and on its site stands the
present Church, which was also opened by Mr.
Middleton.   It cost £5000 and was founded in
1788.   It is a firm and elegant Brick Building,
with a square tower *one hundred* feet high, containing
an excellent peal of *eight* bells, and the interior is so
well constructed, that every person in the congregation
can see and be seen by the Minister.   The appointment is vested in a committee, and is a perpetual
Curacy under Stoke-upon-Trent.   The *Parsonage
House* is neat and small, at the junction of Hanley
and Shelton, near the top of Albion Street, and
almost adjoining the National School.   The present
Curate is Rev Robt. Ellis Aitkens, who possesses
considerable qualifications for his important office.

The *National School* is neat and commodious,
devoid of ornament, and only adapted for utility; but
the *British School*, is a superb edifice, fitted up in
the best manner possible, at considerable expence;
and the upper Room is not exceeded in elegance and
convenience by any Room for similar purposes in the
county.

In the vale below Waterloo and Woodwall, are
Water Works, whence, from a copious spring, a very
powerful Steam Engine forces up the water into the
reservoir on the top of Windmill Hill. a most elevated
spot; where the water filters, and is thence conveyed
in cast-metal pipes to supply not only Hanley and
Shelton, but even Cobridge, Burslem, and. adjacent
places, with a tolerable quantity of good water.
These were established at the sole expence of a private
person. John Smith, Esq. and doubtless, will ultimately well compensate him for so public-spirited an
undertaking.

Near the Water Works has been very recently erected a large Paper Mill, on the most improved principles, by Messrs. Foudrinier. The immense quantity of tissue paper consumed in the manufactories, for printing and wrapping up porcelain and Pottery, may be a sufficient warranty for such a speculation; and as the parties are of great notoriety for their experience and practical acquaintance with the most valuable processes and machinery, little doubt need be entertained that this establishment will be successful. On this property formerly was got the Peacock Coal, much softer then the cannel; it most vividly represents all the colours of the most glowing feathers of a peacock's train, whence it borrows its name.

On the east, below Windmill Hill, is Prospect Place, the elegant residence of Wm. Ridgway, Esq. whence is dispensed with beneficence and urbanity, assistance and consolation to the afflicted of the neighbourhood. The prospect is very delightful and extensive; and by the energies of the patriotic proprietor, the whole of the vicinity has been converted from a rude and demoralized part of Hanley, into a beautiful, cleanly, well ordered hamlet. The advantages will result to society in general, not only at present, but in periods after the present owner is gone to enjoy his endless reward.

A little above the Church, is the modest mansion of Joseph Mayer, Esq. well known as one of the best Linguists of the European Tongues, in the district; and deservedly esteemed very highly for his many public and private virtues. Preserving the noiseless tenor of his way, without ostentation or profusion, his bounty is dispensed among the deserving poor, and his aid readily afforded to every benevolent

institution. Adjoining is the manufactory of Elijah
Mayer and Son; (or in fact, of the son only, the
father having died many years ago, which has long
maintained a very high station in the scale of manufacture, for the excellence of the Queen's Ware and
Brown Line Ware there fabricated. But it is now
notable for a species of Porcelain manufactured only
here; and concerning whose properties the author has
not yet obtained particular information. Mr. Mayer,
the elder, was the son of Mr. M. of the High Carr,
who was unfortunately overtaken by the tide in crossing
the sands near Ulverston, and perished along with
some others. Mr. M. was some time an extensive
merchant in Holland, and settled in Hanley a short
time after his marriage. He was respected by all who
knew him; and the benefits of his liberality yet flow
to persons in the neighbourhood.

The Old Hall manufactory, (long the scene of
the chief manufacture of Crouch ware, and White
Stone ware Salt glaze, in Hanley, under different persons, the latter especially, of Mr. Whitehead, who
erected the *New Hall*, in Shelton,) is now the upper
part of the extenive manufactory of Job Meigh and
Son. Here are Flint Mills, and all the appendages
necessary for a large establishment; and here may be
seen the worthy relict of the late, and mother of the
present proprietor, in an advanced age, rendering
every help in her power, for promoting the regular
processes and benefit of the concern. Her matronly
beneficence is enjoyed by numbers, not only of her
dependants, but of others rendered objects of com-
passion by misery or affliction. C. Meigh, Esq. is
esteemed for his firmness and decision of character, the
Arts have not a more liberal patron, for his means;
nor the poor and defenceless a more firm protector.

His modesty and candour are of general notice; and his friendship has never been known to be affected by the vicissitudes of fortune; nor has his kindness been withheld when the suffering could be alleviated.

At the top of Albion Street is Bank House, a very handsome residence, occupied by its proprietor, Job Meigh, Esq. who is for his philantrophy and liberality justly regarded as one of the worthies of the district, to whom the Inhabitants generally submit any important subjects of reference, in confidence of having strict impartial decision awarded to them.   Also is the gentlemen to whom, in 1823, His Royal Highness the Duke of Sussex presented the Gold Medal of the Society of Arts, for Mr. Meigh's giving to the public a *Glaze* for Common Pottery, entirely free from the deleterious qualities of the usual lead glaze.   On the opposite side of the road is a very good house, with a handsome Portico, belonging to Mr Wm. Parker; a merchant connected with the Continental Markets; and considered among the respectable Inhabitants, not engaged in the manufactures of the district.

The *Bethesda Chapel*, belonging to the Connection of Methodists which separated from that body in 1797, must be noticed, not only because it is equal in elegance and dimensions to any place of Worship for Dissenters in the Kingdom; but for the liberality of its Trustees, honourable to their Christian profession, in readily permitting it to be used by other Christian Sects, whenever there are important occasions for soliciting extensive aids of public benevolence.   Connected with this Chapel, is a large Building for educating near *One Thousand* Children on the Sabbath day, by gratuitous Teachers; and supported by the liberality of the congregation, and some other donations. It must also be stated, that in the town are *eight* other chapels, with which are Sunday Schools, for the various professors of christianity. In Vine Street, Shelton, Messrs. Bentley and Wear, eminent engravers, have a fine Gallery of Paintings, including some of considerable value, the productions of early Artists; but useful to the district as a Depot of the works of resident artists. To this exhibition persons are admitted on very moderate terms. Near here is a proof how much a great part of Shelton is undermined by the collieries, which have been many years in operation; and seem likely to continue. The Coal Mines under all the Copyhold Lands within this Manor belong to the Duchy of Lancaster, and now yield a considerable revenue, being worked, extensively for the consumption of the Potteries, by the Lessee of the Crown, Lord Viscount Granville. Very recently have many of the houses in Joiner's Square, or Eastwood, sustained great injury by the colliery there; some fell, others were taken down, and have been rebuilt; and a part of the Land, which formerly was excellent pasture Land, is now a mere tract of holes and hillocks.

We have mentioned Hanley and Shelton as one town; but it must be understood, that they are separate and district liberties, or villes, for purposes connected with the highways, &c. and only the inhabitants of each place transact that part of public business. Etruria also is one part of the liberty of Shelton; as is likewise that part of Cobridge which belongs to the parish of Stoke-upon-Trent. In 1800, the two liberties had in them *thirty-four* Manufactories, varying in size, for the different kinds of Pottery and Porcelain; but on the sites of some of these, dwelling houses are now erected; and there remain *twenty-six*, (*thirteen* in each liberty,) of which about twenty continue to receive that share of public patronage they endeavour to deserve. The principal of these are known as E. Mayer & Son, J. Meigh & Son, Dimmock & Co. Toft & May, J. Keeling, W. Hackwood, T. Taylor, & J. Glass in Hanley; and in Shelton, I. & W. Ridgway, Hicks, Meigh, & Johnson, Henry Daniel & Sons, J. Yates, Hollins, Warburton, Daniel, & Co. Messrs. Sherratt, Founders and Engineers, Salford, Manchester, have near the Canal a Branch Establishment, for the convenience of the Potteries.

In Shelton, is the elegant mansion of R. Hicks, Esq. a gentleman who connects with sterling piety a most unbounded benevolence of disposition. Here the destitute find relief, the distressed find consolation, and the miserable, sympathy and protection. The Manufactory adjoining produces excellent porcelain and pottery, of the various kinds; and is creditable to the parties Hicks, Meigh, & Johnson. It stands on the site of that where Mr. R. Baddeley first made the *Blue* printed ware; and which subjected him and his brother to the highest censure for extravagance, in having a manufactory covered with *tiles*, instead of *thatch*; and for being the first who erected *four* hovels behind, instead of only *two*.

The Manufactories of Messrs. J. & W. Ridgway, are situated, one at the bottom of Albion Street, the other at Cauldon Place, Shelton. The former occupies the site of that where Mr. Werner Edwards, made Pottery and Colours for the first Enamellers, but is greatly extended. That at Cauldon Place is very extensive; and most judiciously arranged to diminish expence in the several processes. Situated on the banks of the Cauldon Canal, opportunity is enjoyed for receiving coals and all materials, and for forwarding all packages, by the canal conveyances. The Proprietors enjoy justly merited celebrity for their unabating energies to promote the general improvement and welfare of the Parish. Possessed of considerable talent, and enjoying a full share of public confidence, they have always been among the most zealous and ardent alleviators of the sufferings of the distressed; and careful guardians of the public or parochial funds. Wishful to ameliorate the condition of mankind at large, they are ever found second to none in liberality and perseverance. And we may add, they are a blessing to the neighbourhood, and posterity will long hold their memory in grateful admiration.

At the top of Shelton, in a state of repair to be regretted by persons fond of the antiquities and literary character of the country, stands Shelton Old Hall, a venerable half-timbered mansion, built in the form of a long cross †; the birth-place of the poet Elijah Fenton, and now the property of Sir Thomas Boughey, a descendent of the family of Fenton. Near this spot, is to be commenced, in the present year, the erection of a new and extremely *Large Church*, by Funds supplied by a grant under a recent Act of Parliament for supplying different populous districts with accommodation for religious worship according to the rites of the National Church. Cauldon Place, the residence of J. Ridgway, Esq., is a regular, capacious and elegant structure; enjoying a very pleasing prospect, and surrounded by plantations judiciously arranged to preserve every thing essential, and veil whatever would disturb the interesting landscape.

Near, is Shelton Hall, a spacious edifice, the residence of W. Bishop, Esq., one of the directors of the British Gas Company; who have, in the lower part of the town, only a short distance from here, most extensive and commodious *Gas Works*, for making the quantity required to supply the public lamps, many of the Shops, and some of the Manufactories, in Burslem, Hanley, Shelton, Stoke, Fenton, and Lane End. As the charge for this accommodation is very moderate, for some time the proceeds did not pay interest for the capital expended; but now, the more the advantages of pure and good gas become known, the demand proportionably increases, and there is great probability of the speculation proving alike advantageous to the public and its proprietors.

Near the Gas Works, is a very large Laboratory for the making *Copperas*; the property of G. Birch, Esq. of Cannock, and Mr. J. Jones, of Newcastle. Large beds of martial pyrites are formed, and supplied regularly from the Collieries in the vicinity; whence runs the liquor required by Six Large Boilers. The article here produced, has long been regarded as of excellent quality, by the Dry Salters, Printers, and Dyers of Lancashire; to whom it is regularly forwarded by canal.

ETRURIA is a long street of about 120 houses; for whose advantage are erected, at the northern extremity a capacious School Room, on the British and Foreign School Plan; in the centre is another School Room, used also as a Preaching Room, for Methodists of the New Connection; and at the lower end is a neat Chapel, for the Wesleyan Methodists.—The Manufactory is not only capacious, but well adapted for all requisite purposes of the manufacture.   It

E

possesses an extensive front wharf, besides two branch
Canals for secure conveyance of the Materials to
the interior. And a very powerful Steam Engine is
employed to perform numerous important services calculated to diminish manual labour. Etruria Hall the
edifice on the Northern Bank eminence, was erected
by the celebrated founder of Etruria. It has a truly
elegant appearance, viewed from the opposite eminence at Basford Bank. The interior is very capacious,
and the numerous apartments are well adapted for
convenience and utility; but all bespeak the neatness
and absence of ostentation, so constantly observed by
its eminent proprietor. The outbuildings are on a
large scale; the gardens very extensive: but the whole
is now unoccupied, (tho' recently employed as a Board-
ing School, for which purpose it is most excellently
adapted;) as its worthy owner, the second Josiah
Wedgwood, now resides at Mare Hall, a superb and
almost princely mansion, for elegance and capacious-
ness, distant from Etruria about seven miles.

STOKE, PENKHULL, AND THE VICINITY.

STOKE-UPON-TRENT was long the Parish Town of
the district; but now is regarded solely by itself; and
has its Market, and Town Hall, a neat structure, well
adapted for public purposes; and under it are lock-ups,
and a place to hold the public Fire Engine.

Erdeswick says, "Stoke being one of the best
parsonages in the country, it is a marvel (so many
religious houses being near it,) how it escaped in all
ages the covetousness of them. — It resting still according to the first institution of parsonages, not appropriated."

The Parish of Stoke contains Hanley, Shelton, Penkhull, Fenton Vivian, Fenton Culvert, Longton, and Lane End, Towns in the Potteries; with the Liberties of Clayton, Seabridge, Basford, Botteslow, Bucknall, Eaves, and Bagnall, appropriated chiefly to agriculture.

By Act of Parliament, in 1805, Newcastle and Burslem, and Bucknall with Bagnall, were formed into separate Rectories distinct from the Rectory of Stoke, but receiving from it, a stipulated annual sum.

The Old Church, dedicated to St. Peter, a venerable and spacious stone edifice, of the later Saxon Style of architecture, and the mother Church of eight surrounding churches, in a circuit of several miles, is doomed to be taken down; and its materials, for many centuries (probably eight) devoted to the worship of the Triune God, may be appropriated to worthless purposes. On the ground is a stout grave stone with this inscription, Sibil Clarke, aged 112, 1684, Henry Clarke, aged 112.

In the Church are some monuments to the memory of the Fentons, of Newcastle, maternal ancestors of Sir T. F. Boughey, Bart. and the following epitaph commemorates the virtues of the late Josiah Wedgwood, Esq.:

> " Sacred to the Memory of
> JOSIAH WEDGWOOD, F. R. S. & S. A.
> Of Etruria, in this county,
> Born in August 1730,
> Died January the 3d 1795:

" Who converted a rude and inconsiderable manufacture into an elegant art and an important part of national commerce. By these services to his country he acquired an ample fortune, which he blamelessly and reasonably enjoyed, and generously dispensed for the reward of merit and the relief of misfortune. His mind was inventive and original, yet perfectly sober and well regulated. His character was decisive and commanding, without rashness or arrogance. His probity was inflexible, his kindness unwearied, his manners simple and dignified, and the cheerfulness of his temper was the natural reward of the activity of his pure and useful life. He was most loved by them who knew him best; and he has left indelible impressions of affection and veneration on the minds of his family, who have erected this monument to his memory."

The following account of former sittings in Stoke Old Church, will preserve an evidence of the primitive distribution of seats in regard to rank, age, and worth, as well as the former separation of the men from the women in places of public worship.

April 3d, *Anno Domini* 1634.

" By virtue of an order made by Robert, (by the Divine Providence of God,) Lord Bishop of Coventry and Lichfield, *John Mainwaring*, rector of the Parish Church of Stoke-upon-Trent, in the county of Stafford, William Allen, and William Hill, Churchwardens; their and others their assistants, with the consent of all or most of the parishioners, have placed the ancient householders of the said parish in the seats in the said church as ensueth.

Lichfield July 12*th*, 1664.—

" If this be the right copy of the order of my worthy predecessor the Lord Bishop *Wright*, I confirm it, appointing that the elder parishioners, according to their deserving, be seated and preferred before the younger.

"JOHN LICHFIELD AND COVENTRY.

"'The names of the parishioners of *Stoke-upon-Trent*, appointed to place the parishioners in their seats, that have [so done] by common consent, and [whose arrangement was] allowed by my Lord Bishop of *Coventry* and *Lichfield,* Anno Domini 1668.

" *Imprimis.*—Robert Clayton, Thomas Tittensor the younger, Thomas Barratt, Thomas Murhall, John Bucknall of the Gate, John Bucknall of Bentiley, Robert Hunt, John Brown, John Hill, Thomas Ames, Henry Brookes, and Richard Meire, who have placed the parishioners as followeth:

" *The South Side—Men's Seats.*

" 1. *Churchwardens* for the time being.

2. Thomas Hunt, Gent. John Brown, Gent. Thomas Fenton, John Lovatt, and Thomas Lea.

3. William Bagnall, John Machin, Richard Lovatt, Sir Richard Leveson's tenement, and Robert Bagnall.

4. William Hill, Thomas Hill, and Mr. Bentiley.

5. Mr. Terrick, Richard Broad, and Mr. Keeling.

6. John Malpass, John Boulton's tenement, and William Simpson.

7. Richard Nichols, Thomas Turner, and Roger Dale.

8. John Brown, John Brown, John Dale, & John Prickett.

9. John Doody, John Bowyer, and Nicholas Lovatt.

10. Randle Woodcock, Thomas Fenton, and Roger Machin.

11. William Knight, John Proctor, and Benson's Heir.

12. Henry Stevenson, Nicholas Lovatt, and John Wright.

13. Thomas Tittensor, Richard Beech, and Randle Bagnall.

14. Roger Tittensor, Randle Woodcock, & Thomas Machin.

15. Roger Wood, Mary Shaw, and George Hales.

16. John Pattison, Wright's house, John Machin de Lane.

17. John Stevenson, Francis Lycett, Hanley's de Hanley.

18. Richard Boulton, John Barratt, and Dawson's house.

19. John Biddulph, William Hall, and John Crockett.

" *North Side—Men's Seats.*

" 1. Thomas Smith, Gent. and Thomas Bucknall, Gent.

2. William Allen, Ridghouse, John Hill, and Roger Machin, senior.

3. Thomas Serjeant, Gent. Mr. Bradshaw, John Murhall, and John Wood.

4. At the *Wall*, Roger Machin, jun. Thomas Rawlins, John Adams, Ottiwell Jolley, and John Machin.

5. George Hanson, John Machin, and Thomas Bucknall.

6. Richard Cartwright, William Beech, and Thomas Pare.

7. Thomas Tittensor, Richard Thorleys, and Brassington's.

8. Richard Meire, Robert Cross, and John Leigh.

9. Thomas Machin, John Boulton, and Robert Whilton.

10. William Allen, for tenement, William Allen de Hulme, and John Beech.

11. Sir William Bowyer, for Craddock's, Watson's, and Anthony Keeling's.

12. Bentiley's de Laund, Richard Walklott, and John Poulson.

13. John Wedgwood, Richard Trevin, and John Smith.

14. John Wood de Ash and tenement, John Bowyer, and John Plant.

15. John Austin, Laurence Naylor, and William Cowap.

16. John Stevenson, Gilbert's house, and John Boulton.

17. Thomas Walklott, John Leese, Jeffry Steel.

18. Lewis o'Land, Hugh Mare, and Francis Pool.

19. Jeffry Meire, Richard Cartwright, and William Beech.

20. John Adams, William Murhall, and Thomas Ames.

" North Side—Women's Seats.

"1. Roger Bradshaw, and John Allen, Roger Bradshaw hath the Form end.

2. Thomas Murhall, Wood de Ash, Austens de Ash, and Allen's de Hulme.

3. John Machin de Bucknall, Boulton's house de Bucknall, William Adams de Bagnall, Hanson's house, John Beech de Bentiley.

4. Richard Poulson, Laurence Sherratt, Randle Booths, Iohn Hill of Shelton, Randle Bagnall of Eaves.

5. Robert Whilton, John Hitchcock, John Bucknall, of the Gate, Thomas Lovatt, of the Hole-house, Richard Walklott, of Berry Hill.

6. Thomas Ames, Thomas Hanley of Hanley, the whole form.

7. Hitchin of Lane, George Fenton, Robert Hill, and Francis Craddock.

8. Richard Meire, German's house, Edmund Vice, Richard Hewett, and Thomas Pare.

9. Richard Mear, Thomas Turmore, the house of Wright

and Hanley, Richard Walklott, for Hanley-hey's; Thomas Tittensor, for the Over-house, Thomas Wood claimeth the same.

10. Parker's house, Boulton's house, John Bradshaw, and Thomas Bagnall.

11. Thomas Fenton of Boothen, Thomas Ames, John Hanley's of the Penkhull.

12. Thomas Barrott, John Rowley, of Shelton, Hugh Wood, and Stephen Fenton.

13. Spooner's house, Richard Tunstall, and John Hankinson.

14. Roger Harrison, William Harrison, Jeffry Meire, and Roger Cowap.

South Side—Women's Seats.

"1. Thomas Bucknall, and Richard Serjeant, George Fenton claimeth the same.

2. Thomas Ames, John Turmore, Brassington of Moor-hall.

3. Henry Brooks, Bartholomew Bowyer, Richard Lovatt, and Widow Bentiley.

4. Robert Clayton, Thomas Dawson, John Lovatt, the house that is holden of Garnitt and Benson a seat, Horne's land a seat, John Trinley claimeth the same.

5. Robert Hunt, Roger Bagnall for Longton house, Whiston's house, Roger Bagnall of Clayton, for Longton house, the 4th seat; Richard Aston claimeth for German's land.

6. John Kendall, William Machin, and Thomas Lovatt.

7. Thomas Machin, John Proctor, Henry Lovatt, of Eaves, John Kendall, Thomas Tittensor claims the same for Fenton's house.

8. John Brown, T. Broad to Hill, and John Brown for his tenement.

9. Widow Hordern, Thomas Tittensor for the lower house, Hugh Machin.

10. Widow Bagnall, Mr. Egerton, Peter Knight, and John Woodcock the fourth seat.

11. John Hammersley, Richard Kendrick, William Barratt Thomas Machin claims a seat for Bate's house.

12. John Dale, John Hitchin, James Hudson, Ralph Bucknall, and John Pulsbury.

13. Hugh Thorley, Roger Fox, John Simpson of Clayton, Widow Febkin, and John Simpkins.

14. Widow Stevenson, John Bourn, and Roger Dixon. Richard Aston is unplaced and Robert Pyler. Also the young maids are to kneel in the short forms.

"Eccleshall Castle, 26th April, A. D. 1634.

"Being fully informed by such as I have caused and required to survey convenient and commodious sittings and placing of the parishioners, of the parish of *Stoke-upon-Trent,* in the county of *Stafford,* and finding no just opposition against the same, by any of the parishioners aforesaid, I, Robert, *(by Divine Providence)* Lord Bishop of *Lichfield* and *Coventry,* do well approve the Order, by parcelling and seating of the said parishioners aforesaid, and by these presents allow, ratify, and confirm the same whatsoever the Rector, Churchwardens, and parishioners have done therein, until just cause shall be shewed to the contrary. In witness whereof I have hereunto set my hand, and caused my seal episcopal to be hereunto placed at the time and place abovesaid.

"ROBERT LICHFIELD AND COVENTRY."

"THOMAS GOODFELLOW, *Clayton,* } Churchwardens for the
"JOSEPH BOURNE, *Ford Bays,* } Year of our Lord 1772.

Some obscurity in the above document appears at the beginning, by the position of the subsequent confirmations in 1664 and 1668, whether the list applies to the period of 1634, and afterwards 1668; or wholly to the latter: and some sentences are not clearly expressed, which we have taken the liberty of filling up between brackets according to our judgment. Whatever obscurity might exist, originally, or by copying, the article is sufficient, explicit for the purposes already stated, and which induced its insertion. By some it may be considered not uninteresting in furnishing a list of the names of the ancient householders in the parish of Stoke; and in affording a partial means of judging of the comparative state of the parish in regard to the population in the seventeenth and nineteenth centuries.

Mr. Mainwaring, whose name appears, as Rector, in the beginning of the above instrument, is remarkable not only as an instance of longevity, but for the duration of his incumbency. The following has been handed to us as being an extract from the Parish Register, though it is evidently imperfect:

" May 1692. Johannes Mainwaring, s. T. P. Rector Ecclesie de Stoke sup. Trent: sepult."

" Johannes Mainwaring cum extitissit Rector Ecclesie Stoke p. spatium Quinquaginta et non'm annor' expiravit die et annon s'pra dict."

If Mr. Mainwaring was 59 years rector of Stoke, his age, at the time of his death, could not be less than 83 years. He was succeeded by the Rev. John Repton, who was likewise perpetual curate of Norton-in-the-Moors.—*Pitt.*

In the year 1815, a very handsome and commodious *National School,* for the education of 500 children of the poor in the Principles of the Established Church, was erected at this place, at an expense of nearly £1000. which sum was raised principally by voluntary contributions. It is situated at the east end of and adjoining the church-yard.

The Church now erected at Stoke, is of the Modern or Ornamented Gothic style of Architecture. The Architects and Builders, Messrs. Trubshaw and Johnson, of Haywood, in this County, commenced the erection in March, 1826, and it was completed in August, 1829. The Corner Stones in the East, South, and North Angles at the Chancel End, were laid by the Very Rev. Dean of Lichfield, John Tomlinson, Esq. and the late Josiah Spode, Esq. on the 28th of June, 1826; and in each is an Earthenware Tablet, containing the following inscription, in Bas Relief:

Hanc Ecclesiam Parochialem paucis olìm Sto-
kensem Agellum colentibus satìs amplam, jampridém
octo filiarum, quòquó spectas, prole venerabilem, sed
ipsam demúm nimís angustam, ut quæ Novam Homi-
num multitudinem qui artem Ceramicam exercebant,
non caperet, duplo ampliandam et Situ Antiquo, quá
plús ócto Sæculis per Christum Nomen Jehovæ adora-
tum est, paulúm Relicto quominús sepultis injuria
fiat, Totam á solo Reficiendam curaverunt;—Partìm
Pecuniis ditioribus uìtrò Datis, insignibus inter has
duabus Largitionibus, Unâ Trium Millium Librarum
quas ad Dilectum Opus Dedit Joannes Chappel
Woodhouse Rector, alterâ Quingentarum Librm
quas Josias Spode Montis, Partím Tributis pro Ratâ
Vicatim, Partìm quod Auditu Dignum est, Donatione
per subcesivas Mercenariorum Operas Figulorum vo-
luntariè collatâ.

Extremi in Angulis Lapides Dejiciebantur Vigesimo
Octavo die Junii Anno Nostri Domini Christi
MDCCCXXVI.

Joannes Chappel Woodhouse *Decanus in Cathedra Lichfieldensi*	} Rector.
Joannes Tomlinson, *Clivi Villæ, in hac* *Parochia*	} Patronus.
Josias Spode, Jun. *Fentoni Magni,* *(now of the Mount)* Joannes Kirkham, *Penkhulli.*	} Æditui.

FREE TRANSLATION.

This Parish Church, at first well adapted to the few
scattered Husbandmen, who, in early times, composed
the Inhabitants of Stoke-upon Trent, having given
birth to Eight other sacred Edifices, but at length be-

come inadequate to contain, within her Walls, the New Population, which the Local Manufacture, The Potters' Art, had gathered around her; was rebuilt from the Foundations, on an extended scale, as near to the Spot, where for more than Eight Centuries, Worship to God, in Christ's Name, had been paid, as a regard to the Ashes of the Dead would allow, by means of Resources, supplied;—partly, by the Voluntary Offerings of the Opulent, and among these, most conspicuous a Gift of £3000 from John Chappel Woodhouse, Rector, and of £500 from Josiah Spode, of the Mount; (since deceased) partly, by a Parochial Rate;—and lastly yet most worthy of record, by Contributions arising from the supernumerary Labours of the Working Classes spontaneously bestowed.

The Corner Stones of the Foundations were laid the 28th of June, in the Year of Our Lord Christ, 1826.

The Length of the Interior of the Church, from East to West, is 130 feet, the width, 61 feet; the height to the ceiling, 45 feet; the height of the Tower, from the Ground Line, 112 feet.—The Gallery contains 444 Sittings, and Benches for 300 Scholars;—The Body of the Church contains 508 Sittings, and 420 Free Sittings; so that there is ample accommodation for 1672 persons.

The Expence of the Edifice, and additional Ground for inhumation, Organ, Bells, &c. is about £14000; of which Sum, as mentioned in the Tablet, £3000 was given by the Very Rev. the Dean; besides £700 for a Painted Window in the Chancel, and £500 by the late Josiah Spode, Esq.—To this might be added the Sum paid by the Parish to poor men employed in conveying materials, &c. to raise the New and the Old Burial Ground several feet higher than its previous level.

The Rectory House, usually called Stoke Hall, is now in a course of alteration, by Messrs. Trubshaw and Johnson, to render it a very elegant and commodious residence for the Minister of the Parish, and an ornament, instead of the curate's truly shabby house. We unintentionally omitted, in its proper place, the elegant Rectory House recently built at Burslem; but hope this will supply the notice.

In Stoke proper, are only *five* houses, including the Hall; and of course only a few inhabitants strictly reside in Stoke. But the name is applied to the Town West of the Church. Stoke is in the liberty of Penkhull, on the high road from Lane End to Newcastle. Most of the houses in it, are of comparatively recent erection; and the opening of the New Road to the Black Lion, afforded opportunity for many dwelling houses to be erected on the line; while within the last three years, another range has been raised in the new road to Shelton. We have not been able to obtain information concerning any of the very early potters in Stoke. At the Honey-wall between Stoke and Penkhull, are a number of houses, pleasantly situated on an elevated tract of land, possessing a fine view of the eastern side of the district.

The Trent and Mersey Canal passes near the Church Yard, along which are a range of Wharfs and Warehouses, for Canal Carriers; and the Canal Company have here one of their principal Offices, and extensive Sheds, &c. From Stoke to Lane End they have a Rail Road, on which their Waggons regularly convey materials and packages to the neighbourhood of Fenton, Lane Delph, and Lane End; and return with any Crates, &c. The Canal passes over the Trent at this place, the acqueduct being of three brick arches; and so very level with the adjoining land, as rarely to be noticed by persons passing along that way.

A navigable Canal from the south end of Newcastle town to the Grand Trunk Canal at Stoke-upon Trent, a distance of four miles, was made, in pursuance of an Act, which passed in 1795, wholly by subscription, and affords great accommodation to the town, although it has not hitherto paid much dividend to the proprietors.

The Manufactories here are *Eleven* in number; belonging to these Gentlemen:—Mr. Spode, Mr. Minton, Messrs. H. & R. Daniel, Mr. Adams, Mr. Boyle, Mr. Mayer, and Messrs. Ward and Forrister. But, in extent for the number, and in capital employed, they greatly exceed the like number in any part of the district. Three are void; but they are the smallest in the place.

Along the new road are the Manufactories of T. Minton, Esq. The largest is exclusively appropriated to the manufacture of various Pottery; of most excellent quality, for Blue Printing; and has obtained decided preference in many of the home markets. The other manufactory has been appropriated to the Porcelain departments; and connected with it are a Steam Engine and Mill to grind the materials, and colours. The whole concern is of a regular plan for usefulness, and reduction of labour; and the various articles are entitled to the pre-eminence they have gained. The residence of T. Minton, Esq. is a modest edifice in a retiring situation on the road thro' the town; and here in the circle of a numerous and intelligent family, he enjoys the well-earned reward of his ingenuity and perseverance. He has been inti-

F

mately connected with many of the improvements in
the manufacture, during the present century; possessed of extensive information on the chemical properties
of the earths, and great practical knowledge of the
requisite processes, he has been successful in producing
a kind of Porcelain and Pottery, which continue to
increase in the estimation of the public.   Mr. Minton
as a private member of the community, ranks very high
for urbanity and philanthropy.. The residence of H.
Minton, Esq. is near Hartshill; a very beautiful and
compact cottage residence, enjoying a fine and diversified southern prospect.

Messrs. Daniel's manufactory is wholly confined to
Porcelain of the finest kind, (their Pottery being
made at the Shelton manufactory,) and their methods
of ornamenting, are second to none in the district.
The proprietors are highly respected for their numerous excellencies of character, personal, and as public
men.

In one part of the manufactory occupied by Mr.
Adams, was erected the first Steam Engine employed
to grind Flints. Concerning this engine, we have
obtained the following particulars from the person
mentioned:—Mr. G. Cope, of Milton, states, that
about 1782, he erected a small Foundry on the bank
of the Canal at Milton; and in 1786 constructed a
small atmospheric steam engine, with a cylinder twelve
inches in diameter, open at the top, merely to work
the bellows for his cupola or furnace; he next added
a four-feet flint pan, in which he often ground *Composition* (Growan Stone;) but soon found he wanted
more power; and therefore for the flint pan, he substituted one for glaze, which he ground for Messrs.
Hales & Adams, of Cobridge, and when the power

was not applied this way, he used it to turn a lathe, in which he faced the large iron rollers, by him substituted for others of lignum vitæ, in the Printing Presses he made for Mr. Ralph Baddely, of Shelton; twelve inches diameter, by twenty-four inches in length. These were the first iron rollers in presses used by Blue Printers.—Mr. Cope sold this small engine to Mr. Harding, of Hook Gate, about 1792; at that time busily employed in making rollers and spindles for the Lancashire cotton spinners; and who employed to remove it from Milton to Hook Gate, a person from Colebrook-dale, named Green. This person ascertained for what purposes, and how usefully that engine had been employed at Milton in grinding materials and Glazes; and scarcely had he completed his engagement with Mr. Harding, when he formed another with the late Mr. T. Wolfe, an extensive manufacturer of the common kinds of pottery, at Stoke, to erect a very powerful engine on the same principle, to grind potter's materials; which, on being completed fully answered all the expectations of both parties, and excited others of the manufacturers to grind their own materials.

Nigh to the Church Yard, is the Manufactory of Messrs. Z. Boyle & Son, for Porcelain and Pottery of very excellent quality. Their Residence is a large and handsome edifice on the opposite side of the high road, placed in a small paddock; but most injudiciously situated in the midst of manufactories, whose smoke necessarily proves a continual source of annoyance.

At the top of Stoke, called Cliff Bank, is the manufactory, (now occupied by Mr. Thomas Mayer, a very intelligent potter,) where Mr Daniel Bird first ascertained the exact proportion of Flint required by

the several kinds of clay, to prevent the pottery cracking in the oven; and for which he was first called the
Flint Potter. His remains lie under a dilapidated
tomb at the steeple-end of the old church; and the
inscription mentions that he was by accident killed at
Twickenham, near London.

At a little distance above, on the road to Newcastle, is *Cliff Ville*, an elegant mansion belonging to
John Tomlinson, Esq. the Patron of the Rectory of
Stoke; a gentleman of considerable eminence in his
profession, as a lawyer; and whose name will be
found among the Benefactors to every valuable institution in the district. From this place, the prospect
northward and eastward is one of the most picturesque
and interesting, possible to be imagined.

In the centre of Stoke, covering an area of several
acres, and adapted for the most commodious progres-
sion of the numerous processes, is the Manufactory of
Josiah Spode, Esq., (the third of the name,) in extent
not surpassed in Europe, and possessing the advantages
of canal carriage to its very interior. Here the power of a large Steam Engine, on the most improved
principle of Boulton and Watt, is applied to grind the
materials, and greatly reduce the manual labour of the
slip makers. The manufacture includes every variety
of the finest kinds of Porcelain and Pottery, with all
the ornaments and embellishments calculated to gratify
the desires of the luxurious, and the taste of the con-
noisseur. The important material *Feldspar*, was first
introduced into Porcelain, at this manufactory, by the
father of the present proprietor, and the Porcelain
was, in consequence allowed to be the finest in grain,
and most durable in texture, of any in the district.
The Blue Printed has long enjoyed well merited pre-

ference, for the excellence of the Pottery, the great variety of elegant patterns, and the beauty of the shapes of the different articles. The late worthy proprietor, (of whom a brief account is given in a subsequent part,) was reckless of pains and expence to render all his productions deserving of general patronage, and he was so successful, that in comparatively few years, he amassed an immense fortune, the reward of his endeavours to benefit the community at large.

PENKHULL is now the restricted name of the highland above Stoke, southwestward; and here are a number of very convenient houses for the working classes, of recent erection. The parish workhouse is on this elevated spot; and will be inspected with pleasure by the philanthropist, for the cleanliness and comfort here afforded, to the aged and the infirm, the weak-minded and the destitute. In fact, all the attentions of humanity are supplied to them.

We do not find direct or indirect mention of *Penkhull* in Erdeswick, or Plott; yet at Penkhull, in 1600, were three manufactories for Coarse Brown Pottery; one of which belonged to Mr. Thomas Doody; whose descendants now reside in Tunstall. All these are now no longer seen; ranges of dwelling houses occupying the spot, where the poor *earth potter* was busily employed in fabricating vessels for the neighbouring borough and villages. Here died, in Nov. 1828, Mary Broad, at a truly patriarchal age; the first female ever employed in this district as a *Transferrer* of the impressions from copper plates to Pottery.—A few very old houses remain in Penkhull; in one of which formerly they held the Copyhold Court for the Manor; and this still meets in the Liberty of Penkhull. This suggests the opinion, that the present name *Manor of*

Newcastle, was allowed at first out of courtsey to the newly created Borough, which was taken out of Penkhull Liberty and Stoke Parish.

Conformably to an antient custom of the **Manor of** Newcastle-under-Lyme, within the Duchy of **Lancas-ter**, it is essential that the *original* wills of **copyhold** tenants, dying seised of copyholds, should be **produced** and proved in the Manor court, within a limited time after the decease of the testator, or testarix, in **default** of which the estate is liable to forfeiture.

Below Penkhull, to the south west, is situated the *Lodge*, where resides Thomas Fenton, Esq., (a de-scendant of the family of Fenton, of Shelton,) who to extensive professional acquirements as a **Lawyer**, and a fund of Literary and Scientific knowledge, **joins** great information concerning the Localities of the Potteries. To the kindness of this gentleman the author is much indebted, for some truly valuable information.

In one part of Penkhull, is the *Mount*; one of the best mansions in the district, a spacious and elegant square edifice, with suitable attatched offices, surround-ed by extensive gardens and pleasure grounds, and enjoying a prospect almost unbounded, over the vici-nity and the adjacent counties. Its proprietor is Josiah Spode, Esq. the *third* of the name, and the inheritor of all the virtues of his predecessors. In the several relations of civil and domestic society, his character ranks very high amongst the most worthy of the gen-tlemen with which this part of the country is favoured. Tho' possessed of vast property, his modesty and affa-bility remain unaffected by the elevation of his condi-tion. With a large fund of good sense, liberality of disposition, and considerable knowledge of the world, his acquaintance with the claims of the lower classes upon his sympathy and benevolence, prevents any ostentatious parade from abashing the friendless suitor, and causing him to feel his degraded condition; while the wretched and houseless child of want, instead of being left to pine in hopeless misery, frequently finds here a benefactor and protector. Long may the district be benefited by his benevolence, and the parish of Stoke experience the advantages of his services.

Near to Stoke, over the Trent, on the south side of the high road, is the dilapidated mansion of the late Thomas Wheildon, Esq., at no very distant period, one of the most beautiful and interesting of the neighbourhood. The spot, once the scene of hospitality and domestic felicity, is now covered with briers and noisome weeds, and exposed to the rude blast of every pelting storm. The outbuildings are now partly destroyed, or transformed into small houses for the peasantry. At Fenton-Low are some cottages formed out of the old manufactory, and at this day the property of his heirs.

On the north side opposite the Trent, is the mansion of W. Adams, Esq., of a very early and respectable family at Bagnall, long connected with the manufacture of the district. This gentleman joins with considerable experience, extensive information relative to all departments of the Art; and his productions in Pottery and Porcelain are in deserved estimation.

The Manor House, Fenton, is an elegant and capacious mansion, placed on the summit of a very extensive lawn, and enjoying a delightful and extended prospect to the south and west. The gardens and pleasure grounds are large, and arranged with great taste and elegance. There is a beautiful entrance Lodge at the western extremity of the estate, which latter is extremely valuable for its extent and agricultural produce, and the rich mines of coals, Potter's Marl, and Brick Clay, of excellent quality, spread all beneath its surface. The proprietor is Philip Barnes Broade, Esq., a young gentleman, whose promising talents have already secured for him, at the age of twenty-five, the appointment and re-appointment to the highest authority in the parish, (that of Churchwarden,) with that other gentleman of sterling worth, Josiah Spode, Esq. re-appointed the *fifth* time.

FENTON has indeed been greatly enlarged in population during the present century; and since 1820 many new houses have been erected. Here on the south side is a neat Chapel, for the Wesleyan Methodists. Near is a large Iron Foundry belonging to Messrs. Hancock;—and on the north side are Mr. Felix Pratt's House and Manufactory, on the site where Mr. T. Heath made *dipped* Pottery; and who is mentioned with proper respect for his virtues, is in a subsequent part. The present proprietor is notable for affability and promptitude in alleviating the miseries of the distressed.

On the south side, nearer Lane End, are the two mansions of Ralph Bourne, and William Baker Esqs. The former is neat; but being only a kind of business-residence is without exterior decorations, the proprietor's home being at Hilderstone Hall, a few miles south-east of Fenton. Mr. Baker's residence is spacious and commodious, surrounded with gardens and pleasure grounds, and enjoying a tolerably extensive prospect. The public spirit and private virtues of these gentlemen, have been long known in the district; and are duly appreciated by all persons of discernment and worth. Ready for every good word and work, their benevolence has been exercised to discover objects of commisseration; and their liberality has been dispensed with most laudable extension and promptitude. Almost adjoining are the two extensive Manufactories, and Mill, of Messrs. Bourne, Baker and Bourne; whose productions are in estimation in both the home and foreign markets. One of these is on the site of that formerly the property of Mr. T' Bacchus; but being mostly new buildings, the curious find some difficulty in ascertaining which, if any, of the present establishment, must be regarded as having resulted from Mr. Astbury's introduction of Flint and Biddeford Clay, at Lane Delph.— It has often been a subject of regret to us, to find that very little if any notice had been taken of persons who had served their generation in an important manner, and of facts, which are known to have occurred by the results yet remaining.

In Fenton Lane are several truly elegant Cottage Residences, for persons who have retired from the hurry of business, to enjoy in quiet the honourable reward of their assiduity and genius. At the Toll gate is Heron Cottage, a superb tho' small edifice, the property of Charles Mason. Esq. At Great Fenton are the spacious mansions of Thomas Allen and Henry Cartwright, Esqrs. — and the unoccupied mansion house, belonging to John Smith, Esq., the owner of very considerable property in Stoke Parish, but now resident at Elmhurst, near Lichfield. At a short distance is Longton Hall, the seat of Richard Edensor Heathcote, Esq., M. P. for Coventry. As great alterations are being effected here, it cannot with propriety be particularized at present.

The number of old houses in LANE DELPH, shew it to have been long one seat of the manufacture. There are now a large number of new houses, of a very convenient size and plan for the working classes. And within the last year, the enterprising spirit of a private person, Charles Mason, Esq., has established a regular Market, with Stalls and Shambles, to accommodate this part; which doubtless will be duly appreciated by all those for whose convenience the speculation was undertaken. At the bottom of Ark Lane, nigh Mr. Pratt's, is a Chapel for the Calvinists; and in the New Road is one, commodious and handsome, (with a good school room connected, for the gratutious instruction of children on the Sabbath;) owned by the methodists of the New Connection, formed in 1797. In Lane Delph also are entitled to notice, the House and Manufactory, of Thomas Carey, Esq.. also of S. Ginders, Esq,, and of J. Pratt, Esq. The manufactory of Messrs. G. & C. Mason, for Patent Iron-stone China, is commodious. Here is a Steam Engine of some peculiarity in its construction, by Holford, of Hanley; but we never could get from him, an explicit statement of the nature of the improvement, certainly with a cylinder only the size of a six-horse power engine, this has always done the work of others rated as equal to *sixteen* horses. The front Warehouse is four stories high, is fire proof, and has the most beautiful façade of any in the district. The manufactory where Messrs. Bârker pursued their avocation, is now converted into cottages and a tavern called the Dog and Partridge.

On the East is Fenton Park, where is a Colliery of great magnitude and value; in one part of which is a Steam Engine of about *sixty* horses power, on the best principle, and adapted to work *four lifts of Pumps to raise water from the mines.* Almost close to this, is Broadfield Colliery, also extremely valuable for the extent and depth of strata of its several mines. The spectator may enjoy from the eminence, at Fenton Park, a prospect, at once so rich and greatly diversified, as not to be equalled in this district, and scarcely possible to be excelled in any part of the kingdom. Words will not adequately describe its beauties; they must be contemplated, for the mind to have correct ideas of them. In succession the vision is gratified with viewing Caverswall, Lane End, Blurton, Trentham, Swinnerton and Keel Parks, Clayton, Butterton, Great Fenton and Little, Stoke, Penkhull, Newcastle, Silverdale, Knutton, Apedale, Chesterton, Red Street, Talk, Harecastle Hill, Bradwell, Woolstanton, Basford, Shelton, Hanley, Burslem, Newport, Longport, Etruria, Tunstall, Chell, New-Chapel, Mole Cob, Biddulph, Norton, Brown Hedge, Stanley, Bagnall, Bucknall, and Ubberley, a circuit rich in its natural productions; and the wealth of its proprietors; thickly populated, and supplying means of support and comfort to the industrious classes settled in it.

The FOLEY has only a few Houses, and three Manufactories in it. The Manufactory of Messrs. Elkins, Knight, & Bridgwood, is a new and very complete establishment; having in addition to the customary buildings a powerful Steam Engine and Flint Mill. The productions of this establishment are very superior in their quality, and have obtained celebrity in the markets. The proprietors are gentleman of the most respectable character as tradesmen and members of civil society. Opposite are the House and Manufactory of C. Bourne, Esq., the former the best on this side, for excellence of construction, and elegance of appearance. Connected with it are spacious Gardens; and contigous is the manufactory. At the southern extremity are the House and Factory of the late Mr. Myatt; one of the first persons who received the Wesleyan Methodist Preachers; and in whose parlour the late Rev. J. Wesley stood, while from the window he preached to a vast congregation, when last he passed thro' Staffordshire only a few months prior to his decease.

Golden Hill House is the residence of Jacob Marsh Esq., long esteemed highly for his numerous private virtues as a friend and parent; and for his integrity as a tradesman and master.— Descended from a family long engaged in the manufacture of the different kinds of Pottery, and of the first flint and salt glaze ware, he alone remains to perpetuate the name in his family, and convey to posterity a memento of one of those branches to whom the district owes its elevation. His very compact and well arranged Manufactory is at the entrance into Lane End.

LANE END AND THE VICINITY.

LANE END, the market town at the southern limit of the district, is four miles south-east of Newcastle. For many years it was notable for the great irregularity in the position of its buildings; of every size and sort, from the respectable residence of the manufacturer, to the mud and sagger-hovel of the pauper, scattered over a wide extent of territory. But in comparatively recent times, under the almost magic influence of a prosperous manufacture, improvement has commenced, the buildings are regular in size and position, and the place has risen into a respectable station in the scale of Staffordshire Towns.   Much of of the town and neighbourhood is (like Shelton) undermined by the Collieries, which are yet in a considerable degree of prosperous operation. And about three years ago, W. H. Sparrow, Esq., of Wolverhampton, commenced working a Furnace for reducing the ironstone, found in vast quantities in the Plackett's Brook Colliery; and which promises ample remuneration for the principal expended by the spirited proprietor.—— The traveller from Uttoxeter to Newcastle scarcely has a glimpse of any but its old buildings, along the High Street, and on towards the Foley; hence we have heard it much censured as a poor, dirty, and irregular village, but, the fact is quite otherwise; there are as many, if not more *new houses*, of very recent erection, and as goodly a proportion of respectable tradesmen's residences in Lane End, as in any of the other Towns in the Potteries.

The Church is a recent edifice, having been erected in 1795, in place of a former one principally built and endowed at the charge of the late John Bourne, Esq., in 1764; as already mentioned with Hanley Old Church. It is a Chapel of Ease to Stoke, and was enlarged in 1828, by private donations. The emoluments arise from some glebe land, surplice fees, Queen Anne's Bounty, and a very excellent parsonage house and garden, to the amount of near £200. There is a New Church in contemplation, to be erected in the upper part of the town, by a grant from Commissioners under an Act of Parliament for erecting New Churches.

At the west end is the English Free School, founded in 1766, chiefly thro' the munificence of Mr. Bourne. On the east side is the National School, which will contain 500 children, and was founded through the active exertions of Ralph Bourne, Esq., the site of the land was given by the Most Noble the Marquis of Stafford. When the customary forms had been observed, Mr Bourne shortly addressed the Committee, stating his lively interest in such institutions, and his conviction of their utility, and expressed also readiness to contribute £50 more towards an extension of the School for 1200 children; which sum was transferred towards the enlargement of the Church in 1828, for the accommodating the poor, the Society in London having voted £800, and the Dean of Lichfield given £50. The following inscription was engraved on the plate deposited in the stone:

By
RALPH BOURNE, Esq.
of
Hilderstone Hall, in the
County of Stafford,
The Corner Stone of
THE NATIONAL SCHOOL,
dedicated
to the sacred purpose of Instructing the Poor,
Was deposited
on Monday, June 10, A. D. 1822.

The Papists have at Green Dock a small Chapel, and a school Room attatched, with a neat house for the Priest. There are Six Chapels for Dissenters, of moderate size; and with Sunday Schools for children, instructed by gratuitous teachers.

There are two Market-Places; the one at the four *Lane Ends*, near the Church, is the place for the regular Saturday's Market; which is well supplied with all kinds of marketable produce, meat, and manufactures. Here are permanent Shambles, and Stalls, adapted for the several purposes of Butchers and Tradesmen; and every encouragement and accommodation is given to those who sell,— the produce of the Tolls received from the Stalls, being appropriated to the benefit of the town at large. Adjoining is Mr. G. Forrester's Manufactory, which appears to have been the *first* in which a regular plan for the arrangement of the separate places for the distinct processes was adopted. It is not large, but very convenient.

At the other *upper* Union Market-Place, used only for the *Fairs*, which always are the day after those at Newcastle, there is the Union Hotel, and a spacious Market Hall, usually appropriated to any public meetings of the inhabitants. In the Union Market-Place, is Mr. H, Simpkin's Manufactory, for a superior kind of Porcelain. He is well known for his many public and private virtues, and his house, near Steels Nook, is a beautiful tho' small edifice, with gardens of delightful arrangement for Flowers and Fruit. The other Manufactories belong to Messrs. Mayer & Newbold, J. Locket & Sons, J. Hulme & Sons, Bailey & Co. Bridgwood, Goodwin & Orton, L. Cyples, Martin & Cope, A. Shaw, J. Shaw, T. & J. Carey, and some others. That of J Hulme & Sons is well arranged for every purpose; and has a Flint Mill close adjoining. The Waterloo factory is regular and capacious; well situated for Coals and Marl. Those of Messrs. T. & J. Carey, are well adapted for a considerable portion of Business; and have a powerful Steam Engine and Mill connected with them. In the High Street is the manufactory of Mr. W. Turner; doubtless one of the most experienced Manufacturers which have lived in the district. Indeed we know not of any other who will bear placing along with E.

Wood, & T. Minton, Esqs.—In a subsequent part of this work we have again to notice this gentleman.

On entering Lane End from Uttoxeter, the first House worthy of notice is that of Samuel Jackson Hughes, Esq., a neat and spacious residence, in outward appearance a correct representation of the unassuming character of its owner; who, while possessed of considerable wealth, regards every man as his fellow, and in his relative situation as one of the rulers of the town, is ready in every instance to promote the general good, even when himself has been called to make individual sacrifice. The parish at large, as well as this part of it, will long enjoy benefit from his zeal and patriotism.

At Lightwood, the southern extremity, resides William Bailey, Esq., one of the first who made lustre Pottery, by which, with the branch of Enamelling, himself and partner (W. Batkin, Esq.) have been successful in acquiring very competent fortunes. He is justly esteemed for his piety; and in this neighbourhood his philanthrophy has been evinced extensively during more than a quarter of a century.—And in Steel's Nook is the neat and elegant residence of W. Batkin, Esq. abovementioned. In every Institution for promoting the welfare of Mankind, and especially for ameliorating the condition of the poor, his name ranks among the Benefactors; thus is his liberality known to all men;" and he is an excellent specimen of the followers of the "meek and lowly Jesus." At Green Dock is the residence of John Robinson, Esq., who to the highest character of a tradesman and manufacturer, is allowed to connect a most assiduous energy to benefit the whole Parish. Having several times filled the office of principal Overseer for this part, the zeal and ability he has always manifested, in protecting the helpless, and redressing grievances, has secured the applause of the neighbourhood; while the sincere piety and urbanity of his private life, render him at once a kind and valuable benefactor and friend. On the road to Stoke is the spacious residence of C. Harvey, Esq., now a Banker; formerly a most extensive manufacturer. The House was erected by the late Wm. Garner, son of Robert Garner, of the Row Houses manufactory. Mr. Harvey is well known, and equally respected for his private social virtues, and his public spirit. Mr. J. Carey's House is rather elegant, and has its appearance improved by being placed on an island in a large reservoir, that supplies condensing water for the Steam Engine at the Mill, where are ground flour, and the various materials and colours for the manufactories; and when the engine is working, a single jet fountain throws up warm water several feet high. There are a beautiful small bridge, gates, large cannons, &c. but the whole is exposed to the smoke of the manufactories. The proprietor is highly esteemed for many excellencies of character as a master and friend.

In mention of the virtues of persons in this work, should not cause the opinion to be entertained, that they only are of excellent character in the several places; neither should it be regarded as invidious. Doubtless, as many worthies may be found in the Potteries as in other Towns of the same extent. But we can only truly state what we personally are acquainted with, and we have endeavoured to faithfully discharge our duty to the public.

CHAP. III.

ON THE ORIGIN OF THE ART, AND ITS PRACTICE AMONG THE EARLY NATIONS.

BEFORE commencing the Details of the Rise and Progress of the Art of manufacturing Porcelain and Earthenware in this district, now distinguished by the appellation of the STAFFORDSHIRE POTTERIES; we consider it proper, if not indispensible, to mention briefly such historical collateral facts, as tend to elucidate, in the absence of unquestioned data, the Origin of the Invention, its extensive spread among the most early families, and its preservation to the present day by some of those ancient nations, who are considered remaining branches of the earliest kingdoms.

Invention has always been regarded as the offspring of necessity. Its force and progress in manufactures, are in our days precisely the same as in the earliest times,—from Articles absolutely necessary, to those which are useful, convenient, elegant, and luxurious. And research has ascertained, that in its originating the most valuable and important Arts, the results have been either altogether unexpected, or the primary rude attempts to give palpability 'to the Model in the master's mind.'

The manners of mankind in the early ages, certainly were the most simple possible; their occupations were conducive to social comfort and convenience; and for the promoting of these, culinary utensils, alike requisite and suitable, would be objects of desire to the ingenious, long previous to the construction of the most simple Cottage. As the intellectual powers derive energy from exercise, we cannot help indulging the conjecture, that the Kindling of Fires, the Baking of Bread, the Formation of Butter and Cheese, the working of Metals, and the Burning of Clay into Bricks, were practices coeval with the want of these Articles by the human family. And, while, considered abstractedly, they illustrate the progress of Man in the developement of his faculties, mental and physical, to gratify his wishes, and to multiply and enhance his comforts, they also demonstrate that mankind never were in the imagined condition appropriately designated SAVAGISM.

There cannot be a doubt, that, in the earliest period of human society, Man would soon feel the necessity of possessing Vessels capable of receiving and containing any liquids he might desire to use for food, drink, or occasional refreshment; and also of preserving the superfluous quantity. Indeed, unless we admit that they possessed vessels of different kinds, by which they could convey the liquor to the mouth, we cannot readily account for the prevalent intemperance of the ancients.

Mention is very early made of employing the Skins of animals caught in the chase, for Bottles and Vessels; for which purposes, the important qualities of pliancy and infrangibility well capacitate them. Of their utility and convenience, the difference between our customs and those of the ancients prevents our being adequate judges; even allowing that they might at first appear unseemly to the eyes of Europeans.

The use of different utensils would be suggested by the wish to convey readily to the mouth the substance intended to be taken for refreshment. Hence the early employment of shells of fishes, and the stout rind, husk, or shell of certain vegetable productions; a practice continued to this day in some of the countries where historians regard man as having been at first created; and in the same manner as is the Calabash used now by the Negroes of the West Indies. Conjecture is that Articles of this kind first suggested the excavation of pieces of wood, and even of stone, into requisite vessels.

In the infancy of Society, the pliancy and adhesive properties of Clay would be noticed, and suggest its application to various purposes. In Job, the most ancient author known, (B. C. 2247,) there is mention of the *Impression* of a Seal upon Clay, (xxxviii, 14.) At that period it was a custom, (preserved to the present time, in those countries,) for persons who deposited any substances in a store room, to place on the lock, or hinge, which kept close the cover or door, a lump of soft clay, on which there was impressed the owner's peculiar mark, as the moderns now use a Seal. See Nordern, part 1. p. 72; Pocock, vol. 1, 26. Matt. xxvii, 66.

After houses began to be erected, Bricks were very easily formed of Clay; and during a long series of ages, they were the chief materials used in the construction of Buildings. (Dr. Shaw's Travels, p. 172.) It was only about the time of David that marble was first introduced for the purpose; and learned persons indulge the opinion, that the *Ivory Palaces* erected by Solomon and others, (B. C. 897,) were in fact structures of *White Marble*, (I Kings, xxii, 39, Amos, iii, 15.) History proves that the employment of this beautiful substance for the temples, in Greece, was about seven centuries prior to the Christian era, or cotemporary with the Babylonian Captivity.

Altho' there are very ancient records of the employment of vessels which we call Pottery and Porcelain, we are without any certain proofs by which to determine the era of the invention. Neither can we with propriety assert that the formation of these vessels from Clay was the invention of a moment; but the Art itself, however rude at its commencement, must have been well known at a period so extremely early that no traces could come directly down to us; and a long while previous to even the contemplation of a manufacture so elegant and complicated as our Porcelain.

We have somewhere met with a conjecture, and certainly not a very absurd one, that, from some *Impression in Clay*, originated the Art of Pottery. The first *earthly receptacle* for liquids may have been, the clay affixed to a lock, and dried by solar heat until it was sufficiently hard to retain the condensed dews of the night, or the drops from falling showers; or Bricks impressed while ductile with the *footmark* of some animal, which might be discovered filled with water, from the causes just mentioned; or that might remain after being burned, and be quickly found useful to contain whatever was put into the orifice. From hints more rude have equally important Arts originated and been perpetuated.

The facility with which ductile Clay can be formed into Bricks, and the hardness which it possesses after it has been burned, would soon suggest to those who used it, the application of it in forming various utensils for domestic purposes. The figure and size would accord with the purposes for which they were designed, and correspond to the maker's fancy; but the desire of ease would incite to the abstraction of all superabundant materials from the outside. The importance of the invention, and the simplicity of the principles, would excite in different persons the desire of understanding it; and cause them very speedily to attain some degree of excellence in the practice.—"I think (says Mr. Jacob Warburton,) vessels of Earthenware for the purpose of holding wine, oil, and other liquids, were more ancient than vessels of wood—they would be made with very great facility."

The early families were not the vulgar and ignorant Society—the *mutum et turpe pecus,* conjectured by some persons who aspire to the high and dignified appellation of Philosophers; but, were all certainly in the full use and possession of their intellectual faculties and physical powers; being only a few generations removed from the type of the family, that *perfect man,* first created and endowed as the Vicegerent of Deity.

The most ancient historians mention the Art as having existed from time immemorial; and some traces of it have been discovered in most of those nations which were early formed; and remain with such of those now existing, as retain the civilization of the first ages. Hence we are warranted in concluding that it was practised among all the early families, and retained by them when they were dispersed 'abroad upon the face of all the earth.' (Gen. xi. 8.)

The kingdom of EGYPT is believed to have been founded *Two thousand two hundred years* before the advent of the Messiah. This people, in their union of fable and fact, mention their knowledge and perfection in this Art, and also in the manufacture of glass, (LOYSEL, *Art de la Veriere, p.* 1.) at a very early period of their history. Their Instructor in these, and the various Mechanical Arts, for which they sub-

sequently became famous, they state to have been
Theuth or *Thoth*, (Phenician *Taut*, Greek *Hermes*,
and Latin *Mercury*; See Philo-Byblius, Sanconiatho;
Livy. lib. xxvi, Herod. lib. v. c 7. and Annius of
Viterbrium.) most assuredly one of Noah's sons or
grandsons; Goth *thiot att*, signifying the father of in-
terpretation, and of his people;) Mercury being the
scribe or amanuensis of Saturn or Noah, the father of
all learning; the inventor of all arts, who gave them
improved forms of speech, and introduced Letters for
double communication.

It would be useless to enquire whether the Egyptians did or did not require considerable quantities of
Pottery vessels; but Belzoni's researches indisputably
prove that in very early times it was usual to manufacture them. The practice would be extended by
the increasing demand for various domestic utensils;
and in after ages, in the Upper Egypt, sufficient quantities were manufactured to supply all the Lower district with vessels for home consumptiou and exportation. (Dr. Clarke's Harmer's Observ. i. 90.) The
vessels were so covered with a varnish, or size, as to
be impervious to water; they were then connected
similarly to a float; and afterwards passed down the
Nile to Memphis, where the merchants received them.
They were subsequently filled with water, and finally
transported into the Deserts. (Beloe's Herodotus, lib.
iii. § 6.)

This people believed the doctrine of the trans-
migration of souls, and therefore Vessels containing
spicery were used in their rites of sepulture. And it
is very probable, that the vessels extracted from ancient barrows in our own country, had been deposited
for purposes someway similar. (Borlase's Cornish

Antiquities, 236. Henry's History of Great Britain, ii. 140.) With the mummies have been often found figures, of one shape and size, covered with a blue glaze, much resembling the celebrated Blue Porcelain of the Chinese. If any authority may be attatched to the assertion of Praxiteles, figures of similar materials and formation, first suggested the execution of bronze and marble statues.

There is great probability that the practice of the Art had been extended to different portions of that people, prior to the ingression of the Family of Jacob; (B. C. 1706, Gen. xlvii, 11.) for a many ages afterwards, when the Israelites quitted Egypt, Moses carried away with him correct knowledge of this Art, as well as of many other of the mechanical Inventions. (Levit. vi, 28, Num. v, 17.) And there is no reason to suppose, that, among all that great multitude of industrious people, he alone understood and was able to direct their manipulations.

The earliest Historical Records of the CHINESE, mention the existence of the Art, and its practice in both Pottery and Porcelain, in considerable perfection. In this Empire, and also that of Japan, during the five centuries immediately preceding the Christian era, were manufactured Earthenware of very superior quality, and the elegant and delicate porcelain, (which Britons call *China,* from that nation,) *tse-hi,* formed from the argillaceous earth, by the Chinese called *kaolin,* in quality much like our China Clay, combined with the silecious stone called *petuntse,* same as our Cornish growan stone.

See Macquer's Dict. v. *Porcelain.* Bomare states that these eminently partake of the nature of our China Clay. Vauquelin's Analysis gives

Kaolin——Silex 74, Alumina 16.5, Lime 2, Water 7.5.
Petuntse———— 74, ——— 14.5,—— 5.5,——— 6.

This people are peculiarly remarkable for the care with which they have avoided all foreign intercourse; and thereby precluded every opportunity for strangers to make observations and collect information concerning their manufactures. Father D'Entrecolles had to employ considerable cunning to obtain Specimens of the earths used. Some writers have asserted that the modern productions of this country are inferior to the ancient; but from inspection and comparison of the different very ancient and modern specimens, we are persuaded that little if any alteration whatever takes place in either the quality, materials, or process. The most accredited statements of recent Travellers, mention that at King-to-Ching, in the province of Kian-si, the various Articles for constantly employing *five hundred* furnaces, are prepared by *eight hundred thousand* workpeople.

The excellence and elegance with the perfection of the productions in Pottery by these nations, are calculated to induce the opinion, that in the practice of this Art, sooner than in any other, the early families of Mankind acquired great skill and dexterity.

During a long succession of ages, the PERSIANS have been well acquainted with and practised the various processes of manufacturing Earthenware and Porcelain of truly excellent quality. The Porcelain is formed of an argillaceous earth, which, by firing, becomes altogether like a pure enamel; this is combined with small pebbles, and Glass. The examination of fractured pieces gives a grain as fine in its particles, a transparency as clear, the enamel within and without as soft and pure, and the coating or varnish as exquisitely beautiful, as any of the productions of either China or Japan. Its tenacity is such that it

H

will serve for pulverizing articles, and as it is not easily affected by alteration of temperature, it therefore is formed into utensils in which food can be boiled. There is mention of a vessel having been manufactured at Yezd, which weighed only the eighth part of an English Ounce, yet would contain six quarts of water. (Sir J. Chardin's Travels.) The victorious army of Pompey brought many porcelain vessels from Pontus to Rome. And Harmer, (vol. i. p. 75,) mentions that the King of Persia having been offered some Chinese Porcelain, by the Agent of the D. E. India Company, as a present, regarded it as so greatly inferior to the productions of his subjects, that he treated the offer with ridicule.

Some writers suppose the ware to be named *Porcelain*, from the Porteguese name of a Cup, *porcellana*; that people having first brought this production from China to Europe. Others regard it as a contraction of the French *pour cent annees*, from the supposition that their materials were maturing 100 years prior to being used. But we prefer Whittaker's etymon, (vol. i. p. 55. 8vo. Account of Hannibal's Course over the Alps,) that the name *Porcelain* comes from the herb *Purslain*, which has a purple-coloured flower, like to the ancient china, which was always of that colour.— The English name, *China*, is evidently from the country whence it was brought.

With the Potters of Staffordshire there is a restricted employment of these words.—*Pottery* or *Earthenware*, and *Porcelain* or *China*. All are general terms for a kind of manufacture consisting of certain mineral productions, on one and the same principle properly combined and amalgamated, and ultimately subjected to most intense firing, or baking.

Porcelain, for its semi-vitrification, requires the Silex and Alumina to be tolerably pure; and also for that glassy transparency and semipellucid lustre which constitute its chief characteristic. A large proportion of Silex is used; but the Alumina gives the consistence, which renders the mass ductile while soft; capable of being turned, on the lathe, to any shape, and of retaining its form when being fired or baked in the oven. The fusible materials require to be so adjusted, that only the most ardent heat can reduce them into the requisite state of vitrescence. Pottery seldom has the components in equal purity; they are also more fusible, and fewer in number; neither are they susceptible of the high polish and ornament which distinguishes Porcelain.

The PHENICIANS doubtless were the most distinguished commercial people of antiquity. Near the centre of the south-east coast of the Mediterranean, were situated their most important marts, Tyre and and Sidon. The former is allowed to have been founded by Agenor, the grandson of Nimrod; and from Sidon being so constantly mentioned in connection with it, there is cause to believe that both ports were contemporaneous. From these were exported to the neighbouring states, considerable quantities of glass and earthenware.

We must regard this people as really intelligent, when we reflect, that the computations requisite in their commercial transactions, rendered necessary an acquaintance with Mathematics; their attention to physical geography, and astronomy, caused them to be courageous mariners and enterprizing merchants. producing both wealth and information; and, their taste and genius in forming not only vessels, but figures of remarkable things and persons, while causing the study of sculpture, unhappily superinduced a fondness for Idolatry, that ultimately occasioned their total destruction. Wherever any of the tribes of this people made voyages or journeys for commercial purposes, they not only carried the manufactures themselves, but also information of the processes and manipulations employed. And, wherever they carried glass and earthenware, there will be found some remains of the subsequent practice of the Art.

From this source we regard the GREEKS to have obtained their knowledge of this manufacture. And only on this supposition, can be accounted for, the ignorance of some of their writers concerning the nature of these productions; as Bellacensis and Fallopius; who called them *Stones* and *Semi minerals.*

Herodotus intimates the scarcity of vessels of Pottery among the Greeks, yet in his desire to augment the celebrity of his nation, he appears wishful to have it believed that his countrymen actually manufactured all the Earthenware demanded by the wants of the Egyptians and their neighbours. To those who reflect that Greece was of modern foundation, compared with Egypt and Phenicia, we need merely mention (to shew the error of the historian,) that to a native of Sidon, Cadmus, Greece owes Letters, and perhaps some of the Arts; and such was the general ignorance of that people, that only could their Philosophers obtain the required information in the proper kinds of Knowledge, by devoting a considerable portion of time to study in Egypt, Palestine, &c.

A colony of Phenicians settled at the foot of mount Vesuvius, in Italy, 1000 B. C. assuming the appellation of Etruscans; where they further improved their taste and workmanship under Demaratus, of Corinth, in 660. Here, in a large manufactory, and subsequently in smaller ones, in other parts of the country, they practised the Art with much successful assiduity, that the elegance and perfection of their productions, the taste displayed in the form and ornamental department, and the perfection acquired in the various processes, have scarcely yet been equalled; and obtained for the Potters every possible encouragement, at Rome, and the chief cities of that mighty empire.

W. A. Cadell, Esq. (Journey in Carniola, Italy, &c.) says among much useful and very interesting information on other of the Arts. — "Pliny observes that Etruria was the first country of Italy in which the art of pottery was practised, and that this art was afterwards carried to a state of the greatest perfection there; and particularly, that Arezzo was much celebrated for this kind of manufacture. The ancient Romans made much use of earthenware vessels, called Amphoræ, in which they kept their wine, although wooden casks were employed for the transportation of it from place to place, as appears by the representation of waggons loaded with wine on the column of Antoninus in Rome. In the city of Madrid, at present, *wine is kept in earthen vessels, and not in casks.* It is uncertain whether the antique earthenware vases, decorated with paintings on mythological subjects, were made in Etruria or not; but it is certain that most of them have been found in the kingdom of Naples, and in Sicily. After the revival of the arts in Europe, several ingenious artists in different countries improved the manufacture; Castel franco for instance at Faenza in Italy, in the beginning of the sixteenth century, manufactured the Majolica, (the Italian word for earthenware,) decorated with designs after Raphael and Julio Romano, specimens of which are preserved in many collections. In France, Bernard de Palissy, versed in the chemical knowledge of that age, made great improvements in the art of fabricating fayance. Bötscher an apothecary at Dresden, produced two or three different kinds of earthenware, one of which was of a brownish red colour, semivitrified, and so hard as to receive a polish on the lapidary's wheel, by means of which the pieces acquired a lustre equal to that of glazed pottery; cups and other vessels of this kind are to be seen in the Japan palace at Dresden. In the year 1709, the same Bötscher first composed the white porcelain, in imitation of the Chinese, which is now manufactured at the King of Saxony's works at Meissen. Other manufactories of the same kind have since been established at Sevres, Paris, Berlin, Vienna, Naples, Florence, Vicenza, in Staffordshire, and at Worcester, &c. The decomposed white granite of Limoges, an ingredient which forms the Basis of the French porcelain, as well as the decomposed white granite of Cornwall, are both found to be similar to the Kaolin of the Chinese; with this material, and a fusible stone found in Cornwall, and in other places in Europe, resembling the Chinese Petunse, a porcelain is formed, possessing exactly the same qualities as that fabricated in China. In Staffordshire the English stone ware is manufactured of white pipe clay, much lighter and better glazed than either the Italian majolica, or the French fayance; and in consequence of this superiority it has been introduced into most parts of Europe. Amongst those who have distinguished themselves in the manufactory of earthenware, is Luca della Robia, a Florentine Goldsmith and Statuary, born in 1388. He made heads and human figures in relief, and architectural ornaments of glazed earthenware, *terra cotta invetriata.* These figures were employed in the decoration of buildings, and many of them, the works of Luca della Robia, are seen in the Churches of Florence to this day. They are in a good style of sculpture, the colours of the glazing are white, blue, green, brown, and yellow. The art of making these figures of glazed earthenware, was taught by Luca to his brothers Attariano and Agostino, and was afterwards practised by Andrea his nephew; but the family became extinct in Florence about the year 1560, and the art was lost. Other artists in unglazed terra cotta were, Andrea da Sansovino, master of the celebrated Sculptor and Architect Iacopo Sansovino, and Antonio Begarelli of Modena, whose works were highly praised by Buonaroti, as Vasari relates in his life. Stone ware, after the Staffordshire manner, and porcelain, of a pretty good quality, are made at Doccia near Florence, at the manufactory of the Marquis Ginori. The porcelain earth is not got in the country, but is imported from Vicenza. This establishment has now existed upwards of fifty years. Large vessels of red earthenware are made at Florence, and in other parts of Tuscany, for the purpose of holding oil and other things, some of which are four feet high. They are not made on the potter's wheel, but are formed of rolls of clay, built up one over the other, round a conical form of wood. The large oil jars are contracted at the mouth, and are made in two pieces which are joined whilst the clay is wet. Large earthen jars of this kind are also made in Spain as well as in Rome, and used instead of wooden casks.

The suggestion, that the Etruscans first acquired the Art from the Chinese we cannot favour, for that people took great care to prevent any foreigners benefiting by their ingenuity; and, that there have not

been offered any proofs of a communication existing
between these distant people; which Scaliger is of
opinion, never existed till after the fall of the Roman Empire.

Some writers have supposed the vessels brought
to Rome at Pompey's triumph, and called *vasa, murr-
hina, murrina, murrea,* (Pliny's Natural History, lib.
xxxvii. 2.) were species of *precious stones,* found in
Parthia, of a whitish colour, and variously veined and
variegated, so that in appearance they much resembled
Porcelain. We are not informed how so many vessels
of the same kind and material were found in one place.
And both Scaliger and Cardan, who rarely are of the
same opinion, agree that the Parthians early practised
the manufacture of Pottery and Porcelain; and that
these vessels are really of the latter description. There
certainly is an error in supposing Porcelain to have
been fabricated from pulverized sea shells mixed with
eggs, and buried *eighty* or a *hundred years.* This may
have been a size for the vessels; or the pulpy appearance of the clay may have been mistaken for beaten
eggs; and the shells would improve the pottery by the
small portion of lime added to the ingredients. The
practice of long keeping it under ground to mellow,
is occasionally adopted at the present time.

Mr. Joseph Blackwell, of Cobridge, when recently
at Caltagnone, found a person who manufactures toys
of earthenware, made of brown clay, painted in oil
colours, upon the bisquet which far surpass any thing
of the kind he ever saw in this district; and he purchased two as specimens.—At Calazolo he saw Baron
Judica's Museum, collected at an enormous expense
of time and money, fifteen years, and great part of his
fortune; having by excavations under much of the city

of Acre, discovered a great variety of vessels of Pottery, in the highest state of preservation, which can be proved to have been fabricated from the 9th century B. C. to the 7th A. D. The early Sicilians were celebrated for skill in potting. The beauty of these vases are well known in Italy; and sometimes a very exorbitant price is obtained. For *one*, the King of Naples lately gave 10,000 piastres, (£2200.) The Collection at Naples is superb. For about £50. J. B. could have picked up a collection, which would have been invaluable in the Potteries.

From modern researches on the Trans-Atlantic continent, there is sufficient information acquired to warrant the conclusion, that the Art has a long time been practised to considerable extent, by the natives of the countries up the Black River, and also up the Amazon, Ohio, and Mississippi; and from the remains of manufactories which have been discovered, there is reason to believe that great traffic in these productions must have been carried forward with the neighbouring countries. Two vases are extremely curious by well manifesting the first efforts of human ingenuity in practising a new invention. (Govenor Pownall's Narrative. Archæologia, vol. V. p. 318.) Some specimens very recently discovered in Ross county, are regarded as equal in quality and manufacture to any in Italy.

The fact is indisputable, that the Phenician merchants traded to BRITAIN, for Tin, found only in the county of Cornwall, at a period at least *two hundred and eighty-five years* before the birth of Moses; and from this country were obtained all the supplies of tin for other nations, (Numb. xxxi, 22, B. C. 1456. 1 Kings, x, 22, B. C. 1000, Ezek. xvii, B. C. 600.)

(Boye's Pantheon, p. 140. ref. 9. 6 edit.) In the way of Barter, did these merchants supply our ancestors with the various Articles in request, whether the productions of other nations with whom they had dealings, or the manufacture and produce of their own country. Among these, it appears proper to include Vessels of Pottery; because some yet remain, which are regarded as objects of peculiar interest, from their undisputed antiquity, tho' rude in construction, and irregular in ornament; and which are admitted to have been brought into England, many centuries prior to the Roman Invasion. Commercial interchanges render the nations of the earth reciprocally dependent on each other, in consequence of the transporting their produce and manufactures;—the sources of employment to millions of mankind, who thence are enabled to provide supplies for the temporal necessities and personal comforts of themselves and families.

The convenience of utensils of Pottery, and the ease and trifling expence with which they were fabricated, may be supposed to excite the Britons very early to attempt the manufacture of similar articles. When they first commenced the Art, cannot be accurately determined; but the remains of old potteries, which have been discovered in several of the counties of England, at different times, warrant the conjecture of the period being long anterior to any authentic historical records.

In taking down the (Nunnery Chapel) Church of Farewell, in this County, in 1747, to rebuild it, at an elevation of six feet, and several feet asunder in the south wall, were found three ranges of vessels of very coarse Pottery, covered with thin plaster; the mouths towards the inside of the edifice, and several feet distant; the size of the smaller was 6 in. high, 3 in. over the mouth, and 16½ in. in circumference; the others were 11½ in. high, 4½ at the mouth, and 24 in. circumference. (Harmer's Erdeswick. p. 179.)

In the Philosophical Transactions. vol. xix. p. 319, is an interesting account of an Old Pottery, at Newton, very near Leeds, Yorkshire.   Prior to the Christian era, vessels containing spices and other articles were deposited with the corpses of eminent persons; and urns, vases, and bowls have been extracted from barrows in different places in the kingdom.

An interesting Fact may here be mentioned. — At the mouth of the Thames behind Margate Sands, and in that part called the Queen's Channel, in consequence of fishermen's nets occasionally drawing up, off a shoal, coarse and rudely formed vessels of earthenware, on which was neatly impressed the name *Attilianus;* the public curiosity was awakened, and it was found, that about 200 years before Cesar invaded Britain, a small island was situated in that particular spot where now is the shoal, and on this was a small pottery, supposed to have been owned by the person whose name is so singularly preserved to posterity.

There is mention of Britain by Cellarius, Geography, p. 16; Julius Cesar, 186, 204, Aristotle, De Mundo. cap. iii. p. 614.—Pliny mentions that Tin had been obtained from Britain, B. C. 1847; and if we may place any confidence in the opinion and research of Warburton, (Div. Leg. of Moses,) and the author of Egyptian Antiquities reviewed, our too-frequently disparaged nation was known among " the Isles of the Gentiles." (Gen. x. i, 4.) B. C. 2200.

Altho Britain produces a great variety of *Clays*, as well as all the other materials required in the fabrication of the best Porcelain and Pottery, yet as we do not possess any specimens of exquisite workmanship in these branches, there are no proofs that our ancestors were ever emulous to arrive at eminence in the manufacture. On this account, some persons have regarded the urns and vases as of Roman Origin; but we still incline to think, we may with equal propriety regard them as native productions. We cannot account for the prevalent desire to attribute all excellence to the information relating from intercourse with the Romans; and among the priesthood of the darker ages, this seems to have operated greatly, in disregard of the indisputable fact, that the Britons were a civilized people, before the Romans, or even their city had existence.

We cannot suppose that the early Britons had commercial connections similar to those of our day; nor equal fondness for manufacturing pursuits; nor that studied regard for convenience in domestic arrangements; nor that been perception of elegance connected with comfort, prevalent in the majority of families not of the lowest classes of society, for the last century so constantly progressive. We need not therefore wonder that they did not arrive at greater perfection in the art; for want of stimulus; for exquisite pieces of workmanship in sculpture were produced by the English Artists, proving the existence of adequate genius and skill; yet leaving the working in clay, probably as beneath their attention, or not any way in demand.

CHAP. IV.

THE MANUFACTURE OF POTTERY, PRIOR TO 1700.

TO GREAT BRITAIN, a principal manufacturing and commercial Nation, *the Art of making Pottery and Porcelain,* is truly important; whether viewed as conducing to augment the national wealth, by increasing the value of the mineral productions many hundred fold, providing for national Exports to the amount of more than a Million sterling annually; or as affording unto a large population of mechanics and artizans, a compensation for labour and skill, enabling them with their families to live in comfort, and thereby in some degree increasing the sum of general happiness.

At several places on the European continent, during more than 300 years, have been made the Common Stone ware, glazed with nuriate of soda, and white enamel, whose glaze is a real glass opacous by white oxide of tin.   And we ought not to exclude our countrymen from all merit in this department; for numerous tiles still exist, formed in the latter part of the 15th century, which evince that the processes were well known, and that their manufacture was connected with that of Pottery.

There exist documents which imply, that during many centuries, considerable quantities of common culinary articles were manufactured, of red, brown, and mottled Pottery; easily made from a mixture of different Clays found in most parts of the district; and a fine sort is found in Hanley, and Shelton, which for a long while served the various purposes of the Newcastle tobacco-pipe makers.

I

The manufactories, in early times, were situated at the junction of public roads, for the two-fold purpose of publicity and room; and the fact is demonstrable, that wherever one of these *Sun Kiln Potteries* was situated, a spacious and commodious opening of the road remains; witness in Hanley, and Shelton, Burslem, and Lane End. How long anterior to 1600, these Sun Kiln Potteries existed, cannot now be ascertained; but there were two at Bagnall, Golden Hill, Tunstall, Brownhills, Holden Lane, Sneyd Green, Botteslow, Penkhull, Fenton, and Longton Lane, besides others in the (present) towns. A few of these yet remain in operation, (making the large red brick-like milk pans, flower pots, and other coarse vessels;) one is near the Meir Lane Furnace; another near to the Hanley Market-Hall; a third rather modernized at Golden Hill; a very old one at New Oxford, near Chell, and in other places also.

The *Sun Kiln* is formed usually square, 16 to 20 feet in extent each way, and about 18 inches deep; having at one corner, a smaller place, deeper, and lined with slabs or flags. The Clay, after being brought out of the mine is spread abroad on the adjoining ground, and frequently turned over by the spade during two or three seasons, that it may be well exposed to the action of the atmosphere, (called *weathering*.)—Into the smaller vat a quantity of clay is thrown, and by a proper tool *blunged* in the water by agitation, till all the heavier particles and small stones sink to the bottom; the fluid mass is next poured into a sieve, thro' which it runs into the largest vat, or Sun Kiln, until the whole surface is covered to the depth of three or four inches, which is left to be evaporated by solar action. When this is partially accomplished, another layer, and a third, and fourth are added, until the mass is from 12 to 18 inches deep; and the whole is then cut out, and placed in a damp cellar for use.—In China the clay is left exposed many years, that the materials may be completely disintegrated and decomposed; and after it is prepared, the custom is to let it remain many years before it is employed in the manufacture. Indeed, sometimes the clay used, was first prepared by the grandfather; and frequently by the father.—The properties of the various Clays observed by the early Potters, and the purposes for which they were employed, supply us with the Roman *Names*—*Tasconium* the kind used for Crucibles; *Leucargillion*, a white kind for Furnaces; *Argil*, the brown clay for common Pottery; and *Terra Sigillaris*, the finest grained kind, for *sealing*, as already described. Tho' the names are Roman, we are not to regard that people as our first Potters; because of the numerous proofs to the contrary.

Porcelain Clay, is generally redish white, also greyish and yellowish white, without lustre, or transparency. It occurs either friable or compact, stains the fingers; adheres to the tongue; is soft, but meagre to the feel; and is easily broken. Specific gravity about 2.3. It falls to pieces in water, and by kneading becomes partially ductile. The Cornish porcelain clay consists of 60 per cent, alumina, and 40 silex, originates from the decomposition of felspar, and has the particles of quartz, mica, and talc, separated by eleutriation. The Chinese kaolin also contains mica, and is probably of the same origin as the Cornish. The same remark may be applied to the French, &c. It is, however, by no means certain, that all porcelain clay is derived from felspar, as it varies considerably in its composition and fusibility; all the kinds indeed are infusible at any temperature less than a white heat; but some, especially the Japanese, are refractory in the most powerful furnaces. *Magnesian, or Steatitic Clay*, is almost cream colour; its texture is minutely foliated; it has a slight greasy lustre, takes a polish from the nail. It stains the fingers, is very friable, and to the touch smooth and unctuous When laid on the tongue it dissolves into a smooth pulp, without any gritty particles. It is very plastic, and has a strong argillaceous odour. It occurs in nodules, in a hard cellural hornstone, called soap rock, that forms large mountainous masses near Conway, in North Wales, and originates from the decomposition of indurated steatite. *Clay from Slate*, is ashgrey, passing into ochre-yellow: its texture is foliated; it has a smooth unctuous feel, and its siliceous particles are so small as to occasion scarcely any grittiness between the teeth. It occurs in thin beds lining the bottoms of the peat-mosses, of a white ash colour, deprived of iron and carbon by the acid of the peat. Also in thicker beds at the foot of the mountains, but of a darker colour, and less plastic. *Clay from Shale*,— varies from greyish blue to bluish black: its texture is foliated; it has a smooth unctuous feel, takes a polish from the nail, is excessively tenacious and ductile, with but a slight degree of grittiness. It occurs abundantly in all collieries. A sandy clay, greyer, and more refractory, is procured from the decomposition of the indurated clay that forms the floor of the coal, and is provincially called *clunch*. The Stourbridge clay, from which crucibles, glass-house pots, &c. are made, is of this kind. *Marly Clay*, is bluish, or brownish red: either compact or foliated: it has a soft unctuous feel, takes a polish by friction with the nail, is very plastic, more or less gritty, though less so man the common alluvial clay. It burns to a brick of a buff or deep cream colour, and at a high heat is readily fused. It effervesces strongly with acids, and contains from $\frac{1}{4}$ to $\frac{1}{3}$ of carbonate of lime. It is largely employed as a manure, and when the calcareous part does not exceed 10 or 12 per cent, is esteemed as a material for bricks. *Alluvial Clay*, contains a large proportion of quartz sand, and rounded pebbles of various kinds, showing it to have been carried from its native situation, and mingled in its progress with a variety of extraneous bodies. Three kinds may be distinguished; *viz.* Pipe clay, potter's clay, and chalky clay. Pipe clay is of a greyish or yellowish white colour, an earthy fracture, and a smooth greasy feel: it adheres to the tongue; is very plastic and tenacious; when burnt is of a milk-white colour; is with difficulty fusible, though much more so than porcelain clay, from which it is further distinguished by superior plasticity, and containing sand. It is manufactured into tobacco-pipes, and is the basis of the white or queen's-ware pottery.—Potter's clay is red, blue, or green; with a fine earthy fracture, and a soft, often greasy, feel; it adheres to the tongue, and is very plastic; burns to a hard, porous, red brick; and in a higher heat runs into a dark-coloured slag. When tempered with water, and mixed with sand, it is manufactured into bricks: the varities most free from pebbles, are made into tiles and coarse red pottery."—AIKEN.

Solely thro entire forgetfulness, or total disregard, of the number of sites of Potteries which have been exposed at different times in various parts of the district, can the opinion be entertained, that the whole employment of the people was making *Butter Pots*, only once used, and then discarded, or diverted to other purposes; and being comparatively of little value, were not likely to be either very fine in the material, or excellent in the manufacture. Neither are the facts of their being formed of the coarsest clay, and in the rudest manner, proofs that the Butter pot claims priority of date; because vessels for immediate use would always be invented before others for mere convenience. Whoever will be at the trouble to read the accounts formerly given of this district, will find that at Burslem was a manufactory, called the *Butter Pottery*, because Butter Pots were made there. And Dr. Plott mentions that the greatest *Pottery* is at Burslem, for making their several *sorts* of Pots. — We therefore conclude, that Butter pots were only one branch of the manufacture. There is some incongruity in stating first, that *few* persons were employed;— the quantity of goods manufactured was so *inconsiderable*;—that Butter pots chiefly were made;—and that the *great sale* of the goods was to crate men;—as Dr. Plott asserts.

Curiosity properly so called, does not remain satisfied with mere survey of the surfaces of objects; it strives to pry into their conformation, and comprehend their properties; and rarely does the trouble fail of being amply compensated. In examining Specimens, to illustrate the progress of the Art in this district, we find all the materials are the produce of the vicinity; the Clays are those on the surface, and near the strata of Coal, and the fine sand is from the hilly parts of Baddeley Hedge and Mole Cob. At different successive times the Potters, at pleasure, have varied these, and introduced others; from the coarsest brick clay, only much improved by weathering, blunging, sifting, and drying upon the Sun Kiln, made into vessels, that were without any glaze; to the finer clays formed into other vessels, with a smooth surface, on the inside of which pulverized lead ore was dusted from a linen bag, and the ardent heat of the oven partially vitrified it.

Pliny mentions that Anacharsis the Scythian formed the Potter's Wheel, and taught Greece the Art of Pottery. This may be true, yet not prove that he invented the machine. There is little doubt, that he would learn this Art, in his progress to acquire information by travelling. There is also mention of Potters many ages prior to the time of Anacharsis; and the Potter's wheel was used in Egypt anterior to Greece being colonized. See 1 Chron. IV. 22, 23.—

There is some probability that the *Potter's Wheel* mentioned in Sacred Scripture was much similar to that early employed in this district, and now used at the coarse ware potteries for throwing the large jowls, &c. of common clay, which are circular and have a plain surface. This very simple machine remained unimproved, until about 1750, when a person named Alsager, one of the most ingenious mechanics of the neighbourhood, desirous of rendering the workman able to operate with greater precision and neatness, added those parts which remain to distinguish the present from the ancient wheel. No research has ascertained the time, or the person, to whom must be assigned the truly important improvement of *Turning on the Lathe.* There has been mention, that it was suggested by the method of turning Ornaments from Spar in Derbyshire; and another suggestion is, that Messrs. Elers, (hereafter mentioned,) introduced it about 1692; but as there remain specimens, formed by being turned on the lathe, long anterior to their time, it is deemed proper to leave the subject as we found it.

There are some fractured specimens with partially glazed or vitrified surfaces, which, from the places whence they were obtained under the foundations of old potteries, destroyed almost a century ago—evidently were made in some period long prior to any of those whose era is clearly ascertained. Other specimens fabricated about 1600, are large vessels for liquids, *Jowls, Drink-steins,* with a hole in the lowest

and narrow end, for a spigot or tap; *Bottles, Jars,*
and *Common Butter Pots*, of very coarse and inelegant
workmanship, and highly vitrified on their surface to
prevent their being porous.

By what means the manufacturers produced this
partial glazing or vitrification, we have not been able
to learn satisfactorily; but the fact is undisputable.
It also causes an opinion that a kind of *Saggar* was
occasionally employed, to protect the finer ware. One
idea here presents itself. The antiquity of the name
Sagger, (from the Heb. *sagar* to burn; and to this
day applied as *segar*, to a rolled leaf of tobacco for
burning while its fumes are inhaled,) proves a very
early employment of this utensil, tho' for what specific
purpose we are not now informed. Yet as the name
denotes their use, it is extremly probable that use has
long existed, altho' the proportions of the component
materials requisite to bear the high temperatures of
our bisquet ovens, have been ascertained in comparatively recent days.

Few if any branches of Manufacture equal that of
the Potter in affording opportunities for the exercise
of ingenuity and research. Great are the advantages
of making experiments, to persons of observant habits;
and most of them conduce to general benefit, altho' not
wholly pertinent to the primary purposes of enquiry;
hence we may reasonably suppose that very great improvements would have resulted, had the early manufacturers possessed a share of that knowledge of Chemistry of late so much sought after and cultivated.

A Porrenger, made in 1606, exemplifies the ability of the
thrower, and *stouker*. It is formed of the fine brown clay, with
two loop handles neatly bended; the sides are ornamented
with spots of whitish clay, impressed with a rude cross +, formed by the end of a stick. A Jug which will hold three pints,

is formed of the clay from the coal mines, which improves in colour by being fired ; but is of inferior workmanship to the preceding. The crosses on this are of coarse brown clay. The bottoms of both shew that they were placed on something while in the oven ; and their glaze is from lead ore powder, sprinkled or from a linen bag dusted on the vessels while in clay. There is no proof that they were fired in saggers. A **Water Jug**, of six quarts, is formed of the Brown Clay, in the shape of Lambeth Brown ware ; glazed with lead ore in some particular manner ; and from its singular appearance regarded as anterior to the Reformation. On various parts, very thin lengths of clay, are affixed at the taste of the workman ; on each side is a cross of clay of a different colour ; and in the front, over a cross (†) in a circle, is a human face, with a long beard, of either a monk or a druid.

These exhibit the early attempts at *ornaments*; and are regarded as suggesting the method which still exists, of applying leaves, sprigs, flowers, medallions, &c. *in relief*, and formed of a different coloured clay. The *Stouker* (a vulgarism from *stick*, to place or fasten,) was the workman who affixed handles, spouts, and other appendages, for utility or ornament; and the Potter who could fhen (and even till within the last 50 years) *throw*, *stouk*, *lead*, and *finish*, was a good workman; very few indeed being expert at more than two or three of these branches. The different vessels for domestic use, are variously ornamented, with several loop handles *stouked* to the sides. The Drink Cups, shaped like tall ale glasses, have two handles on the prop; and all are glazed with lead ore. The Butter Pots of this date are devoid of every kind of ornament, and only some are partially glazed on the inside.

One Jug exhibits the mixture of Lead ore with the clay ; the handles are better formed and fixed; but the whole has a palpable roughness, altho' it has evidently been subjected to a very high degree of heat. The bright appearance of the surface might suggest that salt had been some way introduced while in the oven; but the idea vanishes, when we reflect that the consequent decomposition of the argillaceous particles would have rendered the surface more smooth than it is. **Two Butter Pots**, of 1640, made of the common clay, without any glaze, have CARTWRIGHT, in rude letters, on a relief 2 inches in diameter. This was a warranty that the Pots were of a proper depth and weight; for at this time, some were made to answer nefarious purposes, and deceive the dealers.

The common people of the district at the present day, call Irish *Tub* Butter, Pot Butter. The porous pots would imbibe the moisture of the butter, and lessen its weight; and those which were too heavy would similarly defraud the purchaser. So that about 1670, Government officially interfered to compel all manufacturers of Butter Pots, at Burslem, (most unauthorizedly called *the Butter Pot Manufactory*, in a Map of the county published in 1757; tho' neither Speed, Camden, nor Erdeswick so name;) to make them hard in quality, and in quantity to contain not less than fourteen pounds avoirdupois, under a serious penalty for non-observance. This person, Cartwright, cannot have deserved the epithet of "a poor Butter pot maker," by Plott applied to some of those he visited; for there is the proof to the contrary still existing, in his handsome donation of *twenty pounds* yearly to the poor of Burslem, for ever, from the year 1658. Tho' we must not suppose all others equally affluent, we cannot help believing, from this bequest, at such a period, that Burslem contained other potters who were not *poor* men.

"The butter they (the factors) buy by the Pot, of a long cylindrical form, made at Burslem of a certain size, so as not to weigh above six pounds at most, and to contain at least fourteen pounds of butter, according to an Act of Parliament made about fourteen or sixteen years ago, for regulating the abuses of this trade in the make of the pots, and false packing of the butter; which before sometimes was laid good for a little depth at the top, and bad at the bottom; and sometimes set in rolls only touching at the top, and standing hollow below at a great distance from the sides of the pot: to prevent these little country *Moorelandish* cheats (than whom no people whatever are esteemed more subtile) the factors keep a surveyor all the summer here, who if he have good ground to suspect any of the pots, tryes them with an instrument of iron made like a cheese taster, only much larger and longer, called an auger or butter boare, with which he makes proof (thrusting it in obliquely) to the bottom of the pot; so that they weigh none) (which would be an endless business) or very seldom; nor do they bore it neither, where they know their customer to be a constant fair dealer." PLOTT, p. 108, 109.

On Tuesday in Whitsun week, 1824, the late Mr. John Riley, accompanied the author to inspect a curious and beautiful specimen of Brown ware, made at the Green head, Burslem, and in the family of Mr. Richard Keys, almost a century:—The vessel is a QUART DRINK MUG, of a cylindical shape, rather widened but not flanged at the top, with a thin edge. [The body is common clay, with a silecous mixture, (tho' almost a century prior to the introduction of flint,) obvious especially in the handles.] This is by the four handles saperated into four compartments, and four persons might use it, yet each drink from his own place.

The four handles are double looped, and remarkably well *stouked* on; the outer surface has a deep groove, in which is laid a twisted band of the red and whitish clays, the bend of each has a button of whiter clay, & of this is also a hat shaped ornament on the top of each upper loop, near the brim; and under is a small hole for the rarefied air to escape, to prevent each being split while in the oven. Between the handles are ornaments, formed by either white clay slip, left to dry, and afterwards impressed with a carved stick or tool; or else stuck on with a stick, and trimmed to its present form. These are in embossed squares, G R above a dog, 1642 above a deer, M H above a rosette, and a well made fleur-de-lis over a seal of a face; and many drops of a white clay slip on the other parts. The Initials warrant the conjecture that the vessel was designed for being presented by one to the other party. The glaze is chiefly of lead, and much like that used for common Cream Colour; only the excess of quantity gives to the white clay a yellowish teint, much like the inside of gloss saggers. Mr. Riley remarked, that such pottery as this, cannot be fired in an open oven ; and as the bottom exhibits marks of bits of broken pots, on which it was placed in the oven, we must indulge the opinion that it was fired in a sagger.

At no very distant period, it was the custom for the whole of a company to drink out of the same vessel ; and this specimen forcibly recalled the usage. William of Malmsbury says " Formerly the vessels was regularly divided ; for, to prevent quarrels, King Edgar commanded the drinking vessels to be made with knobs on the inside at certain distances from each other ; and decreed, that no person, under a certain penalty, should either himself drink, or compel another to drink, at one draught, more than from one of these knobs to another." Book II. p. 31.

The specimens just described may have been placed within larger vessels for firing, and it is possible that the high degree of heat needful to fire the latter, may have so affected as to vitrify the silecious particles along with the lead. It is now well known that lead and silex will form glass; the lead increasing the fusibility of the silecious materials, and improving their brightness. The introduction of one article after another, is usual in all manufactures; custom soon renders confident the workman who at first was timid; and experience quickly makes him familar with the proportion of the kinds of clay, and other materials required by the different sorts of Pottery.

The employment of different clays for the ornaments, soon suggested their mixture, in this manner: on a piece of clay laid on his bench, the workman very forcibly slapped down another piece, differing in colour, and at times a third piece; the mass was frequently cut thro' with a thin wire (usually brass) and slapped together, until the whole had a beautiful scrolled appearance. And several fractured specimens shew that these mixed clays, often had addition of ochre, manganese, and fine sand, to vary the colour. Some of the specimens of Dishes, Drinking Mugs, Candlesticks, &c. formed of these mixed clays, have great beauty of teint from the mixture, and are rather curious in workmanship, the edges being ornamented much similarly to the old pattern of marble paper. A well shaped half-pint, with a handle evincing much ingenuity and taste, as well as a common shaped Drinking Cup, prove the ability of the workman. The body is elegantly and delicately streaked by the mixture of the different clays; but a rough surface shews that neither had been turned in the lathe, to smooth the outer, nor had there been any attempt to polish the inner surface. The articles made were not as level as those now manufactured, especially the *Flat* Ware; warranting the opinion that saggers were not generally employed. Two circular 20-inch dishes, made in 1650, have *Thomas Sans, Thomas Toft,* in rude letters of different clay. They evince much improvement in the quality and ornaments of the ware. The body is of the common brown and whitish clay; the ledge has a neat border of reticulated shreds of clay, the lower whitish, the upper brown; the central parts have other coloured figures; the intervals are coloured by manganese; and the upper surface only of the whole is glazed with lead ore.

About 1680, the method of GLAZING WITH SALT, was suggested by an accident; and we give the names of the parties as delivered down by tradition. In this as in many other improvements in Pottery, a close investigation of one subject has frequently reflected fresh light upon another; something altogether unexpected has been presented to notice; and not unfrequently from an incident comparatively trivial has resulted a discovery of paramount importance. At Stanley Farm, (a short mile from the small Pottery of Mr. Palmer, at Bagnall, five miles east of Burslem,)the servant of Mr. Joseph Yates, was boiling, in an earthen vessel.

a strong lixivium of common salt, to be used some way in curing pork; but during her temporary absence, the liquor effervesced, and some ran over the sides of the vessel, quickly causing them to become red hot; the muriatic acid decomposed the surface, and when cold, the sides were partially glazed. Mr. Palmer availed himself of the hint thus obtained, and commenced making a fresh sort—the common BROWN WARE of our day; and was soon followed by the manufacturers in Holden Lane, Green Head, and Brown Hills; the proximity of their situation to the *Salt-Wyches*, affording great facility for procuring the quantity of Salt required for their purposes.

At this period, 1670, pulverized lead ore became very commonly used for glazing the vessels; and to prevent the ornamental parts being injured by the fire, and the glaze being discoloured by the sulphureous vapour from the coals, the employment of SAGGERS became general; but they were not prepared of determinate proportions of marl. This was a discovery of much later date.—TILES glazed in this manner, having the initials of persons' names, and dates from 1670 to 1700, may be seen in the fronts of old houses, in the district.

About 1685, Mr. Thomas Miles, of Shelton, mixed with the whitish clay found in Shelton, some of the fine sand from Baddeley Hedge, and produced a rude kind of WHITE STONE WARE; and another person of the same name, of Miles's Bank, Hanley, produced the BROWN STONE WARE of that day, by mixing the same kind of sand with the Can Marl obtained from the coal pits. Other manufacturers soon followed and various kinds of Pottery resulted. Some of the specimens are glazed with lead ore, and others with salt; some have only the inside, others have both sides glazed; and all of them manifest considerable improvement in quality, shapes, and ornamental workmanship.

A Jar has a medallion of William and Mary, red and white roses, some trees, and a yeoman of the guard on each side. A four quart jug has in relief a Bacchanalian scene, a bull bait, a fox hunt, and some trees. The middle part of a punch bowl has four fishes, two Lions, and a flower; and the border is ornamented with three rows of square bits of white clay, placed regularly to form a chequer band. A deep flour Mug, with two handles, has been coated with whitish clay, and then a zigzag scroll, flowers, leaves, and fruits, have been formed by scraping off the other coating. These are of white Stone Ware. The Specimens of the other kind, Brown, are vessels, with the sides ornamented by medallions, and the Initials, WM. WR. AR. beneath a crown.

These improvements caused attention to be given in reference to body, glaze, and workmanship, by the Burslem Manufacturers; and in consequence we find CROUCH WARE first made there in 1690. Indeed we may mention, to their credit, that almost every *new* kind of Pottery, was first made by them, and the successive improvements are mere results of introducing materials of a different kind with most or all of those previously used. In making *Crouch Ware*, the common Brick Clay, and fine Sand from Mole Cob, were first used; but afterwards the Can Marl and Sand, and some persons used the dark grey clay from the coal pits and sand, for the body; and Salt glaze; to each bushel the principal Potters added a pint of Red Lead powder. The specimens are jugs, cups, dishes, &c. some of them so well finished, as to induce the opinion that the *Turning Lathe* was now beginning to be employed. The different clays are used to form figures of animals, &c. with considerable taste and elegance, as already described; and in this manner is ornamented and painted a twenty inch circular Dish, with W. RICH, 1702. None of these have however those neat and varied shapes adopted in the next stage of improvement. This kind of Pottery possesses several excellent properties; tho' not manufactured now in this District. It is cleanly in appearance, of a very compact texture, durable, and not easily affected by change of temperature. There are some curious specimens of vessels fused accidently by the increased temperature after the salt had been cast into the oven. The loss occasioned by the too high vitrification, for some time prevented the observation that an inferior kind of Porcelain was thus unintentionally produced; for the thinnest pieces have semi-transparence, but were regarded as of little value because sooner affected than the other by increase, or sudden change, of heat. Before Lathes were used, the very vulgar epithet of *Arsing* was given to the method of getting the clay out of the under part of mugs, bottles, &c. which was effected by placing the chum on the wheel block, and then while in motion the workman cut it out.

Up to the conclusion of the 17th century, all the kinds of Pottery, whether glazed with lead ore, or with salt, was fired *only once*. The oven was always adapted to the quantity of Articles made during each week; and no manufacturer of that period fired more than one oven full weekly, commencing on the Thursday night, and finishing about mid-day on Saturday. There were about twenty-two ovens then in Burslem, and its vicinity, each with eight mouths, at equal distances; and around those used for Crouch ware, was a scaffold, on which the fireman stood to cast in the salt. This proves the inaccuracy of the statement in Parkes's Chemical Catechism, p. 102,—" this method of glazing earthenware with salt, was introduced into England by two Brothers from Holland, of the name of ELERS, about the year 1700. They settled in the neighbourhood of the Staffordshire Potteries; and it is remarkable that the alarm occasioned by the fumes which spread over the country, obliged them to leave it." It had long been well known, that Common Table Salt, or Muriate of Soda, is immediately decomposed on being gradually poured into a fire; and it was easily believed, and successfully proved, that the result would be similar, was it to be poured into a potter's oven, at a certain stage of the process during a high excess of temperature. The Saggers were therefore adapted to the purpose, by being formed with holes in their sides to admit the vapours, and the ware was so placed in them, that every part might be affected. The muriatic acid, evolved by the intense heat, from the soda, in the form of vapour highly charged with alkaline particles was dispersed all through every interstice of the oven and its contents of saggers and ware, completely covering all, and acting on the small portion of silica, and the alumina of the body, partially decomposed the latter, to which the former united while in a state of lignefaction, and the surface of all the vessels became wholly vitrified. Of most bodies, great heat causes the particles to expand and occupy a larger space; but the fact is indisputable, that the particles of vessels of Pottery, on cooling, are more closely united, and the dimensions of the mass diminished.

The employment of salt in glazing Crouch Ware, was a long time practised before the introduction of White Clay and Flint. The vast volumes of smoke and vapours from the ovens, entering the atmosphere, produced that dense white cloud, which from about eight o'clock till twelve on the Saturday morning, (the time of *firing-up*, as it is called,) so completely enveloped the whole of the interior of the town, as to cause persons often to run against each other; travellers to mistake the ro d; and strangers have mentioned it as extremely disagreeable, and not unlike the smoke of Etna and Vesuvius. But a murky atmosphere is not regarded by the patriotic observer, who can view thro' it, an industrious population, employed for the benefit of themselves and their country, and behold vast piles of national wealth enhanced by individual industry. This temporary inconvenience entailed on the district the character of being unhealthy, but the contrary is the fact; as may be seen every day in the very old persons living; and proved by consulting the Bills of Mortality. It is now fruitful, but old people regard it as less so than when glazing with salt was practised. The vapours destroyed the insects pernicious to vegetation; and altho' fruit was covered with carbonaceous filaments, the labour of cleaning it was amply compensated by the superabundance.

Being now arrived at the date when Dr. Plott visited this district, it is very probable we should incur censure, were we to omit his comprehensive detail of the Processes then practised; we therefore give them verbatim. "The greatest *Pottery* (says Dr. Plott, History of Staffordshire, chap iii. secs. 23-29) they have in this *County*, is carryed on at *Burslem*, near *Newcastle-under-Lyme*, where for making their several sorts of *Pots*, they have as many different sorts of *Clay*, which they dig round about the *Towne*, all within half a mile distance, the best being found nearest the *coale*, and are distinguish't by their *colours* and *uses* as followeth: *Bottle Clay*, of a bright whitish streaked yellow colour. *Hard Fire Clay*, of a duller whitish colour, and fuller intersperst with a dark yellow, which they use for their *black wares*, being mixt with the *Red Blending Clay*, which is of a dirty red colour. *White Clay*, so called it seems though of a blewish colour,

3 K

and used for making yellow-coloured *ware*, because yellow is the *lightest* colour they make any *Ware* of; all which they call *throwing* clays, because they are of a closer texture, and will work on the *wheel;* which none of the three other *clays*, they call *Slips*, will any of them doe, being of looser and more friable natures; these mixed with water they make into a consistence thinner than a *Syrup*, so that being put into a *bucket* it will run out through a *Quill*, this they call *Slip*, and is the substance wherewith they *paint* their *wares*; whereof the first sort is called the *Orange Slip*, which before work't, is of a greyish colour mixt with orange balls, and gives the ware (when annealed) an *orange* colour. The *White Slip*; this before it is work't, is of a dark blewish colour, yet makes the ware yellow, which being the *lightest* colour they make of, they call it (as they did the *clay* above) the *white Slip*. The *Red Slip*, made of a dirty reddish clay, which gives *wares* a black colour; neither of which *clays* or *Slips* must have any *gravel* or *Sand* in them; upon this account, before it be brought to the *wheel* they prepare the *clay* by steeping it in water in a square pit, till it be of a due consistence; then they bring it to their *beating board*, where with a long *Spatula* they beat it till it be well mix't; then being first made into great *squarish* rolls, it is brought to the *wageing board*, where it is slit into flat thin pieces with a *Wire*, and the least stones or gravel pick't out of it. This being done, they *wage* it, i. e. knead or mould it like *bread*, and make it into round *balls* proportionable to their *work*, and then 'tis brought to the *wheel*, and formed as the *Workman* sees good.

‘ When the *Potter* has wrought the clay either into *hollow* or *flat ware*, they are set abroad to dry in fair weather, but by the fire in foule, turning them as they

see occasion, which they call *wharing:* when they are
dry they *stouk* them, i. e. put *Ears* and *Handles* to
such *Vessels* as require them: These also being dry,
they then *Slip* or *paint* them with their several sorts
of *Slip,* according as they designe their *work,* when
the first *Slip* is dry, laying on the *others* at their leasure,
the *Orange Slip* making the ground, and the *white* and
red, the *paint;* which two colours they break with a
wire *brush,* much after the manner the doe when they
marble paper, and then *cloud* them with a *pensil* when
they are pretty dry. After the *vessels* are painted,
they *lead* them, with that sort of *Lead Ore* they call
Smithum which is the smallest *Ore* of all, beaten into
dust, finely sifted and strewed upon them; which
gives them the *gloss,* but not the colour; all the *colours*
being chiefly given by the variety of *Slips,* except the
Motley colour, which is procured by blending the *Lead*
with *Manganese,* by the *Workmen* call'd *Magnus.*
But when they have a mind to shew the utmost of their
skill in giving their *wares* a fairer *gloss* than ordinary,
they *lead* them then with lead *calcined* into powder,
which they also sift fine and strew upon them as before,
which not only gives them a higher *gloss,* but goes
much further too in their work, than *Lead Ore* would
have done.

"After this is done, they are carried to the *Oven,*
which is ordinarily above eight foot high, and about
six foot wide, of a round copped forme, where they
are placed one upon another from the bottom to the
top: if they be *ordinary wares* such as *cylindricall
Butter-pots,* &c. that are not *leaded,* they are exposed
to the *naked* fire, and so is all their *flat ware* though
it be *leaded,* haveing only *parting-shards,* i. e. thin
bits of old pots put between them, to keep them from
sticking together: But if they be *leaded hollow-wares,*

they do not expose them to the *naked* fire, but put them in *shragers*, that is, in coarse metall'd pots, made of *marle* (not *clay*) of divers formes according as their *wares* require, in which they put commonly three pieces of *clay* called *Bobbs* for the ware to stand on, to keep it from sticking to the *Shragers:* as they put them in the *shragers* to keep them from sticking to one another (which they would certainly otherwise doe by reason of the *leading*) and to preserve them from the vehemence of the *fire*, which else would *melt* them down, or at least *warp* them. In twenty four hours an *Oven* of *Pots* will be burnt, then they let the *fire* goe out by degrees, which in ten hours more will be perfectly done, and then they draw them for *Sale*, which is chiefly to the poor *Crate-men*, who carry them at their *backs* all over the *Country*, to whom they reckon them by the *piece*, i. e. *Quart*, in *hollow ware*, so that six potile, or three gallon *bottles* make a *dosen*, and so more or less to a *dosen*, as they are of greater or lesser *content*. The *flat wares* are also reckon'd by *pieces* and *dosens*, but not (as the *hollow*) according to to their *content*, but their different *bredths*."

As some labourers were digging for gravel in the open fields of Litlington, in this county, a few years ago, they discovered the foundation of a wall, that enclosed a quadrangular area of 34 yards by 24, running parallel with, and at the distance of about ten yards from that ancient Roman road, called the Ashwell Street, the line of communication between the Roman stations at Ashwell and Chesterford. Within this area were found a number of quite perfect earthenware urns, of various sizes and forms, containing human bones and ashes; also a variety of pateræ, patellæ, simpula, some with one handle, others with two, ampullæ and lacrymatories of different sizes and shapes. Some of the urns are composed of a red, and others of a black argillaceous earth; those of the red being much the hardest and most durable; many of the black being in a state of great decay, and some of them when disturbed by the spade of the labourer, fell to pieces. There was only one coin found, with the head of Trajan on one side, and on the reverse Brittannia leaning on a shield, above the letters BRIT. The spot of ground upon which this discovery was made, is called, in ancient deeds " Heaven's Walls," and lies at the bottom of a hill, on the summit of which is a tumulus, called " Limbury," and sometimes " Limbloe-hill."

For more than a Century prior to Dr. Plott's visit, at the two Potteries at Red Street, were made considerable quantities of all kinds of Vessels then used; and during the early part of the eighteenth century, the manufacturers there, named Elijah Mayer, (who perished near Ulverston,) and Moss, fabricated greater quantities of Pottery than any others of the whole district. A descendant of one family, subsequently in possession of one of these Manufactories, much wished to impress the notion, that these two had made more than all other Potters conjointly. We may allow a little latitude for family partiality; but having positive proofs of the mistaken views of our correspondent, we can do justice to the merits of the parties.

CHAP. V.

THE INTRODUCTION OF RED PORCELAIN, BY MESSRS. ELERS, OF BRADWELL, 1690.

THAT Messrs. Elers effected important improvements, and extended the knowledge of the processes in the Art, cannot reasonably be doubted; but as much hyperbole has been employed, and great obscurity attaches to the subject, we have exercised much care in the enquiries concerning them; and by means of information from Mr. Richard Broad, now eighty-eight years of Age, whose father owned property nearly adjoining; and also, by other accounts from the

family of Marsh, who occupied the premises immediately afterwards; with corroborative proofs from
specimens still remaining, we hope to supply a correct
account of the persons and their manufacture. The
East India Companies, both Dutch and English, were
now supplying Europe with *unglazed* RED PORCELAIN,
as well as the white kind, beautifully ornamented, and
called *China*. The difficulty of finding natural clays
equally pure with those of China, made it not easy to
imitate the red Porcelain; which was first attempted,
and appears to have supplied the *name*. How the
persons in question came to know that Bradwell would
supply them with a beautiful Red Clay, peculiarly
fine in grain and colour; and also coals for their purposes, with trifling expence and labour, cannot be
ascertained; but such is the fact;—and in the field
west of Brownhills toll bar, at this day, is a vein of the
same clay, occasionally used by the Potters for a *dip*.

About 1690, Messrs. Elers, settled at Bradwell,
(from Nuremberg,) where they had a small manufactory, and according to tradition, another also at Dimsdale, both in very secluded situations, and at a distance
from the public roads; scarcely discernible from
Burslem, and only partially so from the manufactories at
Red Street. Here for some time, the brothers made
Red Porcelain unglazed Tea Pots, merely of the fine
red clay of Bradwell, and a small proportion of the
ochreous clay from Chesterton, to vary the shade;
and also Black Porcelain, or Egyptian, by adding
manganese in proportions agreeable to the dark shade
wished for. The remaining specimens shew that some
degree of success resulted; the price was from twelve
to twenty-four shillings each, they have a fine grain,
and are excellent in form and every quality except
ornaments, (which are coarse and grotesque,) and will

ever manifest the ingenuity and enterprize of their
fabricators. Being extremly jealous lest any purchaser
or visitor should approach the scene of their operations,
between the two factories was preserved a mode of
communication to intimate the approach of any persons
supposed to be intruders. Their servants were the
most ignorant and stupid persons they could find; and
an idiot was employed to turn the thrower's wheel.
Each person was locked in the place where he was
employed; and such was the precaution to preserve the
supposed secret, that, previously to the few work people retiring at night, each was subjected to a strict
examination. In this state the processes were pursued,
when a person named *Twyford*, from Shelton, obtained
employment under them, and had sufficient prudence
to manifest entire carelessness and indifference to every
operation he witnessed or participated

A very singular method of ascertaining all their
processes, is currently reported to have been adopted
by another person named *Astbury*; (known by his acquaintance as very acute and ingenious, and well capacitated to effect all requisite developements.)——
Having assumed the garb and appearance of an idiot,
with all proper vacancy of countenance, he presented
himself before the manufactory at Bradwell, and submitted to the cuffs, kicks, and unkind treatment of
masters and workmen, with a ludicrous grimace, as
the proof of the extent of his mental ability. When
some food was offered him, he used only his fingers to
convey it to his mouth; and only when helped by
other persons, could he understand how to perform
any of the labours to which he was directed. He next
was employed to move the treadle of an *Engine Lathe*,
a very different machine from those of this day, and
by perseverance in his assumed character, he had op-

portunity of witnessing every process, and examining every utensil they employed. On returning home each evening, he formed models of the several kinds of implements, and made memorandums of the processes; which practice he continued a considerable time, (near two years is mentioned,) until he ascertained that no further information was likely to be obtained; when he availed himself of a fit of sickness, to continue at home; and this was represented as most malignant, to prevent any persons visiting him. After his recovery he was found so *sane*, that Messrs. Elers deemed him unfit longer to remain in their service, and he was discharged, without suspicion that he possessed a knowledge of all their manipulations.

Only a short time subsequently elapsed, ere they found that no longer were their operations secret; and mortified at the fact that their precaution had been unavailing; disgusted by the inquisitiveness of the Burslem potters, and convinced that they were too far distant from the principal market for their productions, they at length discontinued manufacture at Bradwell, and removed to a munafactory in the vicinity of London, where a branch of the family now is resident. And, as it is known that an Establishment for manufacturing Porcelain, was in operation at Chelsea, between 1720 and 1730, (the era of Reaumur's analytical investigation of the materials and specimens sent from China,) there is great probability that in this manufactory the Messrs. Elers were concerned.

We have obtained the following information concerning the OVEN which has been mentioned as having cast forth such tremendous volumes of smoke and flame, as were terrific to the inhabitants of Burslem, and occasioned that misunderstanding and persecution which ultimately caused Messrs. Elers to quit their residence:—The Oven itself had *five* mouths, but neither holes over the inside flues or bags, to receive the salt, had any been used by them; nor scaffold on which the person might stand to throw it in. The foundations were very distinctly to be seen in 1808, tho' now covered by an enlargement of the barn. E. Wood, and J. Riley, Esqrs. both separately measured the inside diameter of the remains, at about *five* feet; while other ovens, of the same date, in Burslem, were *ten* or *twelve* feet. Mr. John Mountford, twenty-seven years since; took down the remains of the oven, and he states that the height was about *seven* feet, but not like the salt glaze ovens. It was adapted to fire choice articles; and as the most careful research and enquiry in every direction near the spot, supply fragments of Red unglazed Porcelain, and Blue Pottery, (probably made by Mr. Cookworthy, or his relation Mr. Marsh, who succeeded Messrs. Elers, at Bradwell farm; and whose relation, Jacob Marsh, Esq. now resides at Lane End,) there is every probability that only the Red Porcelain, and Black, were made here, as the oven is only adapted for such productions.

We may also mention, that the Salt glazed Pottery of that time, was comparatively cheap; and the oven, being fired only once each week, required to be large, to hold a quantity sufficient to cover the contingent expenses. Hence we find the ovens were large, and high, and had holes in the dome, to receive the salt cast in to effect the glazing. And, had the processes of Messrs. Elers been so terrific, as to cause the Burslem potters to flock to Bradwell, in astonishment at the smoke and flames from so small an oven; there must have been very quickly effected a complete change, for Twyford and Astbury, commenced and carried for-

L

ward, manufactories of Red Porcelain, and White
Pottery glazed with salt, amidst many small thatched
dwellings in Shelton, some of which remain to our day.

CHAP. VI.

PROGRESS OF THE MANUFACTURE FROM 1700 TO MR. WEDGWOOD'S COMMENCEMENT IN 1760.

Prior to Dr. Plott's visit, the manufacturers must
have had a mediocrity of business, as well as regular
methods of disposing of their productions thro' the
country. These were the Coarse Red, mottled and
cloudy, black, and yellow wares. A suitable clay was
used for the body; and other kinds were mixed with
water, and the liquid applied on the surface, to produce many shades of colour, and ornaments much
similar to old patterns of marbled paper.

The Specimens are some glazed with lead, others with salt,
and some wholly without glaze, or in the vocabulary of our
day *dry* bodies; remarkably varied in kinds and appearance,
and the Coffee and Tea pots have shapes varying with the
fancy of the workman ; heart shaped, globose, spheroidal, on
feet, conoid, octagonal, and many other whimsical forms,
with the spouts and handles equally singular and curious. A
spheroidal Tea Pot, which will hold two quarts, has the spout
and handle well fixed on in imitation of a piece of vine branch ;
and on the bend of the vessel are leaves and fruit. Another
Specimen has some embossed work on it. And some smaller
Tea pots have leaves in white clay. As none of the surfaces
of these have been *turned* in the lathe, we must regard turning as yet only partially introduced. The Ornaments *in relief* were formed by scraping away with the point of an iron
nail, the superfluous mass when dry, of either the body or dip,
leaving the representations of flowers, &c. a little raised on
the same principle as the sculptor cuts away the superabun-
dent mass of materials.

Dr. Plott mentions, that at this time a tobacco-pipe maker, of Newcastle, named Charles Rigg, employed to make very good Pipes, three sorts of clay, a *white*, and a *blue*, which he has from between Shelton and Hanley green [now Filcher's and Kirkham's marl pits,] whereof the *blue* clay burns the *whitest*, but not so *full* as the white; i. e. it shrinks more." p. 121. Some of the *Red* was of the kind now frequently seen in best Flower Pots; of rather a dark teint, but beautiful grain, because the clay had been passed thro' fine hair sieves.

At this time also were made the first attempts at the ware now called *Egyptian Black*; by employing the black clay only for jugs and tea pots; which being rich with basaltes, and saturated with oxide of iron, became very black when fired. Several specimens are ornamented with figures, in other clays, of leaves, and fruit; and a small white tea pot has these in black clay. Some of the black tea pots are glazed, but not all; and the *stouking* branch seems improved in all the specimens. In 1820, very near the front of the Burslem Free School, at the depth of almost *ten* feet beneath the surface of the then existing highways, which were being lowered for public convenience, were found two Butter Pots, of 1645, and several other specimens of early pottery, in a hole from which clay had been taken formerly, and which had been filled with refuse articles. One is a jet black tea pot, globose in shape, with three mole feet on the bottom, evidently of clay with some manganese, and finely glazed with lead ore; the spout, handle, and feet, fixed in a superior manner. None of these exhibit any of the *white dip* or *wash*, so prevalent in 1710; and therefore probably it had not been introduced when they were buried.— This kind of ware was much in request about 1740, and Thomas and John Wedgwood manufactured great quantities, long before they erected the Big House.

In the Egyptian Black Clay of the present day, a proportion of *Car* is introduced; it is an oxide of iron suspended in the water drained from the Coal Mines, and procured thus:— Being of a specific gravity greater than that of water, it forms a sediment at the bottom of the channel of the stream that conveys it from the mine: when a considerable quantity is thus lodged in a certain space, the stream, to that extent, is diverted from its usual course; and the car is thrown out of the channel, from whence the water has been turned off, upon the adjoining banks; where it remains till dry. Sometimes small pits or ponds are made on the adjoining banks, and the car is scooped from the bottom of the channel, and thrown into them, without diverting the course of the water. When it is sufficiently dry, it is sold at the rate of one guinea per cart-load. Being very useful for Busts, &c. Mr. Josiah Wedgwood, prepared it of a superior quality in grain, and blacker in colour; and obtained a patent for its entire application. His numerous beautiful productions of this body remain unrivalled. But the patent was given up, in consequence of Mr. Palmer, of Hanley, satisfactorily proving, that the articles had been used some time before Mr. Wedgwood commenced business.

At the time we are now noticing, any manufacturer who was a Freeholder, in Burslem, without molestation exercised his (then supposed) right of taking clay, or coals, or both, from any uninclosed or unenfranchised land in the liberty, at any time, and in whatever quantity he might require; and this right (which was well remembered by many persons alive in 1803,) was exercised to so great an extent on the Sneyd Estate, (then the property of Parker, Earl of Macclesfield,) that only was a stop put to the practice, by the Earl paying a considerable sum for enfranchising the Estate. Prior to using the Salt Glaze and Biddeford Clay, all the clays and much of the coals for the twenty-two ovens, weekly filled with Crouch,

Glazed Black, Mottled, Cloudy, Moulded, &c. were obtained from holes in the streets and sides of the lanes; and all of these are not yet filled up with refuse articles.

Coals were known before the arrival of the Romans, who had not even a name for them, though Theophrastus describes them very accurately, at least three centuries before the time of Cæsar; and as then known to workers in brass.—Brand observes that they were not mentioned under the Danish usurpation, nor under the Normans, but were known in the reign of Henry III. In 1366 they were prohibited in London as a nuisance, but used in the Palace in 1321, and became soon after an important article of commerce. In 1512 they were not always used, because not having got to the main *stratum*, people complained ' that they would not burn without wood.'— The best were then sold at 5s. a chaldron, a bad sort at 4s. 2d. Excepting blacksmiths, they were used in the seventeenth century, under the name of *sea coal*, by the lower orders, who could not afford to buy wood; and in sacks upon men's backs they were hawked about the streets.

The native clays are all metalliferous, each having a portion of oxide of iron. But the clays from Dorset and Devon, used by the tobacco-pipe makers, have all their impurities extracted before they are vended to the purchasers. In the present day, it is well known that every coloured clay has its tinge from a metallic oxide, and that pure clay is white. During this period, and a considerable time subsequent, the Clays from the south of England, were called *Chester Clay*, because received here from that city. They possess every property requisite for their designed purpose; being extremely white when fired, owing to being scarcely impregnated with oxide of iron, which would make the ware yellow or red in proportion to the quantity in the clay.

Mr. Twyford commenced business near Shelton Old Hall, the seat of Elijah Fenton's family; and the

3 L

only known specimen of his manufacture, is a jug made for T. Fenton, Esq., at this day in the possession of a descendant of the same name, residing at the Lodge; below Penkhull; of whom we may observe that great professional ability is in him joined with philanthropy, and a readiness to accelerate every meritorious enterprize.

Mr. Astbury commenced also in Shelton, near Vale Lane, at first. And both these persons made Red, Crouch, and White Stone Wares; using lead ore glaze for some vessels, and salt for those of more value. Mr. Astbury very soon began to employ the Pipe Clay, from Biddeford, mixed with water, with which the inner surface of culinary vessels was washed, and when fired, had a white appearance, different from the smoky hue of those glazed with lead ore, and also from the grey brick-like colour of the others glazed with salt. This excited him to further endeavours; the pipe clay was levigated until only the finest particles were suspended in the water, forming a liquid substance like cream; he also tried this clay and the Shelton marl, for his white ware, with such success, that he soon rejected the native clays entirely, and made *White Dipped* or *White Stone Ware*, by a very easy transition from the Crouch ware.

Mr. Thomas Heath, of Lane Delph, in 1710, made a good kind of Pottery, by mixing with his other clay a species obtained from the coal mines, which by high firing became a light grey; and his Pottery is of a durable kind, not easily affected by change or excess of temperature. Mr. Heath is still remembered by very old persons in Lane Delph. — He lived to a very advanced age, and left behind him the character of being a truly good man, a kind and benevolent master, and a blessing to the neighbourhood. His three Daughters were married to persons who afterwards became celebrated potters.—Mr. Neale, of London, Mr. Palmer, of Hanley, (a descendant of Mr. Palmer, of Bagnall, and the proprietor of a manufactory above the Chapel,) and Mr. Pratt, of Fenton; one of whose descendants, at the present day, occupies the premises since erected on the site of Mr. Heath's manufactory. He also used the Wash of Pipe Clay, first practised by Mr. Astbury; as is seen on a circular fourteen inch dish of the author's, long time the property of a family a Swinnerton, and one of a set made as a specimen of this new kind of ware. The upper surface is tolerably even, and only a very few minute holes (air bubbles) appear in the dip; but the under surface is spotted with them, and exhibits the coarse materials of the body. We cannot help regarding it as a fine specimen of the first attempts at *White Ware*, and *Blue Painting* upon the face. The effect is pleasing, tho' the outline is very rude. In the landscape; mere lines or strokes form the edifice; (like school boys' first attempts at design,) the clouds seem formed by the fingers' end, and a soft rag or sponge; the two human figures are finely contrasted; a very tall thin woman, in the costume of the time, walking with a low stout man wrapped in a cloak.

About this time also was first made the STONE WARE, (in imitation of the kind made in various places on the European continent,) by mixing common pipe clay with the fine grit or sand from Mole Cob. This kind was whiter than any before made; it is very durable, and will bear any degree of heat uninjured; hence, its great demand for chemical purposes; and Macquer's high eulogium, "the best common stone ware is the most perfect Pottery that can be; for it has all the essential qualities of the finest Japanese Porcelain." We may here observe, that with the exception of whiteness, whereon depends its semi-transparency, both appear to have internally the same grain; give similar sounds if struck when properly suspended; have similar density and hardness to give fire with steel; will boil liquids without breaking; and are not fusible;—hence we conclude, that if the clay, from which stone ware is made, were free from heterogeneous colouring matters which prevent whiteness and transparency on the ware being fired; were the vessels carefully formed, all proper attention to the various processes of the work paid, and a fine glaze employed over the whole, it is believed that such stone ware would be as perfect Porcelain as that brought from Japan. Probably the quantity of silica and argil found in this rock at Mole Cob, (which is an interposed bed of sandstone,) approximating closely to the compound which Potters call Clay, and of which Pottery is made, may be the cause of the fine grit preventing biscuit pottery from adhering while being fired; and also of strengthning some kinds of Pottery, and Saggers. It is brought to the manufactories in a pulverized state; poor children resident nigh where the grit rock crops out, break off masses, and with wooden mallets pound the pieces, until sufficiently fine to pass thro' a sieve of a certain size. Iron hammers would perhaps injure the grit, by the particles which would intermingle during the pulverization.

A mere accident at this time (1720) caused another and important improvement. Mr. Astbury being on a journey to London, on horseback, had arrived at Dunstable, when he was compelled to seek a remedy for the eyes of his horse, which seemed to be rapidly going blind. The hostler of the tavern at which he stayed, burned a flint stone till quite red, then he pulverized it very fine, and by blowing a little of the dust into each eye, occasioned both to discharge much matter and be greatly benefitted.   Mr. Astbury, having noticed the white colour of the calcined flint,—the ease with which it was then reduced to powder,—and its clayey nature when discharged in the moisture from the horses eyes,—immediately conjectured that it might be usefully employed to render of a different colour the Pottery he made.   On his return home, he availed himself of his observation; and soon obtained a preference for his ware, which produced considerable advantages.   The specimens warrant the conclusion that he first employed the flint, (after it had been calcined and pounded in a morter,) in a mixture with water to a thick pulp, as a *wash* or *dip*, which he applied to give a coating to the vessels, some time before he introduced it along with the clay into the body of his ware.   For which method, a person, a few years afterwards, obtained a patent, and some time used it. That Mr. Astbury was eminently successful, we conclude from the comfortable independence enjoyed by Mrs. Smith, his grand daughter, who died at Lane End, in 1816, and her son Thomas Smith, who died there in 1823; and who gave part of this information. The old lady, frequently in her garrulous moments, amused the younger portion of visitors to herself, or her son, with anecdotes of the very *kind attentions* she often received from certain persons who afterwards became opulent manufacturers.   A widow Astbury, of Lane Delph, was married by Mr. Thomas Bacchus, of that place; who made Cream Colour, and Blue painted ware, and after her death, he married a person skilled in painting ware, and an intimate acquaintance of the Miss Mayer, married by Mr. Robert Wilson, of Hanley;—and this Mrs. Bacchus, afterwards resided in a house adjoining that person's manufactory, until her death at an advanced age about the year 1809.

Mr. Astbury died in 1743, Aged 65, and is buried on the south side of the old Church, in the angle formed by the two paths.   And at a short distance is the grave of his Son Thomas Astbury, of Lane Delph.   And very near there is the Tomb of Mr. John Fenton, the father of Elijah Fenton, near the Chancel door, of very excellent workmanship; but the epitaph, written by the poet, cannot now be traced. The family of Fenton must have been very respectable, for they were possessors of a large tract, still called Fenton, bounded by Longton, Botteslow, and Penkhull; and including 1600 acres.—The portion of property still in the family, came to the present Sir T. F. Boughey, of Aqualate, by his Grandmother, the Lady of Sir Thomas Fletcher.

This part of the Church Yard seems to have been especially secured by the *elite*' of the parish; probably because less affected by the overflowing of the Fowl-Hay-Brook than the northern quarter, for most of the stones register some person of importance. And tho' rather out of order here, yet we shall be more easily excused for noticing in this place, than pardoned for wholly omitting, the following observations:— Henry Clark, being 112 years of age when he died, in 1684, in the reign of the Abdicator James, and four years prior to the landing of William of Orange, and the Glorious Revolution of 1688; the mind very naturally reverts to the events which occurred from the era of his birth, which must have been in the 14th year of Elizabeth, to that of his demise.   He lived at the eventful period of the estblishment of the Protestant Faith in England, and destruction of numerous religious Institutions and Monasteries, in the reign of Elizabeth, James 1st. Charles 1st. and the Civil Wars and Commonwealth, (a most critical time, and during which by the fanatics, the Abbey at Hulton was destroyed completely, if not by the agents of Henry VIII; while Stoke Church probably was spared because of its very poor appearance.) He witnessed the Restoration and reign of Charles II, and the early attempts of James again to return to the Communion of the Church of Rome. He must have heard of Mary of Scotland's confinement at Tutbury Castle; being about fifteen years old when her decapitation was perpetrated at Fotheringhay Castle. The old Inscription was almost effaced, when two of the parish servants, Josiah Austin and Samuel Davis, paid a stone cutter to sink the letters, which are now very *large and deep.*

John Machin, Gentlemen, of Botteslow, was 71 years of age at the time of his death in 1713; consequently was born in the year 1642; and probably the Pottery at Botteslow was given up, during the disturbances of the Civil Wars. Only on this supposition can we account for Mr. Machin being called *Gentleman.* His Son Thomas lies near the Chancel door, under a plain slab with a Latin Inscription:—"Thomas Machin, Nuper de Botteslow, (in hac Parochia) Generosus, Qui obiit. Vicessimo 1 mo de Novembris. Anno (Salutis humanæ 1747, Ætatis ejus 64." Thomas's Brother Henry Machin, lived at the *Yew Tree House,* near Longton Hall, and was buried in 1719, aged 73. The family is very ancient, and one of the most respectable in the parish; and for the accommodation of its members, with those of other places contiguous,

in their attendance on Divine Worship, a paved foot-
path was made in the old Road from Stoke thro' Fenton to Bucknall, (*Abbey* ley or *Upper*) Ubberley, and
Hilton Abbey. The Mansion is very ancient, and
yet, with the application of a comparatively small sum,
it might be rendered both picturesque and elegant.

Stoke Old Church, is placed on the gravel bed
formed by the eddy of the floods at the junction of
the Fowl-Hay-Brook with the Trent; and as the
opening of deep graves constantly exposes great quantities of well rounded pebbles, there is reason for believing that the foundations rest on the bed of pebbles
left here by different floods. Little doubt can be entertained that the whole of this beautiful valley was a
large bason of water, that opened for itself a passage
at Handford; and at length below Stone; occasioning
the constant recession of the waters, till all were
drained, to Knutton Heath and Chesterton in one
direction; to Harecastle Hill in another; and in the
line of the Trent, to Norton, Endon, Bagnall, and
Ubberley. If the structure be of the age usually attributed to it, *eight centuries*; and its heavy and durable style of architecture, proves it to have been erected
when it was customary to build Churches equally
strong with Baronial Castles;—its erection to the
combined energies of a race of Angles, Saxons,
and Danes, or their offspring by intermarriages; and
at a time prior to the invasion and consequent parti-
tion of Lands by the Norman Banditti. We are led
to conjecture that its early ecclesiastics were not *very
literate*, and that their few record were transmitted to
their superior, by whom the most important might be
forwarded to the diocesan, and thence to Rome; and
the others consigned to the shelves of a cell in some
monastery; for no traces of history afford any clue by

which to ascertain the era of its foundation; neither is there on any part of the venerable fabric discernable outline of scroll or tablet for an Inscription; tho' had there been any such, of even moderate depth, the durable nature of the materials would have preserved it for our gratification.   On the south side of the tower may be seen the breast, wings, and web feet, of a swan or goose; and a small portion of a similar carving is visible on the north side; probably mementos of the great numbers of aquatic fowl then frequenting the ground, and which proved a source of benefit to the persons employed in the edifice.   But the absence of every ostentatious relic, warrants the conclusion, that its erection was more with a design to benefit the district, than to gratify the ambition of the founders. Concerning the peculiarities of the style, there was a spirited controversy, which instead of eliciting truth, generated personal rancour and dislike.   Certainly a little reference to early northern history, would have precluded the supposition of the *Goths* being brought into England by the Saxons; for the latter were only a small tribe of the vast hordes of wanderers who bore the former name ages prior to the Roman Invasion, and their name became a bye-word for whatever was less polished than the whims of the admirers of Greece and Rome supposed every thing ought to be.   There appears an overlooking of a material fact connected with the edifice; the outside is of a different style altogether to that of the interior; and of a much more recent date; for which we cannot account on any other principle than regarding the outside as having been very much altered during the repairs it has evidently received at different times.   There obtained a preference of the style adopted in the architecture of the Saracen's, by those *religieuse* who returned from the Wars in Palestine; and they made all their repairs of old

Churches, as well as their new edifices, some way accordant to this predilection. However, the Church is a very excellent specimen, in its present state, of the Parish Church Architecture of the twelfth and two subsequent centuries.

The eastern side of the tower shews that the first roof was very pointed; and the courses of stone work also prove that the present roof, covered with lead, is not of more than two centuries duration. The different style of architecture adapted in the Chancel, causes an opinion that it is of a more recent date than the body of the Church; which, entered thro' the south Porch, presents the eye with massive and durable columns supporting the arches of the nave. The windows of the transepts have been removed to make room for large square ones, wholly destitute of elegance; and the *present* vestry is truly shabby. At the west end of the south aisle, the attention is arrested by a massive Font, a rude block of granite, sculptured for the reception of water, in which, during many generations, infants were by immersion or sprinkling (at the discretion of the priests) initiated into the visible Church of Christ; or the vessel of consecrated water was placed, for the devout to dip the finger and sprinkle the brow prior to prostration before the Altar. But we favour the former suggestion, because it can be filled with water by a tube from the roof thro' the Canopy over it; and by another beneath it can be cleansed and emptied into a subterraneous Channel.

We may also further notice, that, in Burslem Church yard is an old stone coffin, and three Grave stones, on each other, the uppermost having the inscription 1300; and on another 1494. It has been conjectured that these came from Hulton Abbey; but it is equally probable that they are relics of the former *Burslemites*. No reference has been made to a Cemetry at the Abbey; and the fact of Burslem having belonging to the Lordship, will warrant the opinion that the defunct members of that fraternity, were brought to Burslem for interment.—No doubt need be entertained that Burslem Church served as the place of religious resort for the inhabitants of that part of the parish of Stoke; and probably suffered delapidation, at the same time as the Abbey with which it was immediately connected. Norton Church, of much more recent date served for that angle; as did Bagnall for the Moorland angle. We find Hulton Abbey nearly central in reference to these Churches; it was situated in the vale below the Birches, and between Bucknall and Milton; was founded by Henry of Audleigh, in 1223, for Cistertian Monks; and its value at the Dissolution was £89 10s. 1d. per annum, when its lands were granted to Sir Edward Aston, of Tixal. As scoriaceous substances, and very old Pottery have been found among the ruins, it is no great stretch of the imagination, to regard, as very probable, that the Monks were supplied from Burslem with *Crockery* of different kinds; or that they were occasionally employed in forming it for their own purposes. Very near the Abbey, the Coal *crops* out, and as both clay and coal were close to the spot, they had very little obstacle to indulgence in branches of experimental investigation, very usual among them, and by which society has been much benefitted. From this central residence the persons who had to perform the religious services, might readily proceed to the several Churches around, in the paths still marked out by stone Posts, of the same kind, shape, and apparent age. From Burslem Church, passing thro' Hot Lane to Sneyd Green, then by the Birches Farm to the Abbey; and marked still by land known as Church or Abbey Lands;

of part whereof is the grange Farm, where appears to have been a secluded spot, or cell, to which the monks might retire from the Church or the Abbey, on their way to Wolstanton; and probably the origin of the old Chapel already mentioned. And their line of road is by Blakelow, Bucknall, Botteslow, Trenthay, to Stoke Church, or thro' Shelton, by Hartshill, to Newcastle. On many of the old Stones is a +, to call the attention of the pedestrian to his religious profession, wherever he might be proceeding, and whatever superstition might be in the practice, the moral effect could never be prejudicial; as this would interrupt his train of thoughts, and might suggest correct procedure even after previously cogitating improper designs.

The following instance of longevity is entitled to notice:—Mr. William Willett, of Little Eaves, near Hanley, died September 8th, 1827, aged 105. He was born in the eighth year of the reign of George the First; and had lived thro' all the very interesting period of the establishment of the present dynasty on the English Throne. He had witnessed the rise of Burslem, Hanley, Shelton, and Lane End, from a few scattered houses and potteries, to the high eminence of the chief Towns in the county for size and opulence. The abortive attempt of the Chevalier, or Pretender, in 1745, he well remembered; also the inhuman act of Mr. Murrall, of Bagnall, in skinning one of the sick Rebels left there, and endeavouring to get the skin dressed as Leather; for which, on the return of his comrades from Derby, they emasculated Mr. Murrall between Biddulph and Congleton; and for which, he never after was known to enjoy a comfortable day. Mr. Willett was of some talent as a mathematician; and his chief pleasure in his latest days, was the solution of difficult Arithmetical questions. Having lived at the time of altering the Style, in 1752, he often amused friends with the following fact, designed to try their credulity;—when he was thirty years of age, he was one of a party of sixteen couple met at Endon on the *third* of September, 1752, who commenced dancing early in the evening, while he played on the violin; this amusement was continued by the whole party without any other intermission than merely for refreshment, he playing and they continuing tripping on the light fantastic toe, till day break of the *fourteenth* day of the same month. His sight was a little injured; but his mind was vigorous almost to the last, when the weary wheels of life no longer could revolve, and his body returned to its kindred dust.

About the year 1783, the towns of Burslem and Hanley began to assume some degree of importance; if we may judge from the following circumstances:— There being an intention on the part of the respectable residents of Hanley and Shelton, to obtain a Charter for the Potteries, in anticipation of such a favour, on the 18th September, Ephrain Chatterley, Esq. was appointed Mayor of Hanley and Shelton, and a Corporation was empannelled while the parties were excited by the libations they had sacrificed to Bacchus. On this occasion, seventy Gentlemen dined at the Swan Inn, whose Names we have obtained from the Register of the Meetings, which were subsequently presented annually with the side of a Buck by the Marquis of Stafford; and with Game, Fish, and Fruit by Sir Thomas Fletcher.—This Originated the HANLEY (CORPORATION or) VENISON FEAST; continued to the present day. The initiation of each Member consisted then in swearing fealty to the body, and drinking *a yard of wine*, i. e. a pint of port or sherry, out of a glass one yard in length. The Register mentions whatever peculiarities distinguished each *novice*; but these being of trifling importance to that of the List of Names first entered, we preserve the last to gratify the descendants or connections of the parties, who at that time formed the *Elite* of our citizens of the district, when the present Towns were mere hamlets, or scattered but enlarging Villages:

E. Chatterley, Esq. Mayor.
W. Smallwood, Recorder.
Rev. T. Middleton
Mr. T. Adams, Newcastle
Mr. John Heath, Hanley
Rev. Tomlinson, Newcastle
Mr. Horwood, Trentham
Mr. T. Twemlow, Shelton
Mr. T. Hales, Cobridge
Mr. W. Fowler, Newcastle
Mr. J. Yates, Shelton
Mr. R. Baddeley, ditto
Mr. S. Hollins, ditto
Mr. J. Baddeley, ditto
Mr. J. Mare, Hanley
Mr. J. Beckitt, Newcastle
Mr. R. Griffin, New Inn Mill
Rev. W. Fernyhough, Stoke
Rev. B. Adams, Newcastle
Mr. Clowes, Longport
Mr. R. Badnall, Leek
Mr. J. Heath, Hanley
* Mr. H. Booth, Stoke
Mr. J. Hollins, Newcastle
Mr. C. Cotton, Burslem
Mr. W. Brittain, Hanley
Mr. J. Adams, Newcastle
Mr. Daintry, Leek
Mr. R. Heath, Newcastle
Mr. J. Emery, ditto
Mr. G. Taylor, Hanley
Mr. T. Payne, Newcastle
Mr. Payne, Hanley
Mr. S. Perrey, ditto
Mr. J. Massey, Newcastle

Mr. Wilson, Newcastle
Mr. Royle, Wall Grange
Mr. A. Hassell, Shelton
Mr. R. Mare, Hanley
Mr. C. Bagnall, Shelton
Mr. Caldwell, Newcastle
Mr. C. Chatterley, Shelton
Mr. H. Baker, Hanley
Mr. Bagshaw, Newcastle
Mr. J. Shorthose, Hanley
Mr. V. Close, ditto
Mr. F. Pearce, Teignmouth
Mr. Dewint, Shelton
Mr. S. Mayer, Hanley
Mr. J. Lakin, ditto
Mr. F. Keates, ditto
Mr. W. Mellor, ditto
Mr. R. Sims, ditto
Mr. W. Tittensor, Shelton
Mr. F. Lander, ditto
Mr. J. Yates, ditto
Mr. J. Simpson, ditto
Mr. Endsor, Newcastle
Mr. C. Whitehead, Hanley
Mr. B. Godwin, Cobridge
Mr. Robinson, ditto
* Mr. Adams, ditto
Rev. G. Harper, Macclesfield
Mr. S. Chatterley, Hanley
Mr. T. Wright, Shelton
* Mr. J. Glass, Hanley
Mr. J. Whitehead, ditto
* Mr. J. Keeling Perry, ditto
Mr. J. Mayer, Swan Inn, do.
Mr. L. Bennet, Dimsdale

Those marked with an Asterisk, (*) yet survive, 1829.

On the celebration of the Election of Chief Constable of Burslem, November 8, 1824; E. Wood, sen. made the following observations;—He first adverted to the increase of the town in wealth and population, within his recollection, having commenced Business in 1784. In reference to the Public Market, and the Hall, he remembered well the place when it was without either; the first attempt at a Butcher's stall, was the loan of a door unhinged and placed on two old saggers at either end; and for some time this was continued, until an improvement took place, by boards being placed on crates; next a set of shambles were erected, but very weak in materials, though covered over; which caused them to become a complete nuisance; and many of the boards having been at sundry times pilfered, on the occasion of the celebrated battle of Copenhagen, the stalls were pulled down and destroyed. The towns people next used more eligible stalls; and the Market had risen into a state of equality with any in the county. He mentioned that at their early Constable's Feast, the regulation dish was a *boiled Leg of Mutton* and *Turnips*, which custom continued many years; (and was at this meeting resolved on being continued at all future Dinners on this occasion;) but with the improvements in the markets came the improvement in the feast; and some truly ominous indications of forthcoming ruin were, in the opinions of some sage and cautious persons, connected with the extravagance of a *Roast Goose*, in addition to the Leg of Mutton, with the *Giblet Pye* in the Centre of the Table. Up to this day, however, ruin had not yet prevented their partaking the blessings of the season at this Anniversary; there was a dinner of equal abundance to all their wishes, and which might vie with the social board of a Nobleman: the various luxuries of Flesh, Fish, and Fowl, a remove for delicacies of game; a desert crowned with pine apples, garnished with grapes, spread on capacious tables in a most elegant public Room, and waiting to be enjoyed by the most respectable Inhabitants of the town and neighbourhood.*

The following Resolutions will shew the Manner of convening a General Meeting of the Potteries for Public Purposes:—

At a very numerous Meeting of Inhabitants of the different Towns in the Potteries, held at Hanley, December 12, 1817, John Edensor Heathcote, Knt. Chairman.

"In order to obviate the difficulty which now exists, in regard to the mode of calling Public Meetings of the Inhabitants of the Potteries at large;—

It is proposed, resolved, and agreed, that in future, all Public Meetings convened by, and in the joint names of the Majority of the Head Constables for the time being of Burslem, Hanley and Shelton, Stoke, Fenton, and Lane End,

---

* The following genuine anecdote may illustrate the emphatic mention of the *roast Goose:*

On swearing in of different special Constables for the Township of Tunstall in 1823, one of the worthies present on the occasion, and who was honored with the title of " King of Tunstall," thus addressed their worships, (Geo. Tollet and F. Twemlow, Esqrs.) " Tunstall, your worships is the head of Burslem; and yet it so happens that Tunstall Court is held at Burslem; and the Court dine at Burslem: but we have lost nothing but our dinners—our honor remains. I'll tell your worships how it happened. We had *bad Cooks* at Tunstall, who *boiled the goose* instead of *roasting* it; and we have been *roasted* on this subject ever since; but, blow me tight, your honors, if Tunstall is not the head of Burslem still!"

shall be understood and considered as regularly convened; and that such Head Constables be recognized as the authorized organs on such occasions, and as the proper persons to whom Requisitions may be addressed for calling Public Meetings from time to time; the same to be held at Hanley, as the most central, and usual place of Meetings for the Potteries at large."

But in Hanley, we want a large Room adequate to receive the probable number of Persons on such occasions.   Most public meetings have taken place in the market-place; and *the weather* has not been always favourable.

About 1725, Mr. Thomas Astbury, a son of the person already mentioned, commenced business at Lane Delph; first using a different kind of marl with the flint, which so varied the teint of this improved pottery, that he named it *Cream-coloured stone ware*; and this was further improved by using only the whitest native clay, and flint ground at Mothersall mill.   The specimens seem merely thrown on the wheel, and finished to a polish by the dexterity of the workman.   Some are of a red body, with white ornaments, and glazed with lead ore; and a flour mug, dated 1730, has on it a tulip, rose, and auricula, fairly designed and executed.   The information we have received is, that the first factory was where the Lane Delph Market-Place now is.—The old hovel, whose outside was almost covered with grass, was removed in 1823.   It is also stated that the younger Mr. Astbury erected part of the premises now the property of Mr. S. Ginders.

The Flint employed is the kind common on the south-east coasts of England, as Brighton, &c.   It contains much pure silex, with a large proportion of oxygen in a most condensed state; and so readily does it unite with alumina when both are in a fluid state, that it is employed in various proportions; even to the amount of one fourth of the mass of the body of Porcelain and earthenware. When first it was introduced, the potters put it to calcine in their ovens when fired; after which it was pulverized in large iron mortars, by men, and then passed thro' a fine hair sieve. These processes were, however exceedingly laborious, and extremely deleterious; every possible precaution employed being ineffectual to prevent great quantities of the finest particles of the silex floating in the air of the apartment, and being inhaled by the workmen, producing the most disastrous effects, by remaining on the lungs in spite of every expectorant, causing asthma, and often premature death.

Now, however, the flint is calcined in a small kiln, much like those for burning limestone rock; and is ground in water by the power of a water-wheel, or a steam engine. After being calcined, the nodules are thrown under *Stampers*, to be broken. These are wooden beams, shod with iron on the lower end, and moved vertically in a frame, so as to fall with great force down on the flint laid on a strong grate. A circular vat is made of strong boards, in diameter from seven to fourteen feet, and firmly connected by iron hoops; in the centre of the bottom is fixed a step in which acts the gudgeon of a vertical shaft moved from the upper end, on each of whose four sides is fixed a well constructed paddle, bearing and carrying round in the vat large masses of tolerably pure chert, (a very hard silecious rock;) while the bottom is paved with smaller chert stones. Into this vat the calcined broken flints are thrown, and covered with water; and by abrasure they are ground till the water is a thick whitish pulp, which is then brought into a vat, and either used in the *slop* state, or dried upon a kiln into a fine powder. A few years ago, an inferior chert, containing much carbonate of lime, being used, caused considerable loss to the parties; and hence great care is exercised to prevent calcareous rock being used in grinding the Flint.—It has been suggested, that if the flint was thrown while red hot into the water, it would be rendered more brittle, and be stamped and ground in much less time.

Considerable difficulty attaches to most inventions at first; and we find great incertitude concerning the several persons, who were at this period endeavouring to discover a more eligible method than mere manual labour to reduce the calcined flints into a powder proper for potters to use. We find *Stampers* first used instead of mortars, at what was then called Machin's Mill, Burslem, by a person whose name we have not been able to learn.

The merit of inventing the method of grinding Flint in water, as far as we have been able to ascertain, must be shared by John Gallemore, of Millfield gate, Lane End; Joseph Bourne, of Beamhurstley or Bemersley; James Brindley, the celebrated engineer; and Edward Bedson, a glazier, from London.—Among the papers left by Mr. Thomas Daniel, we find mention that Mr. Gallimore erected the first mill for this purpose, at Cookshut Green, only about two miles from Bemersley; afterwards a second at the Meir, near the Furnace; and another at the Ivy House, near Hanley, the property of Mr. Astbury; and subsequently of those who have since become proprietors of the manufactory in Shelton, once owned by him:—

Messrs. Baddeley, and now Messrs, Hicks and Meigh; Gentlemen who rank very high in public estimation for the numerous excellencies of character which add peculiar lustre to opulent employers. Had this ingenious man Gallemore, not indulged in ebriety, a considerable property would have resulted from his labours; but equally with several other persons of genius concerned in improving the manufacture, his intemperance nullified the advantages which would have accrued to his family, and the benefits were enjoyed by others. He died in 1802, almost one hundred years old.

Mr. Joseph Bourne died in June, 1825. Frequently has the conversation with him and the author turned upon his share of the merits of this invention, and subsequently with his Sons. He constructed the mill-work for grinding the flints, at both Cookshut Green, and the Ivy House mills; but he also stated, that Mr. James Brindley, his neighbour, with whom he was intimate, suggested very important improvements, constantly adopted in all the mills since erected. It is to be regretted that opportunity was not sought, to prevail on the old gentleman to walk to a mill, and give a detail of the particulars.

Concerning Mr. Bedson, we have the authority of Mr. William Sherratt, the elder, of Milton, (father of the gentleman, who in 1790, in company with Mr. Bateman, erected the extensive Iron Foundry, in Salford, Manchester,) in a memorandum, that the first attempt at grinding flint in a slop or wet state, was at the Ivy house, by a small water wheel. Mr. John Mountford, (already mentioned,) was near 50 years of age when he repaired this mill in 1803; and his account is subjoined. While Mr. Bedson was employed in painting Trentham Hall, some observations he heard, led him to consider the possibility of grinding Flint, in a manner similar to painters' colours. He first used a large iron vessel, cast for the purpose at Meir Heath furnace; on the bottom of which, as a kind of pavement, two iron balls, sixty pounds each were driven among the flints just covered with water. The abrasion of the iron among the flints, being found injurious to the ware made with it, was soon abandoned. Mr. John Mountford says, that Rob. Hulme, of Wolstanton, was repairing Holden Lane, and in a certain part he was obstructed by a tremendous Boulder Stone, which was split by gunpowder, and inside which was found a living toad, that was some years preserved in spirits by the Rev. Mr. Middleton, of Hanley. One part of this stone was used by Mr. Bedson as a vat, and it long was a colour pan at the mill. Mr. Sherratt mentions that soon a wooden vat was substituted, and the bottom was paved with flat sided Blue Boulder Stones, on which were driven round Boulders, in place of the iron balls. As these soon become flattened, they suggested, that flat sided stones, as well as a flat pavement, were best adapted for grinding Potter's Materials. Mr. Bedson, was ruined by his ingenuity, like many others in this district; he had borrowed sums from Mr. John Baddeley, Shelton, Mr. T. Whieldon, Stoke, and Mr. Bacchus, Fenton; and tho' he accomplished his designs, yet the benefits accruing from them were never enjoyed by either himself or his connections.

It has often been a cause of wonder that Mr. Parkes has given such erroneous statements, in his Chemical Catechism, concerning many things connected with the Potteries; for he might have obtained correct information, had he sought it; having resided several years at Stoke-upon-Trent. He says "the grinding the flint in water was first practised by the celebrated Brindley;—and the nulls now in use were also invented by him." Brindley applied the Crown wheel to the upright shaft; and Bourne suggested the carriers on that shaft.

Moulds were now made of all the different pieces; for complete Breakfast, Dinner, Dessert, and Supper Services, and much fancy was exercised in forming the Basket-work, Shell-work, Mosaic, Barley-corn, and other patterns, with great diversity of shapes, agreeably to the taste of visitors, and the ingenuity of the workman. The specimens are glazed with salt; and from the accuracy of the ornaments, and the extreme lightness, of Tureens, Dishes, and Sauce Boats, they are supposed to have been *cast* in the moulds, by pouring in a very thin slip, and letting it remain a few minutes, then pouring it out, and refilling with a thicker slip which instantly assimilates with the former, and more than doubled its thickness; a third, and often a fourth dose of thick slip was added, until the vessels had the required thickness; when the mould and its contents were placed a while before a fire, and afterwards they easily separated, and the workman dressed off the seams where the moulds divided, and the spouts, handles, and other appendages were affixed, in the process called "*Handling* and *Trimming*."

In 1732, Mr. Ralph Shaw, of Burslem, availed himself of the method long practised by Mr. Astbury, of using a mixture of flint and clay, to ornament the surfaces of the Pottery; and altho' several other potters were using the same clay as himself, he took out Letters Patent for employing "various sorts of mineral Earth, Clay, and other earth substances, which being mixed and incorporated together, make up a fine body, of which a curious ware may be made, whose outside will be of a true chocolate colour, striped with white, and the inside white, much resembling the brown

China ware, and glazed with salt. The great quantities of salt which must be used therein, will be an addition to the public revenue." The *secret* was, merely *washing* the inside and forming broad lines on the outside of the articles with very thick slip of flint and pipe-clay. To keep his process more secluded and secret, he was accustomed to evaporate his mixed Clays on a long trough in a place locked up, under cover, beneath which were flues for the heat from fire applied on the outside. This also kept the clay free from any kind of dirt; and the idea is supposed to have been gained from the tile-makers' method of drying their tiles in stoves. A pair of Flower Pots, excellent specimens of this person's manufacture, which had been received as a present, from the maker, by his wife's grandfather, were in the Author's possession till very recently. Mr. Shaw became so litigious and overbearing, that many of the manufacturers were extremely uncomfortable, and prevented improving their productions. Not content with the success he experienced, and the prospect of speedily acquiring affluence, his excessive vanity, and insatiable avarice incited to proceedings that terminated in his ruin, unwilling to admit the customary practices of the business, and to brook any appearance of competition; he was constantly objecting to every trifling improvement, as an infringement on his patent; and threatning his neighbours with suits in equity, to protect his *sole* rights; till at length self-defence urged them to bear the expences of a suit he had commenced against J. Mitchell, to try the validity of the Patent, at Stafford, in 1736; and very aged persons whose parents were present, give the general facts of the Trial;—All the manufacturers being interested in the decision, those most respectable were in the court; witnesses proved Astbury's invention and prior usage, of the practice, and a special Jury of great intelligence and wealth, gave a verdict against Mr. Shaw. The learned Judge, after nullifying the Patent, thus addressed the audience: —"Go home, Potters, and make whatever kinds of Pots you please."—The hall re-echoed with acclamations, and the strongest ebullitions of satisfactions, from the potters, to the indescrible mortification of Mr. S. and his family; who afterwards went to France, where he carried forward his manufactory; whence some of his family returned to Burslem about 1750; and, in 1783, Mr. Wedgwood wrote a Pamphlet to prevent Potters emigrating with his Son to France; and others to America.

As this kind of Pottery required placing on bits of stone, to prevent the articles uniting in the oven, it was called *Bit-stone-ware*; and some specimens remain with the bits of stone affixed. Two Saucers, of Mr, Shaw's manufacture, with a fine chocolate outside, and a white inner surface, are fused together, with the bits of stone remaining where they had been placed prior to firing. The accidents from separating the bits from the vessels, caused the invention of Stilts, Triangles, and Cockspurs.

In the early processes of the *White Stone Pottery*, many obstacles required to be surmounted, and the prejudices of workmen presented various impediments. The manufacturers possessed little, knowledge of the chemical properties of the various articles; neither had they any precedents for the kinds, they severally attempted to make. But, as several persons at the same time were endeavouring to produce new and particular kinds, each experienced some degree of success.

Ralph Leigh, (83 years of age, in 1813,) was employed by John Taylor, of the Hill Top, to look after his horses, and was the first man whose wages were raised from 10d. to 12d.

per day. With four or six horses he went twice to Whitfield, or thrice to Norton in a day, for Coals; of which each horse brought 2½ cwt. on its back; along lanes extremely dirty, and roads scarcely passable. At the pit, Coals then cost 7d. the draught, whether 2, 2½, or 3 cwt.; for the colliers *guessed* at the quantity, and did not take the trouble to weigh them.— The charge for carrying each load, from Norton to Burslem, was *three-pence*, (a penny a mile.) Ground Flint was carried in square tubs, *one* on each horse, containing *four* pecks.— During a long time, he carried crates of Pottery to Winsford, and brought back Ball Clay; each of the five panniers carried a crate on a pack-saddle; and a small pannier on each side was used to hold two or three balls of clay, weighing sixty or seventy pounds. Each horse was muzzled, to prevent it biting the hedges, and the roads were narrow and bad, and without toll gates. Afterwards with a cart and four horses he went to Winsford, and delivered his crates the same day; and on the second day brought back a ton of Chester clay to Burslem, which was regarded as very heavy work, owing to the bad roads. He was allowed four days to take crates to Bridgnorth, and bring back shop goods for Newcastle, and a few to the Potteries. He frequently went with crates to Willington Ferry, and returned with Flints, Plaister Stone and Shop goods. He has gone to Liverpool, and also as far as Exeter, before there were regular Carriers. Mr. D. Morris, of Lawton, kept a gang of horses, to bring Clay from Winsford, and Salt from Lawton, to Burslem; these horses also had crates to carry the ball clay, seven in each; which at times were filled with Cream Colour, to be printed by Sadler and Green of Liverpool. He next used a Cart, and afterwards a Waggon, for this purpose, when the High roads were rather improved.

The specimens manufactured by Dr. T. Wedgwood, at that time the principal potter in Burslem, are of good quality, and finely ornamented with embossed work. The bodies, and the shapes, are much varied; Coffee and Tea Pots, of clays compounded and mixed to resemble agate, marble, and other natural bodies, are in various shapes; some glazed with lead ore; and the white, all salt glaze. Had the rising genius of that day been adequately encouraged, doubtless many important improvements would have resulted   The ornaments on some specimens then made, and most of the elegant articles, appear to have been formed by pressing bits of clay into moulds, and after being well smoothed on the surface and edges, they were extracted, and by slip fixed on the sides of the vessel.   Some of these moulds are of brass, very expensive, and much like the large tools used by bookbinders; others are of clunchclay, or *Tough Tom*, not very durable; and of both kinds specimens are yet in existence, found while altering the highways, and digging the foundations for some new buildings in Burslem. In some instances, these ornaments were coloured *blue*, by the workman using a small lock of wool to dust upon them a small quantity of dry smalts, or pulverized zaffre, whose lustre was greatly augmented by the salt glaze.   This method of ornamenting, with that of relief figures in black, and white clay, continued a long time; and doubtless originated the methods of imitating medallions, cameos, &c.

The persons who first made these utensils to produce the ornaments, were then called *Block Cutters*, and the principal person was Mr. Aaron Wood, born in 1717, and the indenture of that period shews that when about fourteen he was apprenticed to Dr. Thomas Wedgwood, distinguished from Mr. Thomas Wedgwood, of the Church yard manufactory, father of the celebrated Josiah Wedgwood, with whom he served his term, and received *four* shillings weekly, when twenty-one years of age; as journeyman, he received *six* shillings weekly, for a further term of five years; having for his ingenuity, and attention one shilling weekly more than was paid to the other journeymen.   When the second term was completed, the great demand for models and moulds of Plaster of Paris, like that brought by Mr. Ralph Daniel, (hereafter mentioned,) found A. W. full employment for different masters; among others, Mr. T. Whieldon, of Little Fenton. As he refused any person working with him he always had a room in which he was locked by the person employing him, and to his son he pointed out a room, at Fenton, in which he produced the best models used by Mr. Whieldon.

"This Indenture, made the three and twentieth day of August, in the fifth year of the reign of our Sovereign Lord King George the Second over Great Brittaine, &c. Anno Dni. 1731, Between Ralph Wood of Burslem, in the county of Stafford, miller, and Aaron Wood his son, of the one part, and Dr. Thomas Wedgwood, of Burslem aforesaid potter, of the other part, Wittnesseth that the said Aaron Wood, of his own free will and consent, and to and with the direction and appointment of his said father, Hath put himself, and doth hereby put and bind himself apprentice unto the said Dr. Thomas Wedgwood, the art, trade, mystery, and occupation of a potter to learn, that is to say, turning in the lathe, handling, and trimming (throwing on the wheel being out of this indenture excepted,) and with him the said Dr. Thomas Wedgwood to worke from the eleventh day of November next, being Martinmas day, for during and until the full end and terme of seven years from thence next ensuing and following, and fully to be compleat and ended, during all which time and terme of seven years the said Aaron Wood, as an apprentice to his said master, will and faithfully shall serve, his secrets shall keepe, his commands lawfull and honest every where shall do, the goods of his said master, hee shall not inordinately waste, nor them to any one lend, without his said masters lycence, from the business of his said master, he shall not absent himself, but as a true and faithful servant shall, during the said terme of seven years, behave and demean himselfe towards his said master and all his. And the said Ralph Wood shall, during the said terme of seven years, find and provide for his said son all sorts of apparrell, whether linen, woollen, or other, as also meat, drink, washing, and lodging, fitting and necessary for an apprentice to such trade as aforesaid. And the said Dr. Thomas Wedgwood in consideration thereof, and of the said seven years service, doth hereby covenant, promise, and agree, that hee, the said Dr. Thomas Wedgwood, shall and will, during the said terme of seven years, teach and instruct, or cause and procure to be taught and instructed, him, the said Aaren Wood, his said apprentice, in the businesse of the potting trade aforesaid, so farr as turning in the lathe, handling and trimming, as much as thereunto belongeth, or the best way and method he can. And the said Dr. Thomas Wedgwood doth also promise and engage to pay unto his said apprentice, the said Aaron Wood, for every weeke's worke done by the said apprentice in the first, second, and third year of his said apprentishipp, the sum of one shilling weekly, of good and lawfull money of Great Brittaine, and for every weeke's worke done by the said apprentice in the fourth, fifth, and sixth year of his said apprentiship, the full sum of one shilling and sixpence, and for every weeke's worke done by the said apprentice, in the seventh and last year of his said apprentishipp, the full and just sum of four shillings of lawfull money of Great Brittaine. And the said Dr. Thomas Wedgwood doth hereby further covenant, promisse, and agree that he, the said Dr. Wedgwood, shall, and will, over and above the weekly wages aforesaid give yearly to the said Aaron Wood, his said apprentice, one new pair of shoes during the said terme of seven years. In witnesse whereof, the said parties aforesaid to these present Indentures have interchangeably put their hands and seales the day and year first above written:

" *Sealed and delivered in*
" *the presence of*
" Sara. ⚹ Wood.
" her mark.
" Jos. Allen.

"Ralph Wood.
."Aaron Wood.
" Dr. Tho. Wedgwood."

Mr. John Mitchell, had his manufactory on the highest land in Burslem, and there being at this time great demand for White Stone Ware, salt glaze, made with Devonshire clay, and flint, (and produced by several who now desisted from using the clays of the neighbourhood,) Mr. M. rapidly enlarged his premises; and as only *one* hovel was still thought requisite for all who made salt glaze ware, the strife among the potters who should excel in the size and height of the hovel, caused him to erect the most enormoursly wide and high one ever attempted to be built. (The largest hovel ever attempted, was finished at Burslem, by John

Shrigley, in 1765, many persons witnessed the laying
of the last brick, but no sooner was this completed,
than the fabric began to crack and open, and in a few
minutes the whole was level with the ground, and the
builders escaped, almost miraculously, by sudden descent. This caused low hovels to be adopted.) The
wages paid to his lathe treaders, usually boys of seven
years of age, were *four-pence* a week; and even in
1766, a good treader had only *six-pence* a week. Mr.
Aaron Wood was engaged by this gentleman as appears by the following instrument, for seven years in
a penal bond of £10. to work during that term, for
Mr. John Mitchell only; (who engaged him, to be the
better able to compete with Dr. T. Wedgwood,) and
to whom also was apprenticed his eldest Son, William.

ARTICLES *of Agreement indented, made and concluded and agreed
upon, the twenty-eight day of September, in the Year of our
Lord One Thousand Seven Hundred and Forty Three, and in
the Seventeenth Year of the Reign of our Sovereign Lord King
George the Second, over Great Brittain and so forth, between
Aaron Wood, of Burslem, in the County of Stafford, Earth-
potter, of the one part, and John Mitchell, of Burslem, aforesaid,
Earth-potter, of the other part, as follows:*

"*First*,—The said Aaron Wood, for the consideration here-
under mentioned, doth covenant, promise, and agree, to and
with the said John Mitchell, his executors, administrators,
and assigns, by these presents in manner following (that is to
say) that he the said Aaron Wood shall and will, for and during the term and time of seven years, to begin and be accounted from the eleventh day of November next ensuing the
date of these presents, abide and continue with the said John
Mitchell, his executors, administrators, and assigns, as his and
their hired and covenant servant, and diligently and faithfully
according to the best and utmost of his power, skill, and knowledge, exercise and employ himself, and do and perform all
such service and business whatsoever relating to the trade of
a earth-potter which he the said John Mitchell useth, as he the
said John Mitchell shall from time to time during the term
aforesaid order direct and appoint, to and for the most profit

and advantage of the said John Mitchell that he can, and shall and will keep the secrets of the said John Mitchell relating to the said trade or business, and likewise be just, true, and faithful to the said John Mitchell, in all matters and things, and no ways wrongfully detain, embezzle, or purloin any monies, goods, or things whatsoever belonging to the said John Mitchell, but shall and will from time to time pay all monies which he shall receive or belonging to or by order of the said John Mitchell into his hands, and make and give up fair accounts of all his actings and doings in the said employment without fraud or delay, when and as often he shall be thereto required. And in consideration of the premises of the several matters and things by the said Aaron Wood to be performed as aforesaid, the said John Mitchell doth for himself, his executors and administrators, covenant, promise, and agree to and with the said Aaron Wood by these presents, that he the said John Mitchell shall and will well and truly pay or cause to be paid unto the said Aaron Wood, the sum of seven shillings of good and lawful money of Great Britain, by weekly payments, for every six days that the said Aaron Wood shall work with the said John Mitchell as aforesaid during the said term; and also shall and will well and truly pay or cause to be paid unto the said Aaron Wood the further sum of ten shillings and six-pence of like lawful money, upon every eleventh day of November yearly, during the said term; the first payment of the said sum of ten shillings and sixpence, shall be made on the eleventh day of November next ensuing the date hereof. And it is further agreed by and between the said parties to these presents, that the said Aaron Wood shall not be from the service of the said John Mitchell above two weeks in any one year during the said term. And that the said Aaron Wood shall not, and will not at any time or times during the said term, work for any other person or persons at the trade of a earth potter, but the said John Mitchell, his executors, administrators, or assigns, upon penalty of paying to the said John Mitchell the sum of ten pounds of good and lawful money of Great Britain. And that the said Aaron Wood shall not have person or persons to work with him in the business that the said John Mitchell is to employ him in but himself only. In witness whereof, the said parties to these presents their hands and seals have hereunto put this day and year first above written.

" *Sealed and delivered in*
the presence of
" J. HENSHALL.
" ANN HENSHALL.

" AARON WOND.
" JOHN L. MITCHELL.
his mark."

Mr. Mitchell was a religious and unsuspicious person; the first who received into his house the Preachers in the Wesleyan Methodist Connection; and tho' he died in very reduced circumstances, yet during some years he was the greatest manufacturer of that day. He had four travellers, Mr. Dean, of Burslem, (afterwards of Bridgwater;) Mr. Dale, of Mole Cob, (since of Exeter;) Mr. Dickens, (since of Plymouth;) and Mr. Bowers, (since of Falmouth.) The practice customary then was, not to take out invoices, or on returning to render an account of the sales; but merely to empty their pockets; after which they received their wages, (*five* or *six* shillings a week,) for the time of the journey; their expences having been paid out of the cash received. Thus each traveller saved sufficient to avail himself of any favourable opportunity to commence business for himself as a dealer in glass and earthenware; and each has been successful, while it is painful to add some of Mr. M's descendants are now in low circumstances in Burslem.

In 1740, Mr. Thomas Whieldon's manufactory at Little Fenton, consisted of a small range of low buildings, all thatched. His early productions, were knife hafts, for the Sheffield Cutlers; and Snuff Boxes, for the Birmingham Hardwaremen, to finish with hoops, hinges, and springs; which himself usually carried in a basket to the tradesmen; and being much like agate, they were greatly in request. He also made toys and chimney ornaments, coloured in either the clay state, or bisquet, by zaffre, manganese, copper, &c. and glazed with black, red, or white lead. He he also made black glazed tea and coffee pots, Tortoiseshell and melon table plates, (with ornamented edge, and six scollops, as in the specimens kept by Andrew Boon, of the Honeywall, Stoke;) and other useful articles.   Mr. A. Wood, made models and moulds of these articles; also pickle leaves, crab stock handles and cabbage leave spouts, for tea and coffee pots, all which utensils, with candlesticks, chocolate cups, and tea ware, were much improved, and his connections extended subsequently, when Mr. J. Wedgwood became his managing partner. He was a shrewd and careful person.   To prevent his productions being imitated in quality or shape, he always buried the broken articles; and a few months ago, we witnessed the unexpected exposure of some of these, by some miners attempting to get marl in the road at Little Fenton. The fortune he acquired by his industry, enabled him to erect a very elegant mansion, near Stoke; where he long enjoyed in the bosom of his family, the fruits of his early economy. He was also Sheriff of the County, in the 26th year of the late reign. The benevolence of his disposition, and his integrity, are honourable traits of character, far superior to the boast of ancestry without personal merit. He died in 1798, at a very old age; and in 1828 his relict was interred beside him in Stoke Church yard.

Of the four apprentices to Mr. Whieldon, three commenced business, and were eminently successful; Mr. Josiah Spode, (the first,) Mr. Robert Garner, Mr. J. Barker, (and his Brothers we believe,)—but Mr. William Greatbatch, a person of great ability, (mentioned again hereafter,) was ruined by a bad debt. The father of William Greatbatch, was a farmer, at Berryhill; and supplied coals to the manufacturers at Fenton, from Botteslow and Colamoor; and among others, to Mr. Whieldon, and Mr. Daniel Bird, on the backs of horses, the roads being then so bad that had a horse stumbled, or missed his step into the holes, he certainly would have fallen, and with difficulty would have been again raised. He received his money every journey, because fearful of the parties.

Mr. Daniel Bird's productions at the manufactory at Cliff Bank, (which Mr. T. Mayer now occupies,) were very lucrative; Agate Buttons, Knife Hafts, and Flint ware, salt glaze, by which he speedily realized a handsome fortune. He was distinguished by the appellation of the *Flint Potter*, because he is believed to have first ascertained the exact quantity of flint proper to be mixed with the clays to form the body of the Pottery.

We shall just notice here, that Mr. T. Mayer has succeeded in a *chef d' œuvre* of the Art of Pottery, by many considered as the best Specimen of Solid Earthenware hitherto produced. It is an Earthenware Table, of truly elegant workmanship, thirty-two inches diametar, on an elegant pedestal of proportionate dimensions; ornamented in a very chaste style, with subject from National History.

Before 1740, two sons of Aaron Wedgwood, Thomas and John, (the one an excellent thrower, the other a most skilful fireman, as lead ore glaze potters,) left their father's service, to commence business for themselves at Burslem, in the manufacture of White Stone Ware. As there was not then an instance of any Master Potter, who did not most diligently apply himself to some branch of the business, usually throwing and firing, their well-known industry, experience, and ingenuity, warranted the expectation of a portion of Success.

The practice of boiling the clay on a *Slip Kiln* being now introduced, the Sun Pans were appropriated as reservoirs of water for the uses of the manufacture; and, as was formerly the practice, all around their sides were thrown, for convenience, or until a proper opportunity for removal, heaps of the broken pots, *potsherds*, (vulgar *shords*,) and much rubbish containing refuse salt, which mixing with the efflorescence from

O

the salt glaze ware, was carried by the water from the falling showers into the Pan or reservoir, and formed a saline liquid. This very important fact was forgotten or not contemplated, by the Brothers, in using this almost saturated water to levigate and mix with their flint and clay; and they sustained loss by their pottery fusing at a temperature much below that of other vitrescent kinds, even tho' glazed with salt; and prior to introducing the glaze.

Thro' a succession of losses and disappointment the Brothers almost resolved to relinquish the manufacture; but having caused some of their ware to be fired in another oven; and they in return firing another's ware in their oven; they found their pottery did not bear the high heat required to vitrify the other. Their investigation ascertained, that the saline particles of the water, with the lime which adhered to the flint stones, rendered their ware very fusible; and that careful sorting of their flints, and pure water, would produce a much better article, with less trouble, and little risk in the firing.

The Manufactures now much improved and widely extended into a source of National wealth, and employment to many thousands of the community, were found to depend on successful chemical combinations of several materials; the principal of which are Clay and Flint, (called, when *pure*, Alumina, and Silica,) at times coloured by oxides and carbonaceous substances which are more frequently united naturally, and have more affinity for each other than any other substances; and of pigments formed of metallic oxides &c. with which the ware is embellished.

Alumina is soluble in every acid; and alone will fuse, when oxygen gas is present, into a hard vitreous substance that will scratch glass; but by strong heat its chemical cohession so diminishes its bulk, that it becomes capable of resisting acids and alkalies. It is found *pure* naturally at Halle, in Germany, and is artificially procured by decomposing Alum in water and carbonate of Ammonia, and washing well the precipitate; but it unites so intimately with water, that even a heat that will fuse iron, leaves of that fluid a tenth of the weight of the earth. The Manufacturers here use Four kinds of Argillaceous Earth, by them called *Clays,* two from the south of Devonshire, *Black,* and *Cracking;* and two from the Isle of Purbeck, called *Brown,* and *Blue.* The *Black* is named so, because the Alumina is combined with carbonaceous matter, which disappears when the Pottery is properly fired. — *Cracking* Clay, much used because beautifully white when fired, has its designation from its contractile property when highly heated, and often cracking in bisquet, when not apportioned with other less contractile clay. The *Brown* likewise is very white, and less contractile than the last mentioned; but some peculiarity prevents perfect adhesion of the glaze, and *crazing* results. The *Blue* is best; it burns white, contracts little, takes a large proportion of Flint, and forms a durable body. And, altho' the opaqueness of Alumina affects the transparency of Porcelain, yet the latter two are occasionally employed in that branch of the Art.

Flint is usually, in weight, a fourth, a fifth, or a sixth part of the mass, which it greatly aids by its transparency. Silica performs a very important part in the composition of many natural bodies; and may be procured *pure* by subjecting nodules of Flint to a high heat, rendering them very brittle by plunging into cold water; next they are pulverized, and mixed with four times the weight of potash, and then dissolving in water, and by an acid taking up the alkali, the Silica precipitates as a white, inodorous, insipid, and insoluble powder, which must be well washed.

For the Finest Pottery there is also used a certain proportion of Cornish or *China* Clay; and likewise of Cornwall or Growan Stone.

The pottery made of flint and Biddeford clay, tho' very white, being liable to crack, when well fired, or suddenly heated; to remedy this, some of the native clays, and the finest white grit from Mole Cob, were used, and much improved the quality of the article, which being comparatively thin saved materials, time, labour, and coals for firing. The Brothers Wedgwood ascertained the kind of clay most liable to *crack*, thence named *cracking clay;* and were excited to further experiments, by some of the vessels made on their new methods, not being sufficiently vitrified; others being well fired, yet not fused; while those of the old body, were completely destroyed; this discovery caused other manufacturers to reject water from reservoirs near potsherd heaps, which were quickly carried off the premises. Rain water, or water from deep wells, now became very important; and the Brothers used only that from Hankerses well, a spring immediately nigh their works, for their different kinds of Pottery. Those made from Clays without glazing, are called DRY BODIES; of which were formed their most elegant and valuable articles. There soon was such a demand for their productions, as to require extra supplies of flint; to grind which Mr. Brindley erected the windmill on the Jenkins, and filled it with machinery to grind flints in water.

Amazed, these Sons of Genius I descry,
Fix on the plastic mass their anxious eye;
Urged by their native energy of mind,
To Model forms aright they feel inclin'd;
Intent on high designs, their fabrile souls,
To shapes unfashioned now direct their tools;
With daring aims, irregularly great,
To raise their Art from its degraded state.

The excellent productions they now sent forth were so much in demand, that they erected a new manufactory, and incurred general censure because of their extravangance in erecting so large a manufactory and covering it with tiles, (all others being *covered with thatch,*) and for erecting *three* ovens, (subsequently increased to *five.*) In like manner, the greatest possible surprize was occasioned by R. & J. Baddeley, erecting four hovels in a row behind their manufactory in Shelton, which they had covered with Tiles (where Messrs. Hicks, Meigh, and Johnson are now manufacturing.) Of the White Stone ware they now made dishes, plates, and common vessels, also some elegant fruit baskets, bread trays, &c. glazed with salt, and probably *cast* in moulds; for the under side of the saucers, and the outside of the cups have different ornaments.

The White Stone ware was varied into a better *Tortoiseshell,* by rubbing manganese upon the vessels before they were glazed; for a different kind ground zaffres were applied with either a sponge or hair pencil; and similar application of calcined copper, iron, and other metals, produced Cauliflower, and Melon ware, &c. In 1750, the Brothers erected near their manufactory, (and now in full view of Waterloo Road to Cobridge,) a Dwelling House, so durable, and on a scale of extent, and a stile of magnificence, so far

3 O

excelling all in the district, that it was called the BIG
HOUSE; and now bears the name, (applied also to its
founders, to distinguish the family from that of the
over house, and that of the Church yard works.) These
Brothers continued their manufactures until 1763;
when they retired to enjoy a very large property, the
reward of their industry and integrity.

Every reader only partially acquainted with the
manufacture, will be aware, that the materials employed in making Saggers, require to be unaffected by
the action of the mixtures in fusion; not fusible by a
degree of heat much higher than what is requsite for
baking the ware, or vitrifying the glaze; and capable
of retaining any shape and size most suitable and best
adapted for the different purposes. The Clays proper
for the kinds of Pottery, differing in kind, quality, and
colour, numerous trials were made to determine the
proportions of marl, sufficiently strong to bear the
weight of the vessels, and sustain the requisite heat.

The ware was varied to the sagger, and the sagger
to the ware, until about 1745, when many different
marls were used for saggers; and for the white stone
ware, the difficulty was long experienced. At length,
it was ascertained, that in whatever heat might be required, *two* parts of Can Marl, mixed with *one* of
Black Marl, would retain their shape. The more the
marl is exposed to atmospheric action, and broken
during the time it lies *weathering,* the better will the
saggers bear most intense heat without cracking. Some
opulent manufacturers find their account in employing
two or three men solely, to constantly work the marl
employed in making the saggers for their manufactories.

Information that the French manufacturers employed moulds of Plaster of Paris, caused some of the

Burslem potters to have moulds formed of Plaster stone; the specimens evincing great ingenuity in the workman, and the prevalent desire to improve the Art.   The correction of this error introduced an important improvement; providing a fresh branch of manual employment, and supplying great facilities for manufacturing the choicest productions of taste and ingenuity. Mr. Ralph Daniel, of Cobridge, happened to visit a Porcelain manufactory in France, where among other information relative to their processes, he ascertained that the moulds were formed by mixing Plaster of Paris in a pulverulent state with water.   He obtained a mould of a large Table Plate, which on returning home he exhibited to all the Potters, and explained the discovery, and its attendant advantage, and quickly moulds were introduced.   The manufacturers were eager to possess moulds, because of the numerous productions which with great facility could be formed in them, yet not be produced by the wheel and the lathe; and others which did not need either; and also the quickness with which the clay acquired, what potters call the *green* state.

The substance, which obtained the name *Plaster of Paris*, because its material was then procured from the hills around that city, is now known to be Selenite, or Sulphate of Lime, mostly called Gypsum; abundant at Chelaston, in Derbyshire, and Beacon Hill, near Newark; and in parts of Staffordshire and Salop.—To prepare it for the use of Masons, Statuaries, and other Artists, for Cornices, Busts, &c. protected from moisture and the weather, the mass is broken small, baked well in a common oven to dissipate much of its water, and then reduced into an impalpable powder;—but for the use of Potters, it is ground by a pair of Stones in a mill, similarly to grain, afterwards submitted to a process, incongruously called *boiling*, on a long trough, beneath which are flues, where it remains until all its water is dissipated, attended by a man, who is prevented inhaling its fine particles by his nose and mouth being protected by a double silk handkerchief. When the mass has been by such process deprived of its water, it is rendered so miscible again with that fluid, that on receiving its own proportion of water, it condenses such a quantity, as almost immediately to become changed into one compact and solid mass. Hence when used, the fluid is quickly poured, into moulds for statues, or busts: and round models or blocks to form moulds for the Potters,— usually for articles not circular, and for teapots, saucers, plates, dishes, &c. This property of so quickly absorbing moisture, causes the plaster moulds to be most peculiarly adapted to the purposes of the Potter; for as the moulds can be kept dry by placing them on shelves around a stove, they very readily absorb the water from the clay impressed into them: and the Articles are more easily *delivered* or quit from the moulds, in a fit state for finishing, than would be conjectured by persons not acquainted with the Art.

The Ethiopians, knew of this property of Gypsum, for Herodotus mentions, that they dried in the sun the bodies of deceased relatives; and then covered each with paste of gypsum, on which subsequently was painted the portrait of the deceased person.

CHAP VII.

INTRODUCTION OF FLUID GLAZE.——EXTENSION OF THE
MANUFACTURE OF CREAM COLOUR.——MR. WEDG-
WOOD'S QUEEN'S WARE, JASPER, AND APPOINTMENT
OF POTTER TO HER MAJESTY.——BLACK PRINTING.——

We cannot ascertain at this day the extent of business carried on in Pottery with the Lead ore glaze,
and in the early time of the Salt glaze.   The Lead
ore glaze continued in many small potteries; but
other manufacturers of the White Stone ware, employed their ingenuity in trials which they glazed and
fired as formerly.   When the ware had been once fired,
called *bisquet*, the workman, with a sponge added
manganese, alone for Tortoiseshell, and with pulverized ironstone added for the darker colours; ochre and
calces of iron and other metals, for *yellow, cauliflower*,
and *melon;* and of copper for green Pickle Leaves;
and with a camel hair pencil added diffrent strengths
of ground zaffers, for *Agate,* for Knife Hafts, and Snuff
Boxes, and by a brush added lead ore and flint glaze,
washing or filling the inside with the glaze, a watery
mixture of lead and flint.   When only Lead ore, with
a little Flint, was applied as glaze, the white clay not
being of the best quality, and the flint so carefully
prepared as in our day, the Pottery had a yellowish
cast, and was named *Cream Colour.*   This method of
making Cream Colour, was practised by many persons,
and different qualities of articles made long before it
received this appellation; (now restricted to the Pottery, which succeeded salt glaze, by *immersion* in the
white Lead *fluid* glaze.)   There are specimens of
Table Plates and Fruit Dishes, made of flint and clay,

in old moulds of the White Stone ware, which after being dipped in the lead and flint glaze for washing the insides of Tortoiseshell, and fired in the old lead glaze ovens, form exactly and identically the first *Cream Coloured* Pottery.

Up to 1740, in each manufactory, all the persons employed were, the slip-maker, thrower, two turners, handler, *(stouker,)* fireman, warehouseman, and a few children, and, to be really useful to the master, and secure sufficient employment, a good workman could *throw, turn,* and *stouk*; and which he practised in each week at two or three different manufactories. But the White Stone Ware, now experiencing such a demand, its manufacture extended the whole range of the district; and the manufacturers introduced the custom of *hiring* each workman to serve only *one* master, and practise only *one* branch of the Art, while workmen for the different branches, were so much in requisition, that persons from distant parts, and especially from the neighbouring villages, were *hired* and settled in the towns, increasing the number of parishioners, and ultimately the mass of parochial burdens.

The increase of workmen, the subdivision of labour in every process; and the dexterity and quickness consequent on separate persons confining themselves solely to one branch of the Art, with the time saved in the change of implements and articles, instead of retarding, greatly promoted the manufacture, by increasing its excellence and elegance. The benefits accruing from the great demand for the salt glaze white stone ware, caused the inhabitants to tolerate the method of glazing, altho' for about five hours of each Saturday, fifty or sixty manufactories sent forth dense clouds of vapour that filled the valleys and covered the hills to an extent of several square miles.

Carlos Simpson, 63 years years of age, 1817, was born at Chelsea; to which place his father Aaron Simpson, went in 1747, along with Thomas Lawton, slip maker, Samuel Parr, turner, Richard Meir, fireman, and John Astbury, painter, all of Hot Lane; Carlos Wedgwood, of the Stocks, a good thrower; Thomas Ward and several others, of Burslem, to work at the Chelsea China Manufactory. They soon ascertained that they were the principal workmen, on whose exertions all the excellence of the Porcelain must depend, they then resolved to commence business on their own account, at Chelsea, and were in some degree successful; but at length owing to disagreement among themselves, they abandoned it end returned to Burslem, intending to commence there the manufacture of China; but soon after their return Aaron Simpson died, the design was relinquished, and each took the employment quickly offered in the manufacture of white stone ware, then sold readily on the day of drawing the oven. Carlos Wedgwood at length commenced making white stone pottery, behind the present Wesleyan Methodist Chapel, which stands on the spot occupied by his house.

At that time the various kinds of Pottery with lead ore glaze, were made at a small manufactory, (which now is that belonging to Messrs. Ridgway, at the bottom of Albion Street, Shelton,) by Mr. Warner Edwards, whose *secret* partner was the Rev. Thomas Middleton, the Minister of (Old) Hanley Chapel. Mr. Edwards's chemical ability exceeded that of all other persons in the district; for he could make the various kinds of Pottery then in demand, and prepare and apply the different colours, to ornament them. He was a careful, shrewd, and very intelligent man, and when he was attacked, in 1753, by the sickness which proved fatal, he presented to the late Mr. Thomas Daniel, (who had been his apprentice, and was then his only private assistant,) a *Drawing Book*, embellished with many elegant Patterns; and on the first leaf is written, by himself—"Werner Edwards's Art of making Enamel Colours in a plain manner." On the blank sides of the leaves, Mr. T. D. wrote, from Mr. Edwards's dictation, the minute instructions and requisite information concerning the several processes, and components for preparing of the different colours; and the prices of the several chemical preparations and minerals, with the names of the persons in London, Manchester, and Liverpool, from whom they could be obtained of the best quality and at the lowest price. Thus the old gentleman rendered more useful to himself, the practical skill in the manipulations already acquired by Mr. D. while he rewarded in the best manner his industry and integrity. This Drawing Book, which we recently inspected, had been surreptitiously copied by some of the colour makers of the district, when it was recovered by the owner's son, Mr. H. Daniel, of Stoke, justly celebrated thro' the trade an Enameller of the greatest ability.

Mr. Aaron Wedgwood, (father of T. & J. Wedgwood, of the Big House, also brother-in-law of Mr. W. Littler, mentioned in the chapter on Porcelain,) soon joined with him and endeavoured to effect some improvement in the salt glaze. Genius and invention have seldom been more usefully employed, than in the improved productions of the Pottery. The united experience, and repeated endeavours of these persons was attended with success wholly without precedent. The transition from washing the vessels or laying the glaze on by a brush, to *immersing* them in the mixture, is both easy and natural. The manufacture of white stone pottery, was rapidly improving, owing to the ascertaining the proper proportions of marl for the saggers, and of flint and clay, for the pottery. And availing themselves of Mr. Astbury's method of *washing* or *dipping*, Messrs. Littler and Wedgwood first introduced a compound of very fusible materials—of certain proportions of ground zaffre with the flint and the clay that composed the body of the pottery; mixed with a determined quantity of water, and varied for the different kinds of articles. Into this liquid the vessels were dipped, while in the state of clay very little dried, and absorbing the water, received a very thin coating of the materials in solution, which when dried and fired in the salt glaze oven, appeared of a fine glossy surface, free from those minute inequalities observable on all the Pottery glazed with salt only. Some excellent Specimens are ornamented by enamelling and gilding; and others having had a little manganese applied, resemble the finest Lapis Lazuli.

The highways of the district at this time and some years afterwards, were in a condition so out of repair, as to be almost impassable. In some instances, by a man was the flint carried from the mill to the manufactory; and in others, by horses, in tubs that would contain four pecks. The chapmen or dealers kept a gang of horses which carried small crates, that were filled with ware, then driven to different parts, and there opened for the inspection of purchasers. The expence of carriage necessarily impeded the extension of the manufacture; yet such is the force of prejudice, that when the Act of Parliament of 1760 for repairing the Roads then made, and opening new ones, was first put in execution, the workmen conjecturing that their Art would be either wholly destroyed, or taken out of the country, rushed *en masse* into open disturbance. Afterwards, carts and waggons were substituted for pack horses; persons were sent to the different places for orders; business was extended, and the district benefited.

The White Stone Pottery was now in demand, and had been improved gradually in quality and work-

manship; but was certainly much restricted, because
the manufacturers were busy making only a small as-
sortment of common articles, of rather inelegant shapes,
and finished upon the wheel and lathe, or by the *stouker*. And tho' of clean appearance, and compact texture, (during the period of fifty years from its introduction to its highest improvement,) it remained devoid
of celebrity, for want of being presented to the public
in neat and varied Articles of utility, formed in elegant
tasteful patterns, as was the French White Stone
ware, with beautiful glaze, supplied to genteel tables
thro' preference of foreign to British manufacture;
and as was the Queen's Ware in the excellent forms
designed by Mr. William Wood.

But the demand having excited among the more
intelligent manufacturers the spirit of invention,—different bodies and glazes were attempted, improved,
and their perfection assiduously pursued, and gradually
accomplished; the Pottery fabricated, tho' inferior to
porcelain in colour and appearance, was nearly equal
in utility and durability; and numbers were eager to
acquire celebrity, by the beauty and elegance of their
designs, and the excellence of their workmanship.

At this time Lane Delph was the chief place in the
southern part of the district. Here, in 1750, William
Edwards made very good coloured Earthenware. Two
Plates of his manufacture, in the possession of Mr.
George Forrister, Lane End, are so truly elegant, that
we might be censured for not troubling the reader with
a description.

They are about twelve inches diameter, made of the whitest
native clays well prepared, and now have a brownish flesh colour. The brim is in basket-work, very well designed and
executed; the bowl part is divided into three compartments

of finely embossed work, on the bend of which is a melon, harp, apple, pear, and two cherries, (whence we conjecture they were dessert plates;) the centre is finely and fancifully scrolled. The glaze has much lead, and is quite green; the center has had a little oxide of iron, or manganese, to give a brownish cast, the green has been partially washed off, so as to appear whitish and very dark green alternately in each compartment. Both plates are cracked, but not crazed in either glaze or body. As these and other specimens of this date, are without glaze on the under surface, we suppose this was done for economy; or was it in imitation of Foreign Earthenware.

Mr. Phillips was also a very eminent manufacturer at Lane Delph. A fine specimen of his manufacture a cream colour Standish for Ink, Sand, and Wafers, made by him in 1760, is now in the possession of Mr. George Forrister, of Lane End; who had used it twenty-eight years constantly; having received it as a present from Mr. Moses Simpson, whose father was a workman for Mr. Phillips. Its ornamental work is very elegant, and it evinces much excellence of material; there is not any crazing; and on the author's suggestion, it is no longer doomed to drudgery, but is preserved as a curiosity. W. Matthews, of Lane Delph, made excellent mottled and cloudy pottery. The drinking mugs are particularly well handled, and finely rolled, but without *spout* or *snip*, as in the similarly shaped vessels of the present day. The article is not any way crazed.

Roger Wood, Esq. of the Ash, three miles east of Hanley, in 1756, erected the manufactory (now occupied by Mr. Sampson Bridgwood, an excellent manufacturer of Porcelain,) on the side of the Brook at the lower Market-Place, Lane End. Here a person named Ford, for some years made common stone earthenware, and brown ware. There were not one hundred houses in Lane End at that time, and very few indeed in Longton liberty. We are told that at this factory the first cream colour was made on that side of the district. Another manufacturer was Moses Simpson, (of the family of Bulky Simpson,) from Hanley; but we have not seen any specimens of his productions. It is remarkable, to the Author at least, that merely the *name* of this person is known in the family circle; his nephew, Moses Simpson, now above seventy years of age, resides in Stafford Row, Shelton, but he only remembers that his Uncle died when himself was a boy.

Opposite to the present Lane End Church, and on the (now greatly enlarged) premises occupied by Messrs. Mayer and Newbold, during many years Messrs. Thomas and Joseph Johnson made salt glaze white stone ware, as well as crouch ware, and other kinds, from clay obtained from the Brickhouse Field, the spot now covered by houses belonging to Jacob Marsh, Esq. The late Messrs. J. & R. Riley, of Burslem, made very respectful mention of the talents and character of these brothers of whose manufacture, a bread-basket, long in the possession of the late N. Jackson, Esq. exhibits proof of ability in the modeller, and excellence in the materials.

About 1756, Mr. R. Bankes, and the late Mr. John Turner, made white stone ware at Stoke, on the spot part of the premises of Josiah Spode, Esq.— Mr. Turner removed to Lane End, in 1762, where he manufactured every kind of Pottery then in demand, and also introduced some other kinds not previously known.—About 1780, he discovered a vein of fine Clay, on the land at Green Dock, now the property of Mr. Ephraim Hobson, of Hanley.

> Purged from their dross, the nobler parts refine,
> Receive new forms, and with true beauties shine.

From this he obtained all his supplies for manufacturing his beautiful and excellent *Stone Ware Pottery*, of a cane colour; which he formed into very beautiful Jugs, with ornamental designs, and the most tasteful articles of domestic use. Some of them are excellent Wine Coolers; others represent different kinds of Pastry, as Tureens, Butter Coolers, &c. and are well calculated to deceive the eye at a short distance. An instance of this deception occurred to the author, being seated in the parlour, where was a Lady's work-basket, which he was led to consider from its appearance as *twig* or willow ware, and was most agreeably surprised, to find it of cane coloured pottery. The deception was not single; for a young Lady, on a visit, had made a similar mistake only the day preceding. Mr. Turner was deputed with Mr. Wedgwood, to oppose the extension of Mr. Champion's Patent— and an agreement was the result; as stated in the Chapter on Porcelain. But in consequence of Mr. Kinnersley's sale of lead being affected by the introduction of Composition, that gentleman entered into partnership with Mr. Turner, to make it at Lane End: and the speculation was to some extent successful. Mr. Turner afterwards erected in the open ground before his manufactory, a machine by which he could turn his throwing engine and lathes. This was open to the inspection of all the potters of the time; but no application of the principle was made, until after steam engines were introduced; as by Mr. Wedgwood, and Mr. Spode. Mr. Turner preserved thro' life the high character of a very kind master, a worthy and intelligent tradesman, and an honest member of the community; and died in 1786, at an advanced age.

About 1750, Mr. John Barker, with his Brother, and Mr. Robert Garner, commenced the manufactory of Shining Black, and White Stone ware, salt glaze, at the Row Houses, near the Foley, Fenton; and where afterwards they made tolerable cream colour. They realized a good property here; and Mr. R. Garner erected a manufactory, and the best House of the time in Lane End, near the old Turnpike Gate. In the possession of Mr. G. Forrister, Lane End, is a very excellent specimen; a Sand Box, which tho' constantly used, remains unaffected by crazing.   The rolling is extremely neat, and the edges shew considerable taste and excellence of workmanship.   It is highly prized by Mr. G., having been his father's; and is well known to have been made near seventy years.   In 1750, the late William Brookes, of Handford Bridge, was placed with these gentlemen, as apprentice to a Turner; and when his term was completed, he was paid *seven* shillings weekly; and labour being now in demand, the custom was to work, for *half a day over time,* while a candle of a certain size burned.   The Lathes used at this time were made in Congleton, because the secret of properly tempering the spindle and collar was possessed only by a smith resident there. In Hanley there resided a very ingenious smith, (proved since to be Mr. John Baddeley, of Eastwood,) to whom the business was suggested.   On a certain day he dressed himself as a potter, with white apron, and also white gloves on his hands, to prevent them being noticed by the smith at Congleton; and having a spindle, &c. with him, he accompanied Mr. W. Brookes, and Mr. Thomas Greatbatch, of Hanley, each having his spindle, &c. to the shop of the mechanic and smith, where he witnessed the several operations, and afterwards practised them at Hanley.   And so careful was he to preserve the secret thus obtained, that, (according to the statement of his daughter, the late Mrs. Poulson, of Stoke,) he frequently performed the most particular operations about midnight, having only the company and help of his daughter. The same Thomas Greatbatch first suggested the movement of an Engine Lathe, to Mr. Baddeley, who was successful in constructing it; and on it Mr. G. was employed many years. The same lathe was sold publickly in 1828; but we cannot ascertain the purchaser.

Mr. John Adams, and Mr. John Prince were manufacturers at Lane Delph, near Fenton Lane, of Red Porcelain, and White Stone ware, salt glaze, and realized large fortunes. The daughter of Mr. Prince was married by one of their turners, the late Mr. John Stirrup, of Cinderhill, near Lane End; and the property he received with her, ultimately rendered him opulent. Another of their turners, Mr William Hilditch, of Lane Delph, gentleman, is now peaceably enjoying the produce of his well directed industry. He is the father of Messrs. Hilditch, China manufacturers, of Lane End. The third turner is Mr. William Shaw, the present Clerk, and Master of the Free School, at Lane End.

Mr. John Alderson, at the manufactory in Stoke, where is now the Top Square; and his Brother Thomas, of the Honey Wall, were successful in making Mottled and Cloudy, and Tortoiseshell, with lead ore and salt glazes, and Shining Black, of a very good quality. A few specimens are kept in the neighbourhood.

About 1760, a son of Mr. Phillips, of Lane Delph, commenced the manufacture of White Stone Ware, salt glaze, at Green Dock, Longton; and he afterwards made tolerable cream colour, at the same place. To his descendants there now belongs some property in

Lane End.   The salt he used, was brought by the old
Huntsman, John Brown, from either Lawton, or the
Wyches, as most convenient for himself.   At this time,
only a good team of horses could draw a cart along
the high road, such was their broken up state; and
not a single one-horse cart was in use on the Lane End
side of the district till the end of the last century.
The Coals were carried in panniers, on mules and
horses; and *four* of these supplied all Lane Delph,
in 1780.   There was a horse-post, to bring the letters from Stone; and the late Mr. S. Forrister well
remembered seeing the postman ride his horse up the
steps into the Warehouse of Mr. Phillips, to communicate some verbal intelligence *first* to that gentleman.

About 1750, another introduction of fresh materials, or a different application of those previously
employed, was beneficial to the person and to the
whole district.   Mr. Enoch Booth, of Tunstall, first
united the Clays of the neighbourhood carefully levigated, in union with those from the South of England,
(Devon. and Dorset.) and a certain proportion of
Flint, on Mr. Astbury's method.   This body he first
glazed with lead ore; next he mixed it with one of
the clays, and then added a little dry calcined flint in
powder; and finally, he used lead and flint in a liquid
state, on Littler's method, but with this difference;
Littler dipped the *clay* ware into his liquid; but Mr.
Booth fired his once, and dipped the Bisquet ware.
There appears little cause to suppose that great improvements took place in the Glaze.   The celebrated
Reaumur had analysed every kind of known glaze,
and published their components, according to his
Analysis, inserted in the old '*Handmaid to the Arts;*'
therefore we may suppose that the different Glazes,
and the methods of glazing Earthenware, were well

known.   The different appearance of the Articles, is admitted to be consequent on the introduction of fresh or new materials into the body or clay, and every such introduction formed a different kind, was attended with beneficial Effects to the individuals themselves particularly, and the whole mass of the manufacturers of the district generally.

This was the first instance of attention being paid to careful levigation of the clay, prior to mixing it with the flint; and also, of proper quantities of Flint and Clay being mixed with a certain measure of water.   The practice now prevails thro' the district; but Slip makers are not sufficiently careful in this department.   By carefully and thoroughly mixing the clay with the water in the blunging vat, all heterogeneous substances will sink to the bottom, and the fine argillaceous particles will remain suspended in the water. The Pottery Mr. Booth made, is very different from that made by the younger Mr. Astbury, at Lane Delph, about 1730, yet like that and other of an ochreous hue, it was called *Cream Colonr* ; and its quality excels any then made.   An excellent specimen is a Sauce Boat,, made in 1768, of a fiddle head pattern, from a mould of Mr. A. Wood's, and enamelled by Mr. John Robinson, then recently come from Liverpool.   The *Flowerers* now *scratched* the jugs and tea ware, with a sharp pointed nail, and filled the interstices with ground zaffre, in rude imitation of the unmeaning scenery on foreign porcelain; and in this art women were instructed, as a constant demand was made on the men for the plastic branches.

In 1751, were made the last improvements of Cream Colour, (prior to those of the late Mr. Wedgwood,) by Mrs. Warburton, of Hot Lane, who had been at the trial of the Patent-right of R. Shaw; and was the mother of Jacob Warburton, Esq.; and also by Mr. John Baddeley, of Shelton, a good potter and very worthy man. The fine appearance of both body and glaze securing to the Cream Colour general approbation, it became the staple ware of the district. Concerning this kind of Pottery Dr. Aikin truly remarked, that "It forms for the table a species of pottery of a firm and durable body, and covered with a rich and brilliant glaze; and bearing sudden vicissitudes of heat and cold without injury; it was accompanied also with the advantages of being manufactured with ease and expedition; was sold cheap; and as it possessed, with the novelty of its appearance, every requisite quality for the purpose intended, it quickly came into general estimation and use." Mr. Parkes allows this eulogium; and yet, in another place, says 'I consider the health of the community must be impaired by the frequent use of earthen vessels which are covered with the common Staffordshire Glaze. The acetic acid will readily dissolve the oxide of lead; hence the boiling of pickles, and the making of other culinary preparations in such vessels must be highly improper.' Chem. Essays, II. p. 90. This gentleman from some splenetic motive, has supplied the public with the most incongruous accounts of Pottery and its connections, possible to be catenated by a person who had resided some years in the parish town of the district. A little research, and candour in statements would have rendered him respectable; and not a subject of disgust to every well-informed Potter.

The Pottery differing in quality and glaze to any before manufactured, trial was made of the adequacy of its glaze to bear fine designs of the enameller. This was first practised by some Dutchmen, in Hot Lane;

who, to preserve their operations secret, had their muffle in a garden at Bagnall, the property of Mr. Adams.   Mr. Daniel, of Cobridge, was the first native who practised enamelling.   Workmen were soon employed, from Bristol, Chelsea, Worcester, and Liverpool, where Tiles had long been made of Stone Ware and Porcelain; and who had been accustomed to enamel them upon the white glaze, and occasionally to paint them under the glaze.   For some years the branch of Enamelling was conducted by persons wholly unconnected with the manufacture of the Pottery; in some instances altogether for the manufacturers; in others on the private account of the Enamellers; but when there was great demand for these ornamented productions, a few of the more opulent manufacturers necessarily connected this branch with the others. At first, the enamellers embellished merely the tasteful productions, figures, jars, cornucopiæ, &c. and the rich carved work on the vessels; then they painted groups of flowers, figures, and birds; and at length they copied upon their breakfast and dessert sets, the designs of the richest oriental porcelain.

The discovery of this kind of Pottery is already mentioned as accidental; and yet with the facts before their eyes, many different persons have wished to claim the merit of being the inventor; in consequence, probably, of each being at the same time busily engaged in experiments to improve both body and glaze of the Pottery he manufactured.   The greater part of mankind are too lazy to think for themselves; neither will they be at the trouble to investigate facts, and consider the credibility of the evidence adduced.   Some wished to ascribe the merit of this invention to the Messrs. Elers, already mentioned; others doubted this, because in the time of William and Mary, as well

as Anne, very excellent Crouch Ware was made in
Burslem, and some White ornamented Ware. The
small size of the oven, whose foundations were then
undisturbed, was also stated as an objection; and considerable difference of opinion existed, until a remarkable occurrence called their attention to themselves,
and caused them to congitate on their own listlessness
and indifference. During the time the other manufacturers were discussing this knotty point of dispute on
the Ale Benches at home, one of the number was making arrangements in London, by which all the merit
of the improvement attached itself unto him. This
was the late deservedly celebrated Josiah Wedgwood,
Esq. The fact is as true as it is remarkable, that the
children of genius appear as eccentric in their situations and dispositions, as are the delights with which
they frequently astonish their compeers; and that many
persons, in subsequent life distinguished for extraordi-
nary productions, of genius or persevering industry,
have been born and educated amidst scenes and circumstances least likely to foster that ability, for whose
exertions they have become notorious. He was born
in August, 1730, in a small tenement near the Church
yard works, Burslem, then occupied and owned by his
father, Thomas Wedgwood. His early education
was very limited; and in fact, scarcely any person of
Burslem learned more than mere reading and writing,
until about 1750, when some individuals endowed the
Free School, for instructing youth to read the Bible,
write a fair hand, and know the four primary rules of
Arithmetic. At the early age of eleven years he
worked for his father, as a thrower; and John Fletcher
remembers being engaged to make *balls* for his master's sons, Josiah and Richard, both throwers, seated
at two corners of a small room, and he placed between
them, for which he was paid *four-pence* weekly, for

the first year, *six-pence*, for the second, and *nine-pence* for the third.   Richard enlisted for a soldier.

I. Fletcher next worked for the brothers, W. and John Taylor, of the Greenhead, about 30 yards above Hankerses Well, and had 2s. per week to turn the lathe for W. T.   He afterwards was apprenticed for six years to these persons, to learn to handle, and stick legs to the Red Porcelain and black glazed Teapots, at 2s. 3d. for the first year, and an additional 3d. each year,—the highest wages then given, and paid him because he had already acquired considerable knowledge of different parts of the business.   He was hired for 5s. 6d. a week for his first year as a journeyman.   At this manufactory was made the first *Posset Cup*, which would contain *five* pints, and was ornamented in the best style of the time.   The workman was Mr. John Broad, of Chesterton, son of the Mr. Broad, already mentioned as intimate with the Messrs. Elers; and uncle of Richard Broad, near fifty years in the service of Lord Crewe.   Messrs. J. and W. Taylor soon built each a dwelling house; the former at the *hill top*, the latter at the top of the Jornell; and then they commenced making White Stone Ware. They mixed for their Red Porcelain clay, one part of Bradwell Red clay, and four parts of the hill top clay. William Taylor, son of one of these persons, was interred at Burslem, Feb. 8th, 1829, aged 90 years. Mr. J. W. continued serving his father, until compelled to desist, from throwing, by a disorder of his leg, (which being much hurt while in partnership, with Mr. Harrison, at Stoke, terminated in mortification, and was amputated.)   He went to reside at Stoke with Mr. Daniel Mayer, (a mercer and draper, whose descendants now reside at Hanley; and who erected the largest and best residence of the time opposite Hanley Chapel, for the business of a Tailor, Draper, and Man's Mercer.)   While residing here, he made and supplied the tradesmen of Birmingham and Sheffield with Earthenware Hafts for Table Knives, &c. in imitation of Agate, Tortoiseshell, Marble, and other kinds; many specimens of which yet remain in the neighbourhood.

Mr. Wedgwood here entered into partnership with Mr. Harrison, a tradesman of Newcastle, (father of the late Mr. John Harrison, banker, of Stoke, ; and at Mr. J. Aldersea's manufactory, he made different kinds of Pottery scratched and blue, then in demand; and probably here began to employ his latent talent for speculation in different articles; for, Mr. H. being unwilling to supply further funds, a separation resulted. He afterwards, in partnership with Mr. T. Whieldon, manufactured Agate Hafts, Ttrtoiseshell and Mellon Table Plates, Green Pickle Leaves, and other useful articles; but this was not long continued; for, as Mr. Whieldon found his manufactory very productive, (and he by it amassed £10,000, a very large fortune in those days,) he was satisfied, and was unwilling to commence the manufacture of kinds of Pottery then in embryo, but continued this manufacture, at Fenton Low, until about 1780.

Mr. Josiah Wedgwood returned to Burslem, about 1760, and commenced Business alone, at the small manufactory (at that time *thatched*, as usual,) to be seen from the bar of the Leopard Inn; very near that of his distant relations, Messrs. T. and J. Wedgwood, and only a short distance from that of his father. Here he continued the manufacture of Knife Hafts, Green Tiles, Tortoiseshell and Marble Plates, glazed with lead ore, for his previously formed connections;

and his attention to their demands soon secured him such a share of business, that he engaged a second small manufactory, only across the high road, and where is the Turk's Head tavern. Here he manufactured the White Stone Pottery, then increasing in demand; and there yet remain of this kind, white Tiles, with *relief* figures, of a Heron fishing, and a Spewing-Duck fountain. This *relief* method was very advantageous, when the Jasper was invented, and the other *dry* bodies used; for the ground could be of any colour, by employing a metallic calc, and the relief figure remain a beautiful white, or any colour deemed requisite.

The brothers T. and J. Wedgwood, of the Big House, were now rapidly retrenching their manufacture; and they wholly retired from it in 1763; a most pertinent illustration, that every man is the *maker* or *marrer* of his own fortune; that, he who depends upon incessant *industry* and *integrity*, depends on patrons the most noble, the most exalted, and who never desert; but are the founders of families, the creators of fortune and fame, controuling all human dealings, and converting even unfortunate vicissitudes into beneficial results. Mr. Josiah Wedgwood continued industrious and persevering; and certainly, there was room then for such a person, in a manufacture gradually rising into celebrity; and in whose several branches he soon acquired eminence. Britain was now destined to behold him render the manufacture of Pottery celebrated in a degree it had never previously acquired; and delineating for himself a Portrait which history will present to the civilized globe, until the mysterious and oblivious mantle of destruction be *thrown* over all mortal productions, and Art, fancy, and fiction, are for ever engulphed in the immortal brilliancy and radiance of truth.

There was increased demand for the *Cream Colour*, made with fluid lead glaze, by Mr. Enoch Booth's method, and which had been much improved in quality by different persons, especially by John Greatbatch, (who made what has long been called the best *China Glaze* applied to cream colour; and also first made for Messrs. Ralph and John Baddeley, of Shelton, their *Blue printed* glaze.)   Mr. Wedgwood therefore commenced the manufacture of improved cream colour, with Greatbatch's glaze; for which he soon had such demand, that he engaged a third manufactory, named to this day, the *Bell Works*, because of a Bell being first used to call the workmen to their labour.   The specimens of his first table plates are excellent; but very shortly afterwards he made such additions and alterations in both body and glaze, as gained for his pottery, deservedly the highest character for excellence.   At the present day it remains unrivalled, tho' by one or two manufacturers almost equalled; and respectable potters declare that the difficulty in making the excellent cream colour for which Etruria is distinguished, has caused several manufacturers, who attempted to imitate it, to desist, and continue their former processes.

Mr. W. about this time opened a warehouse in London, to supply Merchants and Dealers, and as a depot where every article produced by the ingenuity of workmen, might be inspected by the curious.   He had a partner named Bentley, to manage the London Business, said to have united to considerable natural ability, accurate and extensive knowledge of many departments of Literature and Science; and to have possessed a valuable circle of acquaintance of persons celebrated for talent and property, and eminent for skill and research concerning Grecian and other foreign productions of artists, as Patrons of the Fine Arts. From these virtuosi were obtained loans of the finest specimens of sculpture — Vases, Busts, Cameos, Intaglios Medallions, Seals, &c. suitable for the potters' display of ability; and also Prints, and Drawings, of invaluable utility to any person of ingenuity and industry. Some supplied complete sets of oriental Porcelain; and Sir William Hamilton supplied specimens from Herculaneum, which all were successfully and accurately copied by Mr. Wedgwood's ingenious workmen. The production of these imitations of those of Greece & Rome, & the finest designs of antiquity, some of which excelled the original Etruscan productions in colour, elegance, firmness, and durability, being noticed in the current periodicals became known in town and country; and were viewed with admiration at all the Courts of Europe, and demanded by dealers for sale, in Holland, France, Germany, and Russia; and most of the visitors to the Marquis of Stafford, at Trentham, rode over to Burslem, and in later years, to Etruria, to inspect the manufactures. On this account were attributed to Mr. W. by his acquaintance, all the merit in the art of Pottery, of not only all persons who had preceded him, but also of those who were his rivals and contemporaries.

Mr. Wedgwood having had the honour to present unto her Majesty Queen Charlotte, a Candle Sett, made of the best cream colour, and painted in the best style of the day by Thomas Daniel and Daniel Steele; the very neat and clean appearance of the Pottery caused her Majesty to wish for a complete Table Service of the same kind. Patterns of the several pieces were submitted for inspection, and were approved, with the exception of the Plate, (which was the common barleycorn pattern, then making by all the salt glaze manu-

3 Q

facturers.)   Her Majesty objected to the roughness,
(the *bailey-corn work*, as it is called,) therefore this
part was made plain, on the edge was left only the
bands marking the compartments; and being approved
by her Majesty, the pattern was called *Queen's Pattern*;
the pottery was named QUEEN'S WARE, and Mr. W.
honoured with the appointment of *Potter to her Majesty.*
On the service being completed, His Majesty was
pleased to order another; without the bands or ribs,
and only a plain surface.   This alteration the workmen effected to the entire satisfaction of his Majesty;
and it forms the *Royal Pattern*; some little alterations
being made also in the figure of some other articles.
And now under Royal Patronage, Mr. W. had as many
orders for Table Services of *Queen's Ware*, as he
could possibly manufacture, and at prices the most liberal—fifteen shillings per dozen for table plates, and
all the other pieces in the same proportion.   The table plates subsequently made for common use, were
the *Bath* or *Trencher*, from its resemblance to the
wooden platter; then a concave-edge; and recently
the forms have been numerous and various.

Mr. Wedgwood now invented his truly elegant
JASPER, which will bear his name to the remotest posterity.   It is a beautiful and fine pottery, which can
be so coloured with the calc of certain minerals, but
usually cobalt, for blue, that any determined part may
be of the desired colour, and yet leave any other part
delicate and beautiful white.   It is highly useful for
the manufacture of cameos, &c. and profile likenesses
of eminent persons, in which department, a Frenchman,
named *Voyez*, was a most invaluable servant; but at
length was discarded for his nefarious transactions.
Was this the man who divulged the secret of the
Cauk Stone?   Mr. W. about this time commenced

making Busts in BLACK EGYPTIAN; this kind of
Pottery being very appropriate; and his excelling in
fineness and blackness any which had preceded it,
he contemplated securing the manufacture by Letters
Patent; but ultimately relinquished the intention;
because convinced that other persons previously had
made Black Pottery. By using the Jasper and the
Black solely for articles of *nominal* value, purchase-
able chiefly by persons of rank and affluence, the manufacturer was eulogized wherever the articles were
exhibited. Mr. Wedgwood, when become opulent, at
the height of celebrity, was highly exemplary and
praiseworthy ; exciting in the young a laudable emu-
lation to attain the honour and dignity of great men.
Aware of the disadvantages of the district by circuitous and hilly highways, he exerted himself to promote
their improvement; and was partially successful. The
Canal from the Trent to the Mersey was by him boldly
advocated, he cut the first clod, July 17th, 1760, and
acting from his views of benefits likely to result from
it, he promoted it, and derived satisfaction from witnessing its completion, in 1777.

Richard Lawton, (seventy-nine years old, May
1829,) was apprenticed to Messrs. Wedgwood and
Bentley, at the Bell Works, to learn *turning*. His father, Thomas Lawton, made for these gentlemen the
first slip for Egyptian black; and was well acquainted
with the method of making the slip for the Red Porcelain, made by Elers, at Bradwell, many years before;
and by T. and J. Wedgwood, only a short time previously; having been their servant several years. Old
T. L. being intimate with an old man named Bourne,
a bricklayer, resident at Chesterton, near to Bradwell,
obtained from him many tea pots, Red and Black,
dry body, without any kind of glaze, made by Elers,

and preserved by the oldest families of the place ; and which specimens, T. Lawton exhibited to his employers.   From Mr. Bourne, T. Lawton learned further, and informed Messrs. Wedgwood and Bentley, that Elers used only the red clay of Bradwell, and the ochre from near Chesterton, for their Pottery ; — and he likewise had some of the materials brought, which were properly weighed by Daniel Greatbach, one of their foremen, and after being prepared as clay by T. Lawton, were made into articles which suggested their best Black Egyptian.   R. Lawton well remembered seeing many of these specimens ; but never heard that any *glazed* Pottery, by salt, or other materials, was made by Elers for it was the prevalent opinion, that they chose the spot, because of the red clay, and nearness to coals.

About 1765, Thomas Greatbach, turner, at Mr. Palmer's, Hanley, suggested the movements which form the *Engine Lathe*, to the noted lathe maker, Mr. John Baddeley, of Eastwood ; and worked upon it some years afterwards.   Mr. Wedgwood offered *eighty guineas* each for six, provided Mr. B. would not sell any under that price to other persons.   This was not accepted ; Charles Chatterley had two made, on one of which were turned several ornamental vases, &c. given to the author by his father-in-law, after he had carefully preserved them more than forty years.   Mr. W. engaged Mr. Cox, of Birmingham, to make his ; and on the first of his productions, worked old James Bourne, at the Bell works, about 1766 ; at any rate, before the commencement of erecting the present Etruria.

The demise of Mrs. Wedgwood's only brother, brought into the hands of Mr. Wedgwood a further accession of wealth, and he purchased the estate called Ridge House ; below which, on the line of the Canal, he erected the Black Works, in 1768, and the other in 1770.   He also erected houses for his men, and for himself a beautiful Mansion, calling the place *Etruria*, after the celebrated Manufactory of Pottery in Italy. This manufactory having ready conveyance by canal, for Materials and Productions, from and to all parts of the kingdom, in 1771 he removed altogether from Burslem, and here he greatly extended his manufactures, and rapidly acquired a princely fortune.

A person named Leigh, (father to Ralph Leigh, before mentioned,) occupied Ridge House, prior to the Estate being purchased by Mr. Wedgwood. When the Rebels were at Leek (in 1745,) the whole population of this neighbourhood experienced a complete panic. Old Mr. L. was fearful of being killed by the enemy ; and having saved sixty guineas, he hid them under an oak tree, (now standing on the Race Course,) which he shewed to his son, while the tears trickled down his cheeks. In one of the fields of the estate, there was a great quantity of broom *(genista,)* and all the horses, carts, and the *only* waggon of this part, were brought into the broom field, in hopes that the height of the broom would hide the whole and prevent their being seized by the enemy.

The following are two among many honourable proofs of Mr. W's. kindness and integrity as a Master :—Mr. W. Wood, son of Aaron Wood, the modeller, was for some years general modeller for Mr. W. He appears to have been in high favour with his master, for ability and integrity ; and most of the useful articles manufactured at Etruria, are from models and moulds of his production. He worked only for Mr. W. and died in the service of the present worthy descendant of the founder. And we cannot forego presenting the Reader with the annexed Extract from a Letter written some time prior to his death, by Mr. W. Wood, to his son, Hamlet W. and not found till afterwards ; as certainly a most respectful testimonial.

" After having served two years in part of an apprenticeship to Mr. John Mitchell, to learn the art of a flowerer and handler, my father (Aaron W.) and my master agreed to make void the indentures ; and at Martinmas, 1762, at the age of about sixteen years, my father bound me apprentice for five years more to Josiah Wedgwood, to learn "handling and pressing," at the weekly wages of 2s. 3d. 2s. 6d. 3s. and 3s. 6d, each year; however, at the end of my four year's apprenticeship, my father and Mr. Wedgwood and myself agreed that I should serve four years longer as a Modeller, at the weekly wages of 4s. 5s. 6s. and 6s. 6d. each year; receiving 10s. 6d. each year earnest ; but the two last years and a half, my master's bountiful hand gave me 8s. per week, and now and then half a guinea as a present."

Another excellent modeller, and in fact a general workman of first rate abilities, was Mr. William Greatbatch, some time employed by Messrs. Whieldon and Wedgwood ; and who had commenced business on his own account at the manufactory at Fenton, now a small part of the extensive establishment of Messrs. Bourne, Baker, and Bourne ; where he produced numerous articles, of improved patterns and kinds ; and for some time had a most rapid sale of teapots, on which was printed, in black, by Thomas Radford, the history of the Prodigal Son. But heavy losses at length ruined him. His well known abilities caused him to be consulted, and to form the plan, for the New Field Manufactory, then being erected by Admiral Child ; from whom he was to have received a third share of the profits for managing the establishment. Mr. Wedgwood, aware of the talents of his former servant, engaged him, *for life*, at the very high wages of *five shillings* a day, whether at work or play, and a house rent free ; which sum was regularly paid him, to the time of his death, tho' he survived his master; by whom he was so much respected, that most of his sons, and many of his relations, were employed at Etruria.

When the *Barberini Vase* was on sale, Mr. W. regarded it as a subject, a copy of which would be readily purchased by persons totally unable to purchase the original. He therefore continued to exceed each bidding of a Noble Duchess, (Portland,) until the Duke, on ascertaining the motive of this apparently impudent opposition, offered the *loan* of it, for indefinite time, should the opposition be withdrawn; thus her Grace became the purchaser at the Price of 1800 *Guineas*; the original and a fac simile are now deposited in the British Museum.

"Probably the (Portland) Vase was brought to Rome on the sacking of Corinth, by the Consul Mummius B. C. 146; when the statues, paintings, and richest moveables were transported to Rome." Scientific men have been much puzzled about the material of which it is formed;—may it not be an artificial sapphire? The basis of that gem is pure alumina, and the gem can be counterfitted by the chemists." *Ward. Potter's Art, p.* 21. Mr. Turner considers the Vase as having been fabricated thus:—The dark part, or the body, was first formed of glass, which was next dipped into a quantity of white enamel, and the whole was then annealled; and afterwards the exquisite ornaments were cut by the same processes as are adopted for engraving Seals; which would be extremely tedious; and if attempted in our time, would be more expensive for each article than even Mr. Wedgwood's immense biddings.

This Vase, the most exquisite production of antiquity, was discovered in the Tomb of Alexander Severns, who died A.D. 235. It appears to have been formed in the manner Siracides mentions, as being practised by the ancients;—of encasing or covering earthen vessels with glass. First the Vase seems to be very dark almost black blue, which has been immersed into a mass of fluid enamel white; and then the subjects have been cut by the lapidary, similarly to antique cameos on coloured grounds. Messrs. Pellatt and Green, of London, now have a Patent for covering any kind of ornaments, formed of a substance less fusible than glass, with an incrustation of bright clear glass, thus rendering the ornament imperishable. For the preservation of the finest efforts of the artist, this Invention stands altogether unrivalled.

Mr. Wedgwood's *Porcelain* imitation of the Vase, is for its elegance and beauty entitled to all the commendation it has received. In its completion neither expense nor care was regarded; and tho' he sold the *fifty* for Fifty Pounds each to the Subscribers, yet if

Mr. Byerley be entitled to credit, the expenditure exceeded the subscription. The tale of Webber having Five Hundred Guineas for modelling it, is *Parkes's*.— Webber was a draughtsman, and directed the plastic artists, William Wood, and William Hackwood, and others.

Mr. Carver, an engraver, employed by Messrs. Sadler and Green, of Liverpool, having invented a method by which devices from engraved copper plates can be printed upon the glaze, (now called *Black Printing*,) Mr. Wedgwood employed the waggon belonging to Mr. Morris, the carrier, of Lawton, once a fortnight, to take down a load of cream colour to be printed in this improved manner, by Messrs. S. & G. and return with the load previously taken for that purpose. The specimens are beautiful; and a tea service well authenticated to have been sent down in 1767, from the Bell Works, is excellent in quality, and very fine in embellishment. The tea ware required to be painted, was sent for that purpose to Mrs. Astbury, in Hot Lane; which was sold, packed, and sent away from Burslem; and some time elapsed before Mr. W. had the enamelling executed on his own premises. But, the first black Printer in the district, is said to have been Harry Baker, of Hanley, prior to Sadler and Green practising it; and from some plates borrowed from and belonging to a Book Printer.

About this time Thomas Rothwell, possessed of great skill as an enameller, engraver, and printer, was employed by Mr. Palmer, at Hanley, and specimens yet remaining evince considerable ability; but like all the other attempts, they do not equal the productions of S. and G. for Mr. Wedgwood. As several persons were now employed by Messrs. S. and G. Baker, offered his services to any of the manufacturers in the district, as a printer on the glaze of cream colour, in Black, Red, &c. and soon was fully employed. And about this time the late Mr. John Robinson, of the Hill Top, Burslem, who understood enamelling and printing, left the service of Messrs. S. & G. and settled at Burslem, to print for Mr. Wedgwood; but he afterwards commenced business as a Printer in Black or Red, on the glaze, and also as Enameller, for any of the manufacturers; the preserved specimens of his productions, are deficient in elegance. And we may here notice, that the first successful attempt at employing *Leaf Gold*, by way of ornament, was by Sarah Elkin, then a servant of Mr. Wedgwood, at Etruria. When *Blue Printing* was introduced, the enamellers waited upon Mr. Wedgwood to solicit his influence in preventing its establishment. We are informed that he religiously kept his promise, 'I will give you my word, as a man, I have not made, neither will I make any Blue Printed Earthenware.'

Mr. Wedgwood, for many years prior to his death, in the virtuous exercise of benevolence, enjoyed the highest luxury, the most delightful pleasure, which the human mind can participate. Each Martinmas he sent to certain persons in Shelton, Cobridge, and Burslem, for a list of the names, and a full statement of the peculiar circumstances, of poor persons in each liberty, likely to require assistance during the winter; and for supplying them with comfortable Bedding, Clothing, Coals, and some Food, he always furnished adequate Funds. His purse was ever open to the calls of charity, to the amelioration of misery, and the patronage of every philanthropic institution; and his name will go down to posterity with the highest claims on their gratitude, for being a true Friend of Mankind. He had intrisic merit on a real basis; and needs no tralatitions ascription of excellence.   He was a truly industrious potter; he followed the openings of business suggested by the different experiments of himself and other potters; he pushed every successful trial to considerable extent; and his success in business enabled him to employ and remunerate the best workmen, whose utmost ability was constantly excited and directed by his enlarging knowledge.   Thus he raised himself to the acme of his Art; and the public were amazed that a person with so contracted an education, and so little if any advantage over his fellows, had thus been eminently successful as the founder of his own fortune and fame, (immortal as the Art of Pottery,) and in raising himself among the benefactors of man, and the Princes of the people.

CHAP VIII.

INTRODUCTION OF PORCELAIN.——MR. W. LITTLER'S PORCELAIN.——MR. COOKWORTHY'S DISCOVERY OF KAOLIN AND PETUNTRE, AND PATENT——SOLD TO MR. CHAMPION,——AND RE-SOLD TO THE NEW HALL COMPANY.——EXTENSION OF TERM.

Porcelain is known to have been brought into Europe prior to the Christian Era, and yet we are not aware of any manufactories for it being established in Europe until comparatively recent times.   We may regard indolence and ignorance solely as causing incertitude prevalent at that time concerning the materials and processes, for it is now almost a matter of mere opinion, that the finest and the coarsest porcelain, and the best and most common Pottery, differ less in the diversity, than in the proportions, of their component materials. At the commencement of the eighteenth

century several of the European nations were led to
regret that they were unacquainted with the manufacture of an article of merchandise, for which they
had to pay most extravagant high prices to the
India Companies of Great Britain and Holland;
who only brought to Europe, from China and Japan,
the fine whitish porcelain manufactured in those Em-
pires, now become the admiration of persons of opulence, and the ornament of sumptuous tables. There
was consequent a prevalent desire to discover the
materials, and ascertain the processes of the manufacture, in order if possible to rival these productions.
But a fortunate occurance roused the attention of
France to this important object. The Jesuits having
successfully ingratiated themselves with the inhabitants
of China, in attempting to introduce Christianity into
that extensive empire; about the time we now are
considering, Pere Francis D'Entrecolles, by his mild
and affable deportment, and very insinuating address,
so won upon the friendship of those among whom he
had long resided, that he obtained specimens of the
materials, and forwarded them to France, with a
summary description of the processes of the Art. And
doubtless the European manufacturers generally are
indebted greatly to the letters of the Jesuits, and especially this father's interesting account of the manufactory at King-te-Ching; and of the *petuntse* and *kaolin*,
the materials used. The celebrated genius *Reaumur*,
a person of the most philosophic turn of mind, immediately commenced a series of experiments, in which
he was indefatigable, to ascertain the properties of the
specimens forwarded by the Jesuit father, and also to
discover the method of imitating the productions of
the Chinese; which ultimately he accomplished, after
much labour and disappointment; and published in
1727-9, in the Transactions of the Academy of Sciences.

While Reaumur was thus employed in France, Baron De Botticher was equally busily engaged in Saxony, and first produced the white kind of real porcelain in Europe. The Baron professed Alchemy, or the secret of the Philosopher's Stone, for transmuting metals into Gold; and having exhibited to his dupes several specimens, by some means they were shewed to the King of Poland. To gratify the cupidity of this monarch, by compulsory divulgement of the secret, an order was issued for his incarceration in the castle of Koningstein, where he unremittingly continued making experiments. While pursuing this useless research, without opportunity to destroy or mal-appropriate whatever was produced, he found in one of his crucibles, what completely answered his purposes; the intense heat he employed to fuse some of his materials, rendered the crucibles themselves of similar appearance to the white Chinese porcelain; (very probably because of accidentally employing some materials in quality like those used in China;) he carefully repeated the process, and produced white porcelain; which caused Dresden to become the seat of the art. Thus he accomplished a greater object than that for which he was detained; and discovered one which, in value far exceeded that which he was seeking; he greatly promoted the prosperity of the country, not indeed by making gold, but by inventing a new excellent manufacture, which transmutes not the metals, but the *mire* and the *clay* into gold; and the more carefully to preserve the secret among those who were employed in the processes, all the manufactory was rendered impenetrable, and the work people immured as if in cells. At this period also was a manufactory of Porcelain established at Chelsea; and from the circumstance of Messrs. Elers having left Bradwell to settle near London, it is believed that this manufactory originated with them.

The materials forwarded by Pere D'Entrecolles, having been most carefully examined & analyzed similar materials were soon afterwards found in Saxony; the genius of the French chemists was aroused; Reaumur further improved on De Botticher's discoveries; and after unnumbered experiments, and most mortifying failures, not only was the Dresden manufactory, but others in different parts of Europe, established; and eventually have almost rivalled the Eastern productions. The manufactory is in the Albrechtsberg, an ancient castle on a high rock eighty feet above the river Elbe, and employs 510 persons. Condamine regards the porcelain of Florence, as equal to that of King-to-Ching; and with the only defect of its glaze not being a dead white. And Jonas Hanway mentions the excellence of the Saxony Porcelain, and the extreme precaution of the manufacturers to prevent strangers becoming acquainted with their processes. Salt Glaze White Stone Ware, is partially transparent; and with a proportion of phosphate of lime, or bone, added to the Flint and Alumina it would make good and perfect porcelain. There is hence less wonder that De Botticher's crucibles assumed the appearance of Porcelain. It is related, that when Pere D'Entrecolles mentioned to some Chinese, that the European potters had been using some petuntse without kaolin, and could not produce porcelain, he was answered sarcastically that ' the Europeans are a wonderful people, to make a body whose flesh was to sustain itself without bones.' Dr. William Sherard communicated to the Royal Society of London, the statement of the Jesuits; and he also supplied the Museum of that learned body with several specimens of the materials employed by the Chinese Potters. Probably a sight of these materials, (whether Chinese or Saxon, tho' most likely the latter,) and the account given by the

Jesuits, urged Mr. Cookworthy, (hereafter again noticed) a chemist of considerable experience, resident at Plymouth, to investigate the productions of his own neighbourhood; and he was successful in finding in Cornwall, both the *Petuntse* and *Kaolin*, now used in the Chinese Porcelain.

Frederic II. was so wishful to have a Manufactory at Berlin, that when he conquered Saxony, he forcibly transported from Dresden, the artisans, to his own manufactory; and the following device was by him adopted to raise the productions into notoriety, and which ultimately caused its rise to a state of perfection in beauty and elegance, rivalling that of Saxony:— The Jews resident in his dominions being compelled to obtain his permission prior to their marriage, he adopted the condition of a Certificate that the parties had purchased to not less than a stipulated amount of this Porcelain; after which his permission was granted, confident that it would soon be vended among other people.

The close resemblance of very thin pieces of salt glazed white stone ware to foreign porcelain, excited the ingenuity of Mr. William Littler, of Brownhills, (about 1765,) to attempt the manufacture of porcelain; and he removed to Longton Hall, near Lane End, (now the residence of Richd. Heathcote, Esq. M. P.) where he continued his experiments, until his success surpassed all the expectations of his cotemporaries: but there not being much demand for this kind of ware, he sacrificed his Estate at Brownhills, near Burslem, and then discontinued manufacturing porcelain. His chief workman was not only a good practical potter, but a tolerable modeller, named Dr. Mills; who subsequently died in Shelton at a very advanced age.

The precise nature of the composition of Littler's Porcelain, is not known; its defect was inability to bear sudden or excessive change of temperature. Its basis is believed to have been a *frit*, that is, a mixture of the flint and alumina with alkalies, to render them easily fusible, and cause the mass to appear white when adequately fired. The frit has to be ground, and dried into an impalpable powder, which is subsequently mixed with the clay. The specimens, which are well calculated to deceive the eye of the spectator, are cylindrical cups, with handles shewing some taste, a tolerable glaze, and enamelled with flowers, but there are many specks, and the whole has a greyish hue, yet they are calculated to surprise his fellows, by their similarity to foreign porcelain in body, glaze, shapes, and enamelling. Mr. Littler, at a subsequent period, was manager of a porcelain manufactory in Shelton, for Messrs. Baddeley and Fletcher. But this was discontinued for reasons already mentioned, and because expensive. They fired with wood, because the body would not bear coals. Some specimens of this ware, are such close imitations of the oriental porcelain, as to be frequently supposed such by experienced potters of the present day. Mr. Littler became very infirm prior to his death, at a very advanced age, and in reduced circumstances, in Shelton. This Mr. John Baddeley, was son of the flint grinder at Mothersall, and father of Messrs. Ralph and John Baddeley, of Shelton, who first successfully introduced *Blue* Printing of earthenware Table Services.

The clay named *Porcelain Earth*, (or by the English potters, Cornish or China Clay,) of itself extremely white, smooth in grain, & ductile, from which are made the finer kinds of Dresden, Berlin, Sevres, and British Porcelain, appears generally to be derived from the decomposition of the feldspar of granite. In Cornwall are mountains of white granite, partially decomposed; fragments of these are broken up and thrown into currents of water which wash off and carry away in suspension the fine argillaceous particles, which at different places in a cess pool or kind of eddy, subside as a sediment or clay; when the water is drawn off, the solid matter, in the state of an extremely white and impalpable powder, (the *Kaolin* of China) is dug out, dried, and packed in casks. The Petuntse is Cornish *Growan* Stone, which fusing more easily than the earths, closely combines them; an earth long employed for making porcelain, and supposed *pure* clay, proved to be a carbonate of magnesia and silex. The magnesian earth *Steatities* or Soap rock, is occasionally added to fix the infusible materials, and prevent too great contraction by firing.

Mr. Cookworthy, having discovered in what are now called the Cornish Clay and the Growan Stone, similar materials to the *Kaolin* and *Petuntse*, he first attempted the manufacture of Porcelain, and being tolerably successful, he obtained a Patent in 1768, for the exclusive use of those materials in the manufacture of Porcelain and Pottery. He afterwards sold the patent right to Richard Champion, Esq. a respectable Merchant in Bristol, who had been long employed in investigating the properties of Porcelain; he erected a manufactory in that city, in which for some time he pursued his experiments, and ultimately succeeded in bringing to a state of perfection, rivalling the oriental productions; and altho' this is the first real English Porcelain, (for it has the essential property being *indestructible in both body and glaze*; yet he expended a large fortune in erecting the various requsite premises; and after fully completing his scheme, was so

unsuccessful in obtaining a demand adequate to the
expenditure, that about 1777, he sold the Patent to a
Company in Staffordshire:— Mr. Samuel Hollins, Red
China Potter, of Shelton; Anthony Keeling, Son-in-
law of Enoch Booth, Potter, Tunstall; John Turner,
Lane End; Jacob Warburton, Son of Mrs. W. of Hot
Lane; William Clowes, Potter, of Port Hill; and
Charles Bagnall, Potter, Shelton. After this agreement Mr. Champion directed the processes of the manufacture, for the Company, at the Manufactory of
Mr. Anthony Keeling, at Tunstall; but when that
gentleman removed to London, in 1782, a disagreement ensued among the partners; Mr. Keeling, and
Mr. John Turner withdrew and they who continued
together engaged as managing partner, Mr. John Daniel,
Son of the person who introduced Plaster Moulds, and
settled the manufactory at the New Hall, Shelton,
only a short time previously erected by Mr. Whitehead, of the Old Hall, Hanley; on which account the
Porcelain had the appellation of *New Hall China*;
and during the life time of the several partners, the
concern has been carried forward to their great profit.
Mr. Jacob Warburton was the principal Gentleman
to whom the Potteries are indebted for this spirited
introduction of the Porcelain manufacture; even at the
present day a truly important branch of the Trade,
greatly contributing to extend the celebrity, advance
the interests, and promote the prosperity of this very
extensive and populous district.

Mr. Cookworthy was doubtless a person of considerable ability; but according to the information concerning him from relations and Mr. Champion, he was
constantly so very eager in acquiring knowledge, that
he seldom could find leisure to communicate to others
his own stores of information. Hence all there is to

commemorate him, are a few letters and essays in the periodicals of that day; and this discovery of materials for making Porcelain.   Indeed this last will immortalize him; for it is the general conviction of potters, that the greatest service ever conferred by one person on the pottery manufacture, is this of his (by some erroneously supposed to be Mr. Champion's) making them acquainted with the nature and properties of the materials, and his introduction of Growan Stone for either body or glaze, or both when requisite.   Without it, we should want our fine porcelain, so deservedly admired; neither should we have the excellent cream colour, and elegant blue printed, now in constant demand.   This fact shews the real cause of the violent and determined opposition made to an extension of the term when the first Patent expired.   Some time prior to the expiration of the term of the original Patent, Mr. Champion petitioned Parliament for an Act, authorizing its extension for a further period of fourteen years.   The Manufacturers of Cream Colour or Queen's Ware, among whom was Mr. J. Wedgwood, and Mr. John Turner, (and who never had made any Porcelain,) brought forward, as an objection to its extension, the restriction of all others from employing Cornish Stone; (or *Compositson* as it is called,) in the other branches of the manufacture, altho' such advantages were likely to result.   Therefore the Bill when introduced into the House of Lords, was most violently opposed on the part of the potters by their delegates the late Mr. Wedgwood, and Mr. John Turner; whose decided and very active opposition receiving from the late Marquis of Stafford, (then Earl Gower,) his most powerful aid and influence, a very important alteration was made in the body of the Bill; for, while it confirmed to Mr. Champion the sole and exclusive application of the Cornish Clay and Stone for the manufacture of *transparent* Ware, however it might be named, *Porcelain* or any other designation, it allowed the potters generally the free use of the stone in the opacous glazes, and of the Clay in opaque Pottery. The company agreed to supply ground stone from their mill for any manufacturers, not to be used in the glaze of a *transparent* body. Thus to the energetic enterprize of Mr. Warburton and his Colleagues, may be chiefly ascribed the introduction into our Pottery & Porcelain of these valuable materials, indispensible to the improved solidity, durability and texture of the ware, and rendering it greatly superior to all previously manufactured.

Mr. Champion resided in the Potteries until the formation of the Rockingham Ministry in 1782, when he removed to London on being appointed Deputy Paymaster of the Forces, under Mr. Burke, whom he had served in an important manner in promoting the election of that gentleman as one of the representatives of the City of Bristol; and thereby secured the unabated friendship of that celebrated and eloquent Champion of Aristocracy. The enjoyment of the situation however was of short continuance, owing to the dissolution of that short lived ministry; after which his extensive mercantile connections requiring his presence in America, he visited that Continent; and having successfully arranged his affairs, settled at Camden, in South Carolina; where he died in 1787. Many of the manufacturers at this time began to exercise industry and talent in experimental researches into the properties of different substances; which ultimately have changed the materials, methods of workmanship, and nature of the articles produced; have gradually improved the several branches of the Art, far beyond what had been considered possible; and raised the character of their productions with an astonishingly rapid progress; so that in our day, they diminish the importation of Chinese porcelain, and gradually extend their exportation to most nations of the world. The Burslem Potters often rambled to other places where were Potteries, as Derby, and Worcester, acquiring information concerning the porcelain of those places; and afterwards on returning, made trials of numerous kinds. But the perfection to which porcelain is arrived, is not due to the party to whom Parkes assigns it; but to W. Littler, at Longton. Subsequently, the father of the late Ralph and John Baddeley, of Shelton, manufactured good porcelain, then in partnership with the father of the late Sir Thomas Fletcher, of Newcastle; samples of this the author has before him, and it is difficult to distinguish it from good blue and white porcelain from Canton. After Mr. Turner had separated from the New Hall Company, he commenced the manufacture of porcelain, at Lane End; and one of the ornaments he made, is now preserved by Broadhurst Harding, with truly laudable care and anxiety. It is a *beaker*, on which is enamelled, in brown colours, the whole interior of a Pottery. The celebrated modeller Gerverot designed it; and in quality it will still rank very high among English porcelain. Mr. Wedgwood's encaustic painting was in imitation of Messrs. Turner's on white body porcelain.

Jacob Warburton, Esq. was equally respectable for social virtues, great mental ability, and extensive literary acquirements. Some years prior to his decease, he had relinquished the cares and fatigue of business; and having at a late period of life, married for his second wife a person much younger than himself, for whom he had long cherished the most affectionate regard, he retired to his house at Ford Green, near Norton, where, he indulged his fondness for literary felicity, with the true 'Otium cum dignitate.' Possessed of pure benevolence, and sound judgment, his friendship was valued deservedly by every intelligent person in the neighbourhood; and those who were honoured with his intimacy, alone can judge of his correct taste and stores of information. His memory was peculiarly tenacious, and was strengthened by most extensive reading, and a correct oral and legible knowledge of French, Dutch, German, and Italian; the latter being his favourite amusement up to the day of his decease; to which time his mind resembled a pure and brilliant blaze of intellect. On the day prior to his death, (September 19th, 1826,) he enjoyed his usual portion of animal spirits, and commenced a walk to Cobridge, but returned home without effecting his purpose. The next day, while seated on a sofa, he said to a gentleman who was reading to him,—'Do not be alarmed; I feel I am dying,'—and expired without a struggle or a groan, at the age of 86 years. His religious tenets were those of the Church of Rome, but wholly free from bigotry and intolerance, in consequence of his extensive travels and connection with mankind. He was the last of the Potters of the Old School; and from the energies of his character and perseverance, numerous advantages have accrued to other manufacturers. To enumerate his various excellencies is not easy, however they might be adapted to benefit and entertain the reader. Tho' a few years younger than Mr. Wedgwood, yet from the time of that celebrated Potter's commencing Business at Burslem, there existed between the two, the most intimate friendship and confidential intercourse. At a very early period he was engaged in commercial pursuits with his father and brothers, as a manufactu-

S

rer of Pottery; and as salesman for the concern, he several times visited many places on the European Continent. More than 50 years he was engaged in the manufacture, and witnessed the commencement and progress to their present perfection, of those Branches for which the district is now celebrious; and in this period, the most important which Potters have yet known, he contributed to exalt and establish the importance of the Art of Potting, and secured to himself and family a very ample fortune.

CHAP IX.

BLUE PRINTED POTTERY. — MR. TURNER.—-MR. SPODE (1.) — MR. BADDELEY. — MR. WOOD.— MR. WILSON.—MR. SPODE (2.)—MESSRS. TURNER.—MR. MINTON.—GREAT CHANGE IN PATTERNS OF BLUE PRINTED.

About 1770 the manufacture of White Stone Ware, Salt glaze, began to decline, and the Cream Colour with fluid glaze obtained the ascendancy. There were, however, some extensive manufactories continued employed therein, as is proved by the following (strictly *literal*) Copy of a Document, which exhibits the *Scale of Prices* of the several Articles; and is valuable for exhibiting the state of the Business, and the probable rate of profits:

We whose Hands are hereunto Subscribed do Bind Ourselves our Heirs, and Assigns in the sum of Fifty Pounds of good and lawful Money of great Britain not to sell or cause to be sold under the within specified Prices, as Witness our Hands,

This 4th Day of Feby. 1770.

John Platt, John Lowe, John Taylor, John Cobb, Robt. Bucknall, John Daniel, Thos. Daniel, Junr. Richd. Adams, Saml. Chatterley, Thos. Lowe, John Allen, Wm. Parrott,

Jacob Warburton, Warburton and Stone, Jos. Smith, Joshua Heath, John Bourn, Jos Stephens, Wm. Smith, Jos. Simpson, John Weatherby, J. & Rd. Mare, Nicholas Pool, John Yates, Chas. Hassells, Pr. Pro. of Ann Warburton, & Son, Thos. Warburton, Wm. Meir.

PRICES OF DISHES.

Best.		Seconds.	
	s. d.		s. d.
10 inches	3	10 inches	2
11 in.	4	11 in.	3
12 in.	6	12 in.	4
13 in.	8	13 in.	6
14 in.	10	14 in.	8
15 in.	1 0	15 in.	10
16 in.	1 4	16 in.	1 0
17 in.	1 6	17 in.	1 2
18 in.	1 9	18 in.	1 4
19 in.	2 0	19 in.	1 6
20 in.	2 6	20 in.	2 0
21 in.	3 0	21 in.	2 6

Worser Second Dishes half price of Best.

Prices of Nappeys and Baking Dishes.

7 inches	1 6	Seconds	1 0
8 in.	2 0	ditto	1 6
9 in.	2 6	ditto	2 0
10 in.	3 6	ditto	2 6
11 in.	4 6	d tto	3 6
12 in.	6 6	ditto	4 6

Tureens.

Best		Seconds
Large	3 6	2 6
Middle	2 9	2 0
Small	2 0	1 6

Best Stoolpans.		Seconds.
12 inch	1 4	1 0
11 in.	1 2	10
10 in.	11	9
9 in.	9	6
8 in.	7	4

Sauce Boats.

Best		Seconds
	s. d.	s. d.
Large	2 6	2 0
Mixt	2 0	1 9
Less	1 9	1 6
Less	1 6	1 3
Smallest	1 3	1 0

Twyflers.

Best	1 4
Seconds	1 0
Thirds	9
None less than	7
Best Plates	2 0
Best Seconds	1 9
Worser ditto	1 6
A degree worser	1 3
Ditto ditto	1 0

None Sold under 9d. an' not to be Pick'd, but Took as they are put together.

Cups & Saucers Holland Size.		
Mid. White best 10 secds.		8
Small ditto ditto 9 ditto		7
Middle Blue do. 1 2 ditto		10
Small ditto do. 1 0 ditto		8
Three to Piece ware Best 1 4 seconds 1s.		
London Size Cups & Saucers		
Blue and White Best		1 4
Ditto Seconds		1 0
Holland Ware best		1 10
Ditto Ditto seconds		1 6
Covered Toys 6 seconds		4
Handled ditto 4 ditto		2½
Cups & Saucs. 3 ditto		2
Only twelve to doz.		

Butter Tubs and Stands.

Large Best 9d. Seconds 6d.
Middle do. 7d. ditto   4d.
Small do.   5d. ditto   3d.

London Size Cups & Saucers, Best 1s. Seconds 9d.
Irish Size, Ditto and ditto ditto 1s. 2d. ditto 10d.

Sortable white ware, Best 1s. 6d. seconds 1s. 2d.
Covered ware ditto 2s. ditto 1s. 6.
Inlett Teapots ditto 2s. 6d. ditto 1s. 9.

Sortable Blue Flower'd, Best 1s. 10d. seconds 1s. 6d.

No Sortable under 8d. nor Cups and Saucers under 6d.

To allow no more than 5 per cent for Breakage, and 5 per cent for ready money.

To sell to the Manufacturers of Earthenware at the above Prices, and to allow no more than seven and a half per cent, beside Discount for Breakage and Prompt Payment.

The manufacturers now experienced a share of the demand for Pottery by the Continental markets; and some of them visited Holland and Germany, where they obtained such patronage, as convinced them their manufacture was becoming an important Branch of the National commerce. Foreign Connections always introduce improvement in the manners of the parties, and also in the articles fabricated; the results of differing opinions, and varied tastes; which ultimately cause other desires and opinions. Hence great alterations in the shapes of the Articles made, and many new ones were now introduced; and Agents were fixed at most of the places where merchants resorted to purchase British Manufactures.

The chief manufacturers of the improved kinds of Pottery in Hanley, at this time were Mr. Palmer, Mr. Chas. Chatterley, Mr. Wm. Mellor, and Dr. Sam. Chatterley. The two former made Cream Colour, with fluid glaze, and also the dry bodied pottery, then acquiring celebrity. The others are known for

the black pottery; Dr. Chatterley making excellent
Black Egyptian, chiefly for Tea and Coffee Pots; and
Mr. Mellor for the Black glazed or Shining Black,
for the same Purposes, and kitchen vessels; and also
the beautiful *Green Glazed* Pottery, subsequently in
great demand for garden pots, &c. Messrs. John
and Rich. Mayer, were making salt glaze Pottery at
this time—but only their name remains; the site of
their Maunfactory and Residences being now partly
occupied by Hanley Market-Place.

A person in Hanley has had more than sixty years
in her possession a Specimen of Mr. Palmer's ware.
It is a Bread Basket, 15 inches long, 8 wide, and 5
deep; formed to resemble a kind of *reticular* vessel,
the *corded* part being preserved, and the intervals cut
out to form the net-work. It is without any appearance of crazing; the glaze is grayish, and has a sur-
plus of lead. Many extremely beautiful Articles
made by Mr. Chatterley yet remain. We have had
two Candlesticks, near 60 years made, one of bisquet,
finely ornamented; the other glazed, the column very
neatly fluted, the circle beneath the bowl well turned,
and ornamented with rosettes. A fine vase of extremely white bisquet, *pearl* I believe, has some blue
fern leaf ornaments, on the lower parts, and the cover;
and the bands have scrolled work in them. The Blue
is very fine, and particularly strong in quality.

Mr. C. Chatterley was among the first who fixed
an agent in Holland. The late Elijah Mayer, Esq.
was some years Mr. C's representative there. After
some time carrying on the manufacture to great advantage, he admitted as a partner his Brother Ephraim,
who survived him, and secured the property to the
two orphans left by Mr. C.—The manufactory was

3 S

continued by Mr. E. C. until about 1797, when he transferred its business to his Nephews, James and Charles Whitehead, Sons of Mr. Whitehead of the Old Hall, one of the early and most eminent Salt Glaze Potters.

The Manufacturers of the district generally were now excited to unremitted exertions, and these with their previous knowledge, produced those various improvements which have brought the Pottery into repute. The superior kinds now became the medium of ornamental devices; at first in mere outline, and blue painted, rude and coarse; then in imitation of the foreign China, and gradually improved to fine and delicate designs. A specimen is preserved of a quart mug, with a bluish glaze, which was painted by Dan. Steele, in Blue, and well exhibits the defective nature of the process at that time.

But the improvements in the quality of the Pottery, and also in demand for it, caused equal attention or excel in the *Blue Painting* on the Salt Glaze, and a desire to produce *enamelled* on the Cream Colour. The artists then in the district acquired additional skill; and many young women, of good families, were taught the Art; which is now an important branch of the Manufacture. From different Porcelain manufactories in other parts of the kingdom, came Blue Painters and Enamellers, who increased the celebrity of the Productions. Upon the dessert and tea services they copied the designs of the richest Japan and China Porcelain; they also ornamented the relief ornaments of the other articles of taste and fancy. For many months no research availed to ascertain by whom, or the exact time when, the method of *Gilding* in prepared Gold, was introduced; though specimens exist made near fifty years ago, but the gilder and enameller could not be ascertained. At length a few days prior to this part going to press, we ascertained that the merit is due to Mr. John Hancock, of Etruria. In the early practice of *Blue Painting*, the Colours were prepared by merely grinding with a muller on a stone, the zaffres, and the Crystals of Cobalt first brought into this Country by Mr. Mark Walklett, and Mr. John Blackwell, of Cobridge, exceeding fine in quality, and readily used as above. But, the demand increasing, we are informed, that Mr. Cookworthy (already mentioned,) who had been a Painter, and also a Chemist and Druggist, at Bristol, happening to meet an old acquaintance, Roger Kinnaston, also a painter, in very reduced circumstances, fully instructed him in the process of preparing a Blue from Zaffres; and also the whole *Recipe* for extracting the pure metal from Cobalt ores. At first, the ore was calced in the fore-bung of the Potter's Oven; but, about 1772, Mr. K. had an air furnace set up at Cobridge, where for some time, he pursued the making of Blue. All the advantage Mr. K's. family derived from the practice, was a mere livelihood. In the hands of a prudent person, the instruction Mr. Cookworthy had kindly given, would have proved an invaluable source of opulence; many preparers of Blue, in our day, being possessed of considerable wealth; but with Mr. Kinnaston, it was merely subservient to gratifying his Bacchanalian propensities. He sold copies of the recipe for trifling sums, £10. or £12.; and after living in indolent ebriety, he died without honour and in a state of poverty.

We do not apoligize for introducing mention of the following gentleman, altho' not a Staffordshire Manufacturer; but he was the first who practised Blue

Printing, and doubtless the first who manufactured a complete Table Service, (Dinner,) ornamented by that process. The late Mr. John Turner, of Caughley, Salop, having acquired competent knowledge of the processes of the manufacture, and some celebrity as an artist, at the Porcelain Manufactory, at Worcester; on the expiration of the term of his engagement, commenced the manufacture of Porcelain at a place named Caughley, near Broseley, Salop. The excellence of his ware, and the elegance and novelty of his patterns and shapes, gained him such a share of patronage, that he rapidly arrived at comparative opulence. In 1780, he completed the *first Blue Printed Table Service* made in England, for Whitmore, Esq. father of the present Member for Bridgnorth. The pattern was called *Nankin*; and had much similarity to the *Broseley* Tea Pattern, which in 1782, was copied from a *Nankin* pattern, and by Mr. Turner adapted to Tea Services, Thos. Minton, Esq. of Stoke, assisted in the completion of the Table Service, and named the other *Broseley*, by way of compliment to the adjacent town.

The great demand for Blue Painted and Enamelled Pottery, caused an attempt to facilitate the process, by forming the outline on the ware, from a Glue Bat, similarly to Black Printing, which could be readily filled in by the painter. This was first practised by William Davis, for Mr. W. Adams, Cobridge; and from him Mr. Daniel Steele, obtained his knowledge of the process. Davis had learned engraving and copper-plate printing, at Worcester; and had practised Blue Painting and Black Printing in Shropshire, from which he came to the Potteries. The method of printing with glue bats was also practised by Harry Baker, for Mr. Baddeley, of Shelton; about 1777,

and very little progress was made in the practise for
some time. The next stage in its improvement was
employing paper and transferring it to the Pottery;
but in this the printer proceeded very differently from
the present method. The paper was different in texture and quality, and was applied in a dry state. The
Plates were so extremely strong that no delicate shades
were preserved. The specimens have scarcely any
thing deserving the name of a *fine part.* And unless
the printer was very expert in removing the paper
from off the plate the instant it came from between
the rollers, the greatest difficulty resulted; and while
much loss in paper and colour occurred to the master,
the workman both lost his labour for that impression,
and had additional trouble to clean the plate prior to
taking off another. The larger plates were in two
parts, and the impressions were taken at two distinct
times; and lately might have been found among the
oldest Blue Printed ware, twenty inch dishes, painted
at twice, because the paper could not be extracted off
the whole at once with adequate rapidity. The method of damping paper adopted by Copper-plate printers, suggested another improvement; and various
essays were made by different persons, with different
degrees of success. Mr. John Baddeley, of Shelton,
some time employed Mr. Thomas Radford to print
Tea Services by an improved method of transferring
the impression to the bisquet ware; which was attempted to be kept secret, but was soon developed;
and the glaze prevented the beautiful appearance which
attached to the Black printed. This caused J. Greatbatch to improve the Pottery and the Glaze; and, for
Mr. R. Baddeley he formed an excellent body, with
a glaze, containing some growan stone in both, with
a little cobalt in the fritt which formed the glaze.

The elder Mr. Turner first employed a Blue Printer, who used wet Paper. His name was Wm. Underwood, from Worcester; and he lived to a very advanced age. The Pattern Mr. Turner used was the *willow*, designed by him from two oriental Plates, still preserved, and exhibited to the Author by Mr. W. Turner. The border remains, but the other parts are varied a little: the Cottage is altered in shape, and the Figures are less in the copy than in the originals. The workmen who then made *four* Soup Tureens from *two* moulds in a day, was considered a fair workman, and received wages of *ten* to *twelve* shillings weekly; but now, 1819, a mere common workman will use *six* moulds, and finish *sixteen* or *eighteen* daily. Mr. Myatt's thrower, the late Wm. Bridgwood, of Lane End, was expected to average *fifteen score* dozens daily, for which his rumuneration was *fifteen shillings* weekly, house rent free, fire, and the keep of a cow.

Several other Manufacturers now commenced manufacturing Blue Printed Pottery. The late Mr. Jas. Gerrard with Mr. Jas. Keeling, of New Street, Hanley, introduced some improvements in the processes. About 1783, James Richards, John Ainsworth, and Thos. Lucas, an engraver, left the service of Mr. Turner, at Caughley, and engaged with the Staffordshire Manufacturers; Richards and Lucas with the first Mr. Spode (hereafter mentioned;) and Ainsworth with the first Mr. John Yates, of Shelton. These two printers first introduced the Composition called *Oils*, and the method of washing the paper off the bisquet pottery, and hardening on the colours previous to the immersion in the fluid glaze.

Mr. William Smith, an engraver of considerable ability, resident in Liverpool, was engaged to engrave new plates in a superior style for Mr. R. Baddeley, of Shelton; and the excellence of the pottery, with the elegance of the embellishments from plates of finer execution, rendered him unrivalled for some time. But as the method of printing was very injurious to the plates and by waste of paper and colours, much diminished the profits of the Master, Mr. Smith engaged Thomas Davis, of Worcester, to print for Mr. Baddeley, and he introduced other improvements in the operations. The Blue Painters experienced such a diminution of employment and remuneration, that they employed every artifice to prevent its success, but without avail; for the novelty and elegance of the Pottery secured the demand, which has continued to increase; and in this day, 1829, few manufacturers do not practise the art; and many have several presses constantly employed in Blue Printing.

After (the first) Mr. Josiah Spode left the employment of Mr. Whieldon, at Fenton, he was employed along with the late Mr. Charles Harvey, in the manufactory of Mr. Banks, (who resided at Stoke Hall,) on White Stone Ware, and for Cream Colour, Scratched, and Blue Painted. But Messrs. Baddeley and Fletcher discontinuing making Porcelain, at Vale Lane, Shelton, Mr. Spode commenced manufacturing the pottery most in demand. — Cream Colour, and Blue Painted, White ware; and his productions were of tolerable excellence. His family remained resident at Stoke; and Messrs. Banks and Turner separating and Mr. Banks relinquishing business in a short time afterwards, Mr. S. engaged the manufactory, (which subsequently he purchased,) and there manufactured also Black printed, and Black Egyptian. About 1784, he introduced the manufacture of *Blue Printed* into Stoke; on the improved methods success-

fully adopted by Mr. Ralph Baddeley, of Shelton.
The Patterns were—for Table Services what is now
called the *Old Willow*, with a border of a willow and
a dagger; and for Tea Services the *Broseley*, from the
Pattern used at Caughley.   The engraver was named
Lucas, and his first printer was named Richards, from
Caughley.   Specimens of this ware, shew the great
strength of the engraving, and consequent deep blue
of the ware.   The first transferrer Mrs. Mary Broad,
of Penkhull, (recently buried at Stoke,) informed us
that she remembered the first dish printed in Blue, at
Stoke, being long carefully preserved as a specimen. —
He continued to extend his business until his death, in
1797 or 8; and from persons well acquainted with him
we learn, that with his wealth, increased his kindness
as a master, and benevolence to the wretched and in-
digent; and that when he was passed "the Bourne
whence no traveller returns," his loss was regretted,
as a liberal master, a munificent benefactor, and above
all, a truly honest man.

In 1779, his elder Son (the second Josiah Spode,
Esq.) married the eldest daughter of Mr. John Barker, of the Row Houses, Fenton Culvert, with whom
he received, in the whole, a dowry of £500.   The
parents judging this a proper opportunity to establish
a regular London business, alike advantageous to themselves and the newly married pair, the younger Mr.
Spode therefore commenced as a Dealer in Earthenware; and subsequently also of Glass and Porcelain;
and the assiduity he manifested, to gratify the varying
tastes and wishes of purchasers in kinds, quality, and
shapes of the various articles, soon gained him extended
connections, while the excellent Blue Printed pottery
(recently introduced,) supplied by the father, obtained
such preference as to produce a considerable increase

of business. Early in 1797, a very short time prior to the death of his father, the younger Mr. Spode experienced a bereavement, conceivable by those only who have been similarly bereft,—the loss of an affectionate and beloved wife, in child-bearing of a daughter. He never again married; but to his latest hour cherished the remembrance of her virtues, and remained consoled for his loss sustained, by the virtues of her offspring.

Mr. Spode now wholly resided at Stoke, to superintend the manufactory. His Blue Printed ware was the best manufactured; his Cream Colour, excellent; and both remain in high estimation; and the various *Dry* body wares are of superior quality, and the articles made by most experienced and ingenious artists. Each year witnessed his persevering attention, and his generosity kept pace with his prosperity. In one year, prior to the demise of his father, the clear profits of the London business alone exceeded £13,000. The connections gradually increased, after he settled here; and his satisfaction with the attention to his interest by a confidental servant in town, was evinced, by a most substantial mark—a present of £1000; and as a further reward for his assiduity and integrity, by a share in the London Business; still enjoyed by his son.

About 1800, Mr. Spode commenced the manufacture of Porcelain, in quality superior to any previously made in England, and in imitation of that made at Sevres, which it equalled, if it did not surpass, in transparency. For entering on this Manufacture with every reasonable prospect of success, Mr. S. was well capacitated, by the extensive knowledge he possessed relative to those subjects apparently best adapted for public demand, and which seem calculated to

T

ensure quick and profitable returns. At this period, the London Dealers were supplied from Worcester, Derby, and Caughley, with the best British Porcelain; having rich embellishments upon most beautiful patterns of the various Articles. He therefore now incited the ingenuity of his modellers and other plastic artizans, to produce varied shapes of the articles already in use; and to design other new articles, for the approbation of persons of taste. The *Bone Body* Porcelain, which is very transparent, he brought to considerable perfection. He also first used Feldspar, which by being very carefully prepared, increased the excellence of his Porcelain; which in 1821, he further improved in both body and glaze. His enameller, Mr. Henry Daniel, here first introduced, in 1802, the present method of ornamenting Porcelain, in *raised* unburnished gold, much similar to *embossed dead* gold, or *frosted work*, on plate. A Porter Cup then made, is a fine specimen, of Mr. Spode's porcelain, and of the artist's ability. The excellent quality of the Porcelain, the taste and elegance manifested in the patterns or shapes, and the beautiful designs so exquisitely enamelled, insured him, in a comparatively short time, a valuable extension of connections. These will convey his name to posterity as entitled to grateful admiration, and long vie with every similar effort in the plastic art, whether produced by the skill of foreigners, or the genius of Englishmen.

His Majesty George IV. while Prince of Wales, being on a journey of pleasure to Liverpool, in 1806, in company with his Royal Brother, the Duke of Clarence, visited the Marquis of Stafford at Trentham, on the way; where many of the Nobility joined the company. Having often intimated a wish to witness the manipulations and processes of the Porcelain

Manufacture, the opportunity was embraced, and their Royal Highnesses with the Nobility and suite visited the establishment at Stoke. Mr. Spode had so arranged, that all the persons employed, of both sexes, were in their best attire, to manifest their respectful and loyal attachment to the Heir Apparent, and the Family on the throne ; and as the Royal and Noble visitors passed thro' the different apartments, the appearance and demeanour of the working classes, drew forth repeated eulogiums. The Large warehouse, (117ft. long,) was then visited, where were arranged every variety of Pottery and Porcelain, in the most elegant and curious productions, manufactured by Mr. S. whose loyalty and respect were so highly appreciated by the Royal visitor, that Mr. S. received the appointment of "*Potter to His Royal Highness the Prince of Wales.*"

At the commencement of 1823, Mr. Spode was engaged to manufacture a splendid Porcelain Vase, valued at £100, as a present from the Middleton Hill Mine Company to his Majesty. This was completed in April, and was exhibited several days in the large China Warehouse of the manufactory, to some thousand of visitors. Its chasing and enamelling are executed in the first style of the Art ; and the whole is conspicuous for its unblemished beauty, the purity and delicacy of the material, the simplicity of the style, and the splendour of its ornaments. In July, the same year, Mr. Spode completed for the Hon. East India Company's Factory at Canton, a most splendid Table Service of Porcelain, of *thirteen hundred pieces*, valued at £400. to replace the service destroyed by the Fire. The Porcelain was of the finest body made at the manufactory, alike distinguished for its beautiful Parian whitness, and delicate transparency. The larger articles are perfect in the manufacture, and prove that perseverance has overcome the difficulties formerly regarded as insurmountable in producing large specimens of the best Porcelain. The first style of embellishment has not been employed, but a second grade ; yet the appearance is rich and splendid, and equal to any specimens of Dresden Pocrelain. Would it have been believed thirty years ago, that China would receive again specimens of her chief manufacture, from England, where in the course of less than one generation, it has been brought to a state of perfection, almost if not wholly equal to that of the Chinese and Japanese, and certainly superior in ornament to any made in Europe. Thus within little more than the life of man, how great has been the progress of the Art of Pottery. Such an article, as in our day would be made by numbers of workmen for a mere trifle; and for the low price of *one shilling*, in a much superior style, was once a subject at which the *Beau Monde* were called to wonder and admire. An elegant *Teapot*, of Pottery, gracing the side board of Lady Isabella Montague, was the genius of inspiration, anticipating new honours for our country, in Sir Chas. Hanbury William's Poem 'Isabella;' where after describing her Ladyship's morning occupations, and visitors; he introduces one of her admirers, a Mr. Bateman, from Staffordshire:—

> ' To please the noble Dame, the courtly Squire,
> Produced a TEAPOT made in Staffordshire.'
> So Venus look'd, and with such longing eyes,
> When Paris first produced the golden prize.
> ' Such works as this, (she cries,) can England do ?
> It equals Dresden, and excels St. Cloud.'
> All modern China now shall hide its head,
> And e'en Chantilly must give o'er her trade;
> For Lace, let Flanders bear away the bell;
> In finest Linen, let the Dutch excel;
> For prettiest Stuffs let Ireland first be named;
> And for best fancied Silks, let France be famed;
> Do thou, thrice happy England, still prepare
> Thy Clay, and build thy fame on EARTHENWARE.'

The several Slabs, about 16 by 12 inches on the superficies, which were deposited in the respective Corner Stones of Stoke New Church, (viz. one of the BEST PORCELAIN, glazed, on which, in addition to the bas relief Inscription, is a Landscape, in the finest style of enamelling, with an excellent drawing of Stoke Old Church, the Winton's Wood Field, Hanley Church Steeple, and other conspicious objects; with a very elegant embossed border richly gilded and enamelled; laid in the Stone of the North East corner, after the very Rev. the Dean of Lichfield, had placed the stone; one of *rich Brown Porcelain*, with embossed border and foliage, in the South East corner Stone, laid by Mr. Spode; one of *Jasper* similarly ornamented, in the Chancel Stone, laid by Mr. Tomlinson, the Patron; one of the *Patent Stone Porcelain*, in the South

West Corner Stone, laid by the senior Churchwarden Mr. J. Spode; and one of the best *Blue printed Pottery* in the North West Corner Stone, laid by Mr. Kirkham;) were manufactured by Mr. Spode, to transmit to generations far remote, invaluable memorials of the perfection to which the Potter's Art in this neighbourhood had arrived in the early part of the nineteenth century; of which they are characteristic Specimens.

We have already mentioned, that Mr. S. contributed the liberal sum of £500, towards erecting the Parish New Church, at Stoke, but he did not live to see it covered in; his death occurring in July, 1827. Possessed of the highest excellence of character in the relations of civil and social life, volumes concerning his worth were indicated by the grief-worn cheeks of the spectators at his Funeral Obsequies.

While the Printer was arranging the Types of this part, and almost of this identical page, the Author received the distressing intelligence that (the third) JOSIAH SPODE, Esq. had suddenly expired. His invaluable worth as a Friend unaffected by the caprices of fortune, and his integrity as a Tradesman of the highest class, are not surpassed by any survivor; as is well known to those persons best acquainted with him. The numerous personal and pecuniary scarifices he made to aid the suffering Poor in times of peculiar distress, will cause his memory to be embalmed by all who can and dare extol real philanthropy; and to the Author his demise is an almost irreparable loss.

About 1800, Mr. Benj. Adams, of Tunstall, was successful in the manufacture of Jasper, and which would have been more highly esteemed had it been *alone* before the public; but, in this, as well as most other instances, the imitation very rarely equals the original. This Jasper is deficient in the brilliancy of

3 T

teint, fineness of grain, and excellence of workmanship, obvious to every beholder, of that fabricated at Etruria, and that by Mr. Turner. We have not been successful in obtaining any personal notice of Mr. Adams.

Messrs. John and Wm. Turner, (sons of Mr. Turner, before noticed,) of Lane End, for some years with considerable success continued the manufacture of the excellent Pottery for which their father was celebrated. Mr. Turner succeeded in making a Shining Blue glazed Pottery, similar to that of the Japanese Porcelain; an imitation of which had been attempted by Mr. Cookworthy; and was pronounced by Mr. Wedgwood, as a *desideratum*. The specimen preserved is a pint Cup, which, had the ability of the Gilder been as well employed in preparing his gold, as in the execution of the Pattern, would have equalled any of the rich Gilding at this day of the Artists employed by Mr. Spode, Mess. Daniels, Mess. Ridgways, or Mr. Minton. Their Jasper was second to none but Mr. Wedgwood's, and they were not despicable rivals as potters, and in the respectability of their foreign connections. The Black Egyptian made by Mr. Turner as the plinths for his Jasper Ornaments, will bear the polish of the lapidary's wheel, to a degree of exquisite fineness, only to be credited by the persons who have inspected the specimens.

One Cup made by them for the late Viscount Creamhorn, has never been equalled in the district; tho' formed of the common Clay of Lane End. This was once produced by the late Jacob Warburton, Esq. at a meeting of Potters, to shew to what a degree of perfection even common pottery may be carried. It became so estimable in the opinion of its owner, that to prevent the possibility of injury, he had a proper sized mahogany box made for its reception, and in the door is a pane of glass, thro' which alone he permits it to be inspected.

Their principal modeller was Mr. Jas. Luckock, a person of great skill, and most extensive acquirements as an Artist. But their further progress was prevented, and themselves completely ruined, by the political convulsions in France, at the era of the reign of terror; their principal market was destroyed, their property confiscated, and themselves unexpectedly reduced, from a near prospect of great affluence to a state of comparative indigence. Mr. W. Turner happened to be in Paris when the reign of terror was most awful; and the application for Moneys due to him, was returned by incarceration and several examinations— not very pleasant to the free-born Englishman.—Indeed, he acknowledges, that he owes his liberty, and most probably his life, to the interference of the present Marquis of Stafford; whose Physician, Dr. James, and Secretaries, Messrs. Erskine and Hutchinson, were most busily employed to obtain his liberty. And, when, subsequently, the gens d'arme' brought his Passport, he witnessed the infatuation of a bastard freedom, in the most haughty rejection of the douceur Mr. Turner liberally offered to the bearer of so welcome a document.

In 1784, Mr. E. Wood commenced business at Burslem, and continues to the present time. At that time, the best mould maker and tureen maker in that part, was John Proudlove, who was hired by Mr. W. for *three* years, at *twelve* shillings per week. This gentleman has justly obtained the character of *Father of the Pottery.* We can say of him, what is not known to apply to any other Gentleman in the district; that *'he has earned his daily bread by working in every branch of the Manufacture.'* There are still remaining proofs of his skill in the more ingenious departments; and his ability as a Modeller and Sculptor, has long been widely indicated in the very correct Bust he produced of the late Rev. John Wesley. At this day, his manufacture embraces almost every kind of article required by the European and Trans-Atlantic Markets; and his large establishments present the philosophic enquirer with all the processes and manipulations of the Art, in the most improved methods, on a scale of magnificent grandeur. By his acuteness and philosophic comprehension, which rank him among the chief mechanical geniuses of this age, he has so increased the power, successfully obviated the difficulties and inconveniences attending the operation, and so well accommodated to peculiar circumstances the construction of the *Steam Engine*, at the Bichers Colliery, as to effect an astonishing economy in steam and fuel, while preserving the Power so requisite for the operations. The Newspapers of December, 1827, stated that Mr. Warner, of Loughborough, had offered his Engineer £1000. to divulge his discovery of a method of *doubling* the power of the Steam Engine. What merit then attaches to Mr. Wood's leaving his discovery accessible to all mechanical geniuses.

> The explosive Steam's dense Columns here aspire,
> Like gathering Clouds, wing'd by Caloric ire;
> Thro' Valves' alternate, over and below,
> To fill each vacum, they swiftly go;—
> Resistless to the Valves' successive calls,
> The well-packed Piston slides 'twixt iron walls;
> The balanced beam with quick librations, moves
> The Sun and Planet Wheels' revolving grooves;
> Until the' expanded Vapour, as a drop
> Sinks, by the gelid stream's effective stop.

About this time Mr. Robert Wilson, of Hanley, at the manufactory previously occupied by Mr. Palmer, a short distance above the Church, brought to perfection that kind of Pottery, which had long prevented the general use of Porcelain, and from its composition

was called CHALK BODY; of very excellent quality
for fineness of grain, and smooth beautiful glaze, of a
fine cream colour, but not so durable as some of the
other kinds of pottery. For some years this kind obtained the preference in the Dutch Market; and the
manufacture was very advantageous to the parties,
who realized considerable property by it; but the improved quality and mode of ornament of the Blue
Printed in the present day, has superseded most, if not
the whole of this kind.

About 1793, Mr. Thomas Minton connected himself with a Mr. Pownall and Joseph Poulson, and at
Stoke commenced the manufacture of Blue Printed
Pottery, of much excellence of quality, and with additional elegance of Patterns, which speedily secured
considerable celebrity. A few years afterwards, the
manufacture of Porcelain was connected with the other,
and has been attended with success. The manufactory is now the property of Mr. M. alone. The
Porcelain there fabricated possesses great excellence
for fine texture and elegant ornaments; and his Blue
Printed Pottery was, in 1826, so much improved in
its various properties, as to place it at the summit of
the scale of excellence, and secure for it an unprecedented share of patronage. Mr. Minton has been
closely connected with most of the improvements of
the last forty years; and we have already mentioned
his excellent character as a Parent and a Gentleman.

About 1795, a new kind of Pottery, a *dry* body,
or without glaze or smear, was introduced into the
market by Messrs. Cheatham and Woolley, of Lane-
End. It is to the white Pottery, what Jasper is to
the coloured. Not being affected by change of temperature, but very fine in grain, durable in quality,

and of a most beautiful and delicate whiteness, it received the name it still bears, of *Pearl*, from Mr. J. Spode, at that time resident in London. It is used, like Jasper, for the finest description of ornaments; and is in general estimation among all ranks of society. Very few of the different attempts made to produce Pearl of equal excellence to the inventors, have been attended with any success.

About 1802, Mr. Wm. Brookes, engraver. then of Tunstall, now of Burslem, suggested to Mr. J. Clive, a new method of ornament by Blue Printing. The border of the plate was engraved from a beautiful strip of Border for Paper Hangings of Rooms; and many of the manufacturers approved of the alteration. The New Hall Company instantly adopted it for some of their tea services. The following improvement is likewise by the same person;—a certain ornamental border is employed for all the plates, whatever be their size; but every plate has a different Landscape, or Group of Flowers, for the dishes, soups, plates, &c. Indeed, the finest oriental Scenery has recently been transferred to Pottery, by Mr. James Keeling, of Hanley. In the latter part of 1828 he produced a most beautiful dinner service, ornamented with views from the Illustrations of Mr. Buckingham's Travels in Mesopotamia; and the principal manufacturers followed by completing Services of interesting Views of remarkable subjects in Turkey, Persia, and Hindostan.

CHAP X.

INTRODUCTION OF LUSTRE.—AND IMPROVEMENTS, IN POTTERY AND PORCELAIN SUBSEQUENT TO 1800.

The general voice of the district is in favour of Mr. John Hancock, now residing at Etruria, and a person of no mean talents as enameller, (while employed by Mr. H. Daniel, and Mr. John Brown, Enamellers, at Hanley,) having first produced the *Lustre.* We have heard it asserted, that he only introduced here the practice of what had been some time before invented at Derby; which certainly is possible; but the total silence of Derby tradition, discourages the assumption. Mr. Hancock appears to have made the process of *Lustring* of little value to himself; for the recipe could be obtained from him by any person, for a small sum of Money. Hence the great number of persons engaged in the branch; and the varied excellence of their productions. The *Lustre* of our day is a good red clay body, with a fine brown glaze; upon which is laid, for Gold Lustre, a very thin coating of a chemical mixture containing a small quantity of Gold in solution;—also of Copper, for Copper Lustre. The Steel Lustre employs oxide of Platinum in the same mixture instead of gold; and when *Silver Lustre* is made, a further coating of platinum worked in water only, is laid on the steel Lustre. The ware is then fired, and will be good or bad as the glaze and the metals are so. The first maker of the *Silver* Lustre properly so called, was Mr. John Gardner, (now employed by J. Spode, Esq.) when employed by the late Mr. Wolfe, of Stoke; and the

next were, Mr. G. Sparkes, of Slack Lane, Hanley;
and Mr. Horobin, of Tunstall, (now of Lane End.)
A person named Mr. John Ainsley, recently dead,
introduced it at Lane End; and since 1804, it has
been practised with varied success, thro' the whole of
the District.   The *Gold* Lustre is regarded as having
been first produced by a Burslem Artist named Hen-
nys, then resident in London; where for some years
he thus ornamented the Chalk body ware made by
Mr. Wilson, of Hanley.   This Lustre is the *solid*
kind.   The method of preparing a Gold Lustre which
could be applied by the Pencil, is very different every
way; and was discovered by Mr. James Daniel, of
Pleasant Row, Stoke.

Mr. John Hancock, was for time prior to 1800,
employed by Messrs. Turner, of Lane End; and
while there, introduced the method of gilding with
burnished Gold.   The practice originated in a Conversation with Mr. William Smith, Slack Lane, Hanley,
(who possessed the Secret of *Water Gilding,* practised
in Birmingham,) that suggested the application of gold
in a *liquid* state, in place of the leaf gold used upon
size; on the attempt being made, the success surpassed all expectations.   Some persons attributed the
invention to Mr. Henry Daniel; who certainly has
claims for many important improvements in the Enamelling Departments; but so far from arrogating the
merit to himself, he very explicitly avowed his complete ignorance of the person by whom the invention
was made, as well as when or where it occurred; and
only by mere accident was the fact ascertained; Mr.
Philemon Smith remembered having heard the subject
mentioned, and referred us to the person, to whom
the merit is due; and Mr. Turner verified the account.

In 1800, Mr. W. Turner having amused himself with examining by chemical analysis the different strata perforated in sinking a new shaft of a Coal Pit at Milfield Gate, discovered, in what is called the Taberner's (or Little) Mine, a mineral, which by calcination becomes a pearl white, yet unlike other minerals, does not *shrink* by the most ardent temperature to which it has been subjected — 130° of Wedgwood's pyrometer. This is now called *Patent Stone*, in consequence of the brothers Turner having obtained Letters Patent for manufacturing, with it as one material, a real Porcelain, wholly different from any previously manufactured. The stone is very different from the *Iron Stone;* and therefore the present Patent Ironstone China must not be confounded with the other Patent Porcelains, Champion's and Turners'. The late J. Spode, Esq. purchased the right to manufacture this patent Stone Porcelain; and a fine specimen of it has already been noticed, p. 220.

Mr. Fletcher, of Edinburgh, of Sporting celebrity, having given an order to a tradesman at Edinburgh, for a very large Punch Bowl, the order had been forwarded to different celebrated Potters, and remained not executed. Application was ultimately made to Mr. Turner, whose throwers attempted by different processes to accomplish the object; but it was only fully and satisfactorily got into form, by the ingenuity of Mr. William Massey, the Modeller, now resident at Stoke. It holds *twenty-two* Gallons Imperial Measure ; and is now preserved in the Museum at Edinburgh. On its outside is a kind of tablet; on which are beautifully enamelled, a Chinese Town, and the Names of the Persons and Place, as well as the date. The late John Daniel, Esq. mentioned this specimen in terms of the most glowing description.

V

Early in the present century, Capt. Winter having boasted that the Articles of his manufacture, at Tunstall were the only *true Porcelain* made in Staffordshire, experienced no little chagrin, on ascertaining that his ware would fuse at a heat much below that usually required to fire Mr. Turner's, and that while his *contracted* in the same manner as other productions of the district, Mr. Turner's retained its size unaffected in shape or expansion; at which fact, Dr. Hope, of Edinburgh, expressed his surprize, in language most complimentary. But, at the time when most benefit might have accrued to Mr. Turner, in consequence of the celebrity which his Porcelain had acquired, the late Mr. Harwood, of Newcastle, Steward of the late Marquis of Stafford, interdicted any further supplies of the stone indispensibly requisite, under the pretext that the Marquis was offended at the Patent having been obtained, and would not encourage any *monopo'y !*

Singular, indeed, that the manufacture of Porcelain under one Patent, should be prevented in such an authorative and aristocratic manner, (tho' probably the ostensible denouncer was wholly ignorant of the procedure of his agent,) while another person secured great advantages. But the Marquis might have been excited to this procedure, by a remembrance of the opposition Messrs. Turner's father had manifested towards the extension of the Patent Term to Mr. Champion.

In 1810, Mr. Peter Warburton, for the New Hall Company, took out a Patent for Printing Landscapes and other designs, from Copper Plates, in Gold and Platinum. upon Porcelain and Pottery. The appearance is extremely beautiful; but a great oversight in the first introduction of the method, has prevented its acquiring the celebrity to which it is entitled. The Copper Plates employed were those previously used for Black Printing. engraved in a very fine manner, and not containing sufficient oil to receive adequate strength of the pulverized gold. One or two Specimens, from very coarse plates, possess great beauty and elegance. There is every probability that this branch of ornamenting will again be introduced for the bottoms of tea saucers, and sides of the Cups.

In 1821, Messrs. Ridgway, of Cauldon Place, Shelton, introduced a Porcelain of Bone Body, with a new glaze, that surpassed every other kind then produced. And to its excellent quality was added entirely original models of the several articles of Dinner and Dessert Services; (also subsequently used for Blue Printed Pottery,) much resembling the beautiful ornamental Pieces used for Silver Plate, with gadroon edge, and tasteful appendages. On the Table Services first coming into the market, the elegance of the vessels, and excellent quality of the Porcelain, and the Stone China, received general approbation, and obtained unprecedented preference. Other manufacturers speedily followed their steps, and improvement has succeeded improvement, in quality and ornament, to the present day. In 1828, Messrs. Ridgway again placed themselves at the summit of the scale of excellence, in regard to their Porcelain, which is certainly not excelled, if it be even equalled, by any of the European Manufactories. And, with the elegant forms and ornaments, well repays the inspector's investigatons.

About 1822, Mr. Henry Daniel, the enameller, already mentioned, commenced the manufacture of a

different kind of Porcelain, at Stoke; and in 1826, the
Stone China, at Shelton; the shapes and patterns being
of the improved kind, so much preferred by the public.   But, in addition to the various methods of enamelling then practised, he introduced the practice of
laying grounds, of different colours, and ornamenting
them with gilding, both burnished, and embossed, or
frosted work as applied to plate.   His efforts have
been very successful; and the Porcelain fabricated at
the manufactory of H. and R. Daniel, will bear a
comparison for excellence, and elegance of ornament, with that of any other manufacturer.

Early in 1827, Messrs. Daniel completed for the
Earl of Shrewsbury, different services of porcelain of
the most brilliant and costly kind ever manufactured
in the district, and probably more than twice the value of any private order ever received here.   The extent of the order convincing the manufacturers, that
it was his Lordship's noble and patriotic purpose to
stimulate their ingenuity, in making the several articles
as specimens of the perfection to which the porcelain
manufacture is arrived; they acted under this excite-
ment, and the result was, that the productions would
well compare with the choicest specimens of European
Porcelain.   The TABLE SERVICES embraced every
species of article to which modern luxury has assigned
a purpose and a name; and on their several grounds of
Pink and of Green, the highest style of embellishment
which ingenuity could devise and Art execute was
employed to produce a splendid yet tasteful *tout en-
semble.*   The centres of the plateaus have three large
Vases, modelled with a degree of excellence in execution, and of justness in design, that are alike creditable
to the ability of the workman and the principals, and
well adapted to secure the meed of praise from all per-

sons capable of judging of the intrinsic merits of these splendid specimens; and in the elegance of their ornaments in the several departments of chasing, gilding, flower, landscape, and figure enamellings, we are not aware that they have ever been even equalled, not to say excelled, on British Porcelain.

> Designs for these, to meditation's eyes,
> Great Nature most redundantly supplies,—
> Of Models best ! her presence is the source,
> Whence Genius draws augmented fire and force ;
> Of Teachers best ! her precepts give the powers,
> Whence, to Perfection, Art by Practice soars.

Twelve smaller Vases, executed in a similar style, are supporters to the former. And, devoid of extraneous appendage, in the centre of each border or piece, is the Coronet of the Noble Earl, with the motto ' Prest D'Accomplir ;' the inciting Spirit of the Order, which was most speedily executed. The DESSERT SERVICES were altogether original in the shapes, and presented a most splendid and elegant succession of novel and ingenious devices and ornaments; and the TEA SERVICES are of the newest patterns, on which very beautiful subjects of Natural History, in flowers, birds, and foliage, are enamelled with the strictest attention to accuracy and nature; and with the richest embellishments the ingenuity of the Artists could introduce. A TOILETTE SERVICE, en suite, for every Dressing Room of Alton Abbey, in Maroon, or Green, Pink, and Blue, richly gilded, also are a part of the order. The DEJEUNE SERVICE embraces every Article that the refinements of taste and fashion have agreed to connect with this morning repast ; and also the proper Ornaments for the Boudoir, of the most chaste description; all under the particular directions, and agreeably to the taste, of the noble Countess. The ground is a deep Maroon, with embossed and chased

3 V

dead gold foliage, thro' which are traced a series of the finest designs, so as to appear white in the mass of gold, and add to the brilliance of the whole; the edges are strong gold richly burnished; and in the centre is the Earl's Coronet, and a beautiful ellipse of burnished Gold.—On the view of the whole we were equally gratified at the high degree of perfection to which the Art has risen, and the patriotism of the Individual in thus patronizing the manufacture of the district almost adjoining his own residence.

Messrs. James and W. Handley, then of Shelton, about the same time introduced a Porcelain from feldspar chiefly, of very excellent quality; and of this they made several Vases, much larger in size, and truly elegant and original in design, than any before produced. The application was disregarded; else we should willingly have introduced the particulars.

In the latter part of 1828, Messrs. Alcock and Stevenson, of Cobridge, published a series of Busts of the most eminent characters of the present time, executed in the best manner of the Art, in regard to accuracy of delineation and taste and elegance of Workmanship. Many of them being exquisitely finished in dead gold, they are a very chaste, elegant, and beautiful ornament equally for the drawing room or the library.

Very recently several of the most eminent Manufacturers have introduced a method of ornamenting Table and Dessert Services, similarly to Tea Services, by the Black Printers using red, brown, and green colours, for beautiful designs of flowers and landscapes; on Pottery greatly improved in quality, and shapes formed with additional taste and elegance.

This pottery has a rich and delicate appearance, and owing to the Blue printed having become so common, the other is now obtaining a decided preference in most genteel circles.

It is well known, tho' apparently little regarded, that the common or coarse Red Pottery, of which are formed many utensils for cooking food used by the lower grades in the community, is covered with a very pernacious glaze formed by either litharge, or the Potter's lead ore. When vessels of this kind are employed in either baking or boiling food, it is now ascertained, that the lead glaze is very soluble during the time of heat, and that it intermixes with animal fat, or the acid juices of fruits, or vinegar when cold, and that it is partially soluble even when any of these remain awhile in the vessels cold; its effects are thus very deleterious, producing visceral disorders, among the labouring classes, for which they are not able to assign any cause; but for whose alleviation they have recourse to ardent spirits, and thus superinduce the habit of dram drinking. Job Meigh, Esq. having discovered and made public a glaze free from all these bad properties, and wholly superseding the application of oxide of lead for the vitrified surface; and also the body of a better kind of coarse Pottery; by whose introduction and use by the common coarse ware potters, the source of injury to the health and morals of the lower classes would be removed, and yet they be served with vessels innocent yet more durable; the Society of Arts, at their Annual Meeting in 1822 honoured Mr. Meigh with their Gold Medal; and, in presenting it, His Royal Highness the Duke of Sussex highly complimented Mr. M. for his patriotism; and expressed his hope that the valuable discovery would be immediately adopted by those who made such ware; and thereby preclude further danger and injury to the health of his Majesty's subjects, from the poisonous glaze; and he requested Mr. M. to accept his personal thanks. The Glaze is made in this manner:—

Red Marl is ground in water until there is formed a mixture, of the consistence of thick cream; into this, the vessels, when well dried, but not yet baked, are first immersed, for the purpose of filling up all the pores in the surfaces; they are again well dried, and then are *dipped* into the *Glaze*, formed by grinding together in water to the consistence of thick cream, equal quantities of Feldspar, Glass, and black oxide of Manganese; (the last being omitted when the hue is needed of a whitish drab or gray.) The vessels are next dried well, and baked as usual. The composition for the better kind of common Ware, is 4 parts common Marl, 1 part Red Marl, and 1 part brick clay; and the Pottery thus made is harder, less porous, and better adapted for common purposes.

Thus have we endeavoured to trace the various stages of Improvement in the Places and Manners of the Potters, and the practices of their Art, whose Origin, Progress, and present Perfection, have been exhibited, it is hoped, free from exaggeration. We have noticed that the most remarkable efforts of ingenuity have resulted from the intercourse of persons peculiarly circumstanced; and are most vigorous when excited by the emulations, the oppositions, and the friendships, formed while pursuing the same means for personal aggrandizement. How much their rivalships, their jealousy, and even their antipathies, have contributed to the advancement of the Art, it might not be prudent to mention, even was the fact fully comprehended. But doubtless to these are owing the foundation and completion of that excellent superstructure, which, operating thro' successive ages, has at length assumed a station in the Commercial World, never contemplated by the early Potters. If we have not been equally happy in the denouement in every instance, let the reader remember that to understand all the circumstances of so intricate a subject, requires more time and ability, as well as industry, than are possessed by most writers.

CONCLUSION.

It only remains to solicit indulgence for any inadvertencies, and Corrections, for an Appendix, from every friend who can supply them.

FINIS.

INDEX.

W